The Cure

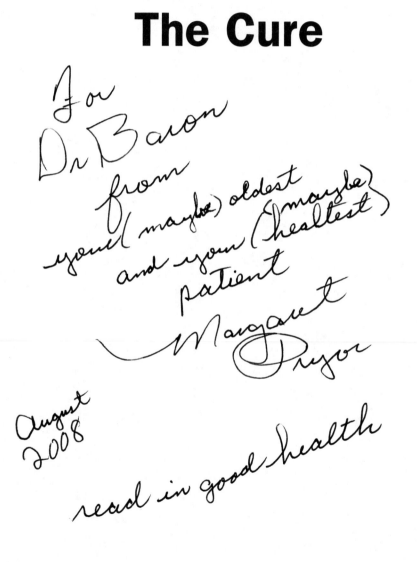

For
Dr Baron
from
your (maybe) oldest
and your (maybe) healtest
patient

Margaret
Pryor

August
2008

read in good health

3039330

The Cure

Geeta Anand
Pulitzer Prize-winning reporter for the *Wall Street Journal*

**How a Father Raised $100 Million–
and Bucked the Medical Establishment–
in a Quest to Save His Children**

Pompe Disease: one of a group of muscle diseases that interfere with the processing of carbohydrates to draw energy from food /a defect in the gene for the acid maltase enzyme (also known as acid alpha-glucocosidase), which affects the storage and breakdown of glycogen / infancy to adulthood / slowly progressive weakness of respiratory muscles. those of the hips, upper legs, shoulders and upper arms; cardiac involvement may occur in childhood form, less common in adults / slowly progressive and less severe in childhood and adult-onset forms; infantile form often leads to death by age 2 / autosomal recessive, or caused by the contribution of a defective gene from each parent

5ml

Do not discard after single use • Sterile

Reorder No. 309603

REGAN
An Imprint of HarperCollins*Publishers*

PEEL

10
EXP 08/2006

For the Crowleys,

who taught me how to live.

For my children, Tatyana and Aleka,

who taught me how to love.

For my husband, Greg,

whose support made this book possible.

Ten percent of the author's net payments from sales of this book will be donated to the Muscular Dystrophy Association.

All insert photographs courtesy of John and Aileen Crowley's personal collection, except:

Pages 4 (top), 5 (top) courtesy of Dr. Priya Kishnani; page 4 (bottom) by permission of *The Journal of Clinical Investigation*; page 5 (bottom right) courtesy of the Easton family; page 8 (top) courtesy of Tony McKinney; page 9 (top) courtesy of Genzyme Corporation; page 15 (bottom) courtesy of the Assink family; page 16 by Don Smith, by permission of *The Record*.

FIRST EDITION

Designed by Kris Tobiassen

Printed on acid-free paper

Library of Congress Cataloging-in-Publication Data

Anand, Geeta.
    The cure : how a father raised $100 million—and bucked the medical establishment—in a quest to save his children / Geeta Anand.—1st ed.
        p. cm.
    ISBN-13: 978-0-06-073439-8
    ISBN-10: 0-06-073439-6
    1. Glycogen storage disease type II—Treatment. I. Title.

RJ399.G58A53 2006
362.196'7480092—dc22
[B]
                                                                    2006048286

06 07 08 09 10 WBC/RRD 10 9 8 7 6 5 4 3 2 1

Contents

Author's Note

This is a true story. All the people and events depicted in this book are real. I researched it over the past five years, beginning with my articles for the *Wall Street Journal* in 2001 and 2003, and continuing in January 2004 when I started this book. Some of the material comes from my own observations, but most of it is based on my interviews with John and Aileen Crowley and several hundred others involved in the Crowleys' lives and in the race to find a cure for Pompe disease. I also relied on scientific literature, corporate records of Novazyme and Genzyme, and newspaper and video clippings. Where I wasn't present, the dialogue and scenes are primarily based on participants' memories of what was said and how things unfolded. Where their memories diverged on important issues, or where I wasn't able to interview a key player, I explained so in the endnotes.

—Geeta Anand

Prologue

John Crowley's hand shook as he hung up the phone in his wood-paneled study in Princeton, New Jersey, and looked up into the expectant green eyes of his wife Aileen. She had been standing beside his desk for several minutes, listening intently. It was a Friday evening in October 2002.

"So what's up?" she asked, her voice carefully neutral, trying not to show the hope he read in her expression.

John paused, absorbing the moment, and then his face broke into a massive smile. "You won't believe it, Aileen," he said, jumping up and walking around his desk to pull her into his arms. "The kids are going to get their Special Medicine. It's finally time. They could start within two weeks! I'm going to Florida on Saturday to get everything set."

Aileen started to respond, but she was interrupted by a screech from behind as they were drawn into a hug. The children's nurse, Sharon, had overheard the conversation from the kitchen, and she ran into the room and threw her arms around the pair.

"Oh, Mister John. I'm so happy," she whispered, squeezing them together tightly. John watched the lines of tension around Aileen's mouth ease and her eyes slowly melt. The three of them stood together for a long time, crying, as even the hardened Aileen finally allowed herself to believe that the grueling four-year fight to save her children was almost over.

John was the first to pull away from the arms and tears. He walked through the kitchen into the adjoining playroom, where five-year-old Megan, in a pink flowered dress, sat in her electric wheelchair, slowly and methodically brushing a Barbie doll's hair. Patrick, four years old, was already upstairs in bed, his ventilator steadily swishing in time with each forced breath. John pulled up a chair and sat beside Megan.

"Megs, you know Daddy's been working on Special Medicine," he said, using the term he had coined for the cure he had so desperately sought to halt the disease that had devastated the muscles of two of his children. Megan nodded her head ever so slightly and kept brushing.

"It's taken a long time to get Special Medicine just right," John continued, "but Megs, now we're done making it, and I've found a special place to give it to you."

At this, Megan looked up. "Where?" she asked, her straight brown hair swaying above her shoulders with her slight movement. She was a pretty girl with dark brown eyes and a porcelain complexion, a square face, and high cheekbones. A plastic tube sprouted from a hole in her neck and led to a pocket behind her wheelchair, where a ventilator hummed steadily, breathing for her. When she spoke, her voice was muffled, almost as if she were speaking from underwater. The weakness in her oropharyngeal muscles—the ones involved in speech[1]—made it difficult to enunciate, but her family and friends could understand exactly what she was saying.

"We're going to give you Special Medicine in Florida, Megs," John said.

His daughter dropped the doll and spun her wheelchair around in pure excitement so quickly he had to pull his foot back to avoid getting run over. Like many five-year-olds, Megan moved quickly and without regard to those around her. But unlike them, she drove a 400-pound electric wheelchair, and he knew she could inflict serious damage. She'd already broken her grandmother's toe, gashed several walls in the house, and torn out a kitchen cabinet.

"Can I go to Disney World?" she asked in her distinct, slurring cadence, eyes imploring in an otherwise expressionless face. As always, John was awed by how much emotion burst from his daughter's eyes. He wondered if this were true with everyone and he just hadn't noticed, or if it were only so in children with Pompe disease who couldn't move any other facial muscles. For them, the saying was genuinely true: their eyes really were the only window into their feelings.

"Yes, you can go to Disney World whenever you want," he said, nodding vigorously.

"Yea," Megan shouted, pumping her arms in the air as high as she could as she sped out of the playroom and into the kitchen, circling her mother and nurse, singing, "I'm going to Disney World." John stood smiling, hands on his hips, relishing his daughter's joy.

Four years ago, when their two youngest children were diagnosed with a disease they'd never heard of, John and Aileen Crowley had been told that there was no treatment. Pompe disease, a rare genetic disorder—so rare that fewer than ten thousand people in the world are born with it—weakens the muscles of patients over time so that eventually they cannot walk, talk, or even breathe on their own. Babies and toddlers diagnosed with the degenerative disease usually don't live past their second birthday.

But John couldn't live without hope. He was a fighter, and he had never in his life accepted a negative outcome without a struggle. In the absence of any other options, he had simply made his own answers: He quit his job as a marketing executive, raised $27 million from venture capital investors, and built a biotechnology company around promising science for Pompe disease. Two years later, he made what was considered by the business community to be an unimaginably successful sale of the firm to Genzyme Corporation, one of the world's largest biotechnology companies, knowing it had the money and know-how to get a drug developed faster than did his own still youthful company. At his insistence, as part of the deal he was named head of Genzyme's program to develop a medicine for Pompe disease.

His intent in making this a condition of the sale had been twofold: first, he truly believed that the urgency he felt as a Pompe parent would help speed a treatment to all Pompe sufferers. Second, he wanted to use his proximity to the drug's development to guarantee Megan and Patrick placement in the first clinical trials—the experiments to test whether a proposed medicine works in human beings as well as it has in animal studies. In these trials, patients are given different doses of a prospective medicine, and tests are administered to measure efficacy and side effects. Based on the results, the Food and Drug Administration (FDA) decides whether a new medicine is safe and effective enough to be sold in the United States. For Megan, Patrick, and millions of others with imminently life-threatening and untreatable diseases, clinical trials offered the only hope.

But despite his position at Genzyme—and in some ways, because of it—John ran into one obstacle after another in his attempt to get the kids treatment. The experimental drug for Pompe proved so hard to make and was in such short supply that spots in the trials were scarce—and weighted toward younger children, who required a smaller dosage for efficacy. On top of this, hospitals viewed John's petitions with a jaundiced eye, wary of the possible conflict-of-interest issues raised by John's dual roles as patient father and director of the Pompe drug development program at the company sponsoring the research. By this point, his journey to help his children had made him a rich man, but money could not cure them. With each passing day, he grew more frustrated as he shipped off the precious enzyme to Europe to treat one sick child after another, wondering if his position at Genzyme was a hindrance, not a help, in his quest to save his kids. While he watched other children grow stronger and healthier, his own children steadily deteriorated. At times, John had been his own worst enemy. He was impassioned, but sometimes so cocky that he overreached, or alienated people who sympathized with his plight.

One whole year had elapsed since John joined Genzyme, and now Megan and Patrick were so weak they couldn't even sit up on their own. Both were confined to wheelchairs and breathing through tubes inserted into permanent holes cut into their tracheas. Megan had recently lost the ability to lift her head, and Patrick was struggling even to grip the little toy action figures he loved to play with. Desperate, John had called a doctor he knew at the University of Florida in Gainesville, Florida, two weeks earlier, asking if he might run a tiny clinical trial for his children. The phone call he had taken earlier that day was from the same doctor, calling to say that he had all of the internal hospital and university approvals to begin treating Megan and Patrick.

John sat back down in his study and dialed Continental Airlines to make a reservation on the first flight out the next day for Jacksonville, the nearest major airport to Gainesville. It was on Saturday of the weekend Aileen's college roommate was getting married, but John believed he couldn't afford to delay for a single day. He knew how easily things could go off track—he'd had his hopes dashed many times before. He needed to get to Gainesville immediately to make sure everything was ready for the trial.

John heard the television set click off upstairs and knew Aileen was going to sleep. Resisting the urge to slide into bed beside her, he put his head in his hands and sighed. He hadn't told anybody—not even Aileen—about the enormity of the challenge that lay ahead.

After all the delays and disappointments of the past year, he no longer trusted his colleagues to push hard enough or fast enough to get his children treated in time. He had approached the Florida doctor without informing anyone on Genzyme's medical team whose job it was to file clinical trial applications and coordinate human experiments. If he could get the Florida trial started, he was gambling that his colleagues would whine and protest that he'd gone behind their backs, but that in the end they wouldn't stop him. "It's better to ask forgiveness than permission," he'd said often enough over the past four years.

It was one minute before midnight on October 4, 2002. Four hours remained before he needed to start the drive to Newark Airport.

"It's better to ask forgiveness than permission," he repeated aloud to himself.

That approach had propelled him through the first thirty-five years of his life. Would it work for him now, in the hour of his children's greatest need?

1. Veritas

On a clear, brilliantly sunny afternoon in June 1997, John Crowley walked to the podium to deliver the Class Day address to his fellow Harvard Business School graduates. At five feet six inches tall, he stood ramrod straight in his navy suit, his dark hair closely cropped and his square face wreathed in a bright, eager expression. Eyes shining, he unleashed a crisp, white smile into the crowd.

John opened a folder containing his speech and paused, relishing the attention of nine hundred fellow graduates and a few thousand of their friends and family members. They filled the metal chairs arranged in hundreds of rows in front of him under a white tent. To his left stood Baker Library, and behind the audience the Charles River sparkled. Across the river, the green-topped cupola of Eliot House, a Harvard college dorm, poked out from behind the summer greenery.

The business school had developed a distinct, close-knit identity since moving in 1927 to its own campus of neo-Georgian buildings. Students spent many hours each day with one another in class, and many more hours together on group homework assignments at night. Friendships born here tended to live on as the students graduated to become a disproportionately large portion of the nation's business and political elite. Many who came here were the sons and daughters of heads of state, ambassadors, and company chief executives; those who didn't start off as part of the elite were likely to join it when they left. Of the nation's *Fortune* 500 companies, some 15 percent of their top three officers came through this business school.

John's family sat in the front few rows of the audience. His mother Barbara sat beside his stepfather Lou and half-brother Jason. In the next row, his six-month-old daughter Megan, a bottle in her mouth, looked up from the lap of his wife Aileen. Automatically, his eyes scanned the seats around her for their two-year-old son John Jr., before he remembered that they had decided to leave him at home with a baby-sitter. But the rest of his tight-knit family was there, including Aileen's parents, Marty and Kathy, and her Uncle Charles and Aunt Jane.

"It is my great privilege and honor to share with you today the many experiences of the past two years and the hopes for the future of what is now and should always be the greatest class in the history of the Harvard Business School," John began. "For those of you keeping count, that's my first attempt to pander to the crowd," he said, looking up and smiling as the audience laughed appreciatively.

"In the one and a half hours that I have to speak with you all today—scared you, didn't I?—okay, in the next *twenty* minutes, I'll do my best to capture what has been for so many of us such a powerful and moving experience both in learning and living."

John's mother nodded, thinking that in his opening, her son had expressed the awesomeness of the moment with enough humor to avoid being annoyingly grandiose. He had always exuded a boyish charm, and others had always seen him as the kind of guy who was almost too good to be true—but *was* true. It was a testament to the high esteem his classmates held him in that he'd been elected to be their Class Day speaker, their representative at this graduation event. He reminded her so much of his late father, a police officer, who had snared her with his wiseass sense of humor the night they'd been introduced by mutual friends at Oprandy's, a New Jersey bar, in February 1966. When the bar closed, he and his brother had sat in her car for another hour, laughing as they regaled her with joke after joke, until her father drove up and knocked on the window, demanding to know why she wasn't home. By April, they were engaged, and they rushed to marry in August because she was pregnant with John.[1]

As she did at every milestone in John's life, Barbara thought of how thrilled his father would have been. She remembered the early morning in

January more than twenty years earlier when she'd sat John, then seven, and his younger brother Joseph, four, side by side on her bed to tell them their father had died. Sergeant John Francis Crowley—after whom John was named—had been found dead at the end of the night shift, apparently of carbon monoxide poisoning caused by a defect in his police cruiser.

She'd left Joe at home and taken John to the funeral at the towering stone St. Cecelia's Catholic Church in the town of Englewood, New Jersey, where she'd been married, her children had been baptized, and both sons would serve as altar boys. Thousands filled the twenty-five rows of dark wooden pews and spilled onto the street outside. Sergeant Crowley, the son of an Irish immigrant rubber factory worker, had grown up in the ground-floor apartment of a four-family brick house on Prospect Street, a few blocks from the church where he was being eulogized at age thirty-five. In stories in the local newspapers, friends and colleagues remembered him for his sense of humor and his pride in being a cop. Sergeant Crowley "was so proud to be a cop that nothing else was important to him," Police Chief Thomas Ryan told one newspaper.

Little John Crowley had listened intently in the front row as the priest addressed the homily to him, telling him there was no way he could understand why God had taken his father from him so young, but that now it was his responsibility to help take care of his mother and his family. After his father's coffin, draped in an American flag—Sergeant Crowley had also been a U.S. Marine—was carried down the twenty-two marble steps, John had instinctively saluted. Everyone assumed his mother had prompted him to do so, but in fact it was his father who had taught the boy the proper way to honor the departed. Now, as the boy saw the officers saluting the coffin, he did too. Then a lone bagpiper played "Amazing Grace."

Sergeant Crowley loved the police force, but he was at least as devoted to his children. When his wife was in labor, he had rushed home to change into a suit so he'd be appropriately attired to receive his firstborn into the world. When the doctor came into the waiting room to tell him he had a son, Sergeant Crowley passed out in his excitement. It had been his dad, coming off the night shift, who drove John to his first day of kindergarten. As if it weren't grand enough to arrive at school in a police cruiser, John had pushed the buttons so the lights and siren sounded as he got out of the car. John accompanied his dad on weekends when he made extra cash hauling people's junk to the town dump. A former Special Forces Marine, Sergeant Crowley had filled his son's imagination with stories of soldiers' heroism and patriotism. He told John he was going to the Naval Academy when he grew up. John still had the picture his dad had taken holding him as a newborn, with his shotgun, baseball bat, football, Marine uniform, and a toy motorcycle cop arranged in front of his bassinet.

"Your father would want you to grow up strong like him," John's mother had told him and his brother Joe many times as they grew up.

John took on the responsibility of being her eldest son and confidant—more so than she had ever intended. By second grade, he was helping her keep track of their savings, adding up the numbers in her checkbook and balancing the columns. By ninth or tenth grade, he would emerge from his bedroom with charts he had drawn showing the progress of the family's few shares of IBM and recommending new investments. Mother and son had developed a relationship so intense that even after he left home for college, they spoke almost every day on the phone.

Barbara and her late father, Frank Francis Valentino, a building superintendent, insisted her boys go to college, even though neither of their parents or grandparents had studied beyond high school. For each of her sons, she had saved $20,000 to help pay for college. Not only did John graduate from Georgetown University's School of Foreign Service, but with a year and a half at the Naval Academy in between, he had gone on to earn a law degree from Notre Dame, and now an MBA from Harvard.

Watching him onstage today, Barbara thought for the hundredth time how differently children could turn out. Her father used to call John "governor," even as a little boy, and then turn to her younger son Joe and say, "You're a good boy—I wish I had the money to buy you a gas station." Joe, who did not attend the graduation, had struggled since his father's death, always seeming to be the one who ended up in trouble. The boys shared the same playfulness—in fact, Barbara privately thought Joe was far funnier, but the younger boy was a little reckless. He was now working as a police officer in Baltimore, but he carried two other sets of business cards, one saying he was Senator Ted Kennedy's personal assistant, another claiming to be a talent scout for Paramount Studios. Which card he pulled out depended on the type of woman he was trying to impress. When it came to his brother, John spent half of his time worrying about Joe and the other half regaling his classmates with tales of Joe's latest antics.[2]

Barbara wondered what was next for her John. She had never known someone as driven, intense, and emotional. Fellow freshmen at Georgetown University nicknamed him "Admiral," a reference both to his leadership potential and the Navy ROTC uniform he wore even to class. At Harvard, his study group mates teasingly called him "Senator Crowley," because of his oratory skills, confidence, and popularity. At Georgetown and Notre Dame, he had studied hard but socialized little and made few friends. But at Harvard Business School, he seemed to have found a new equilibrium. He stayed out late drinking with his classmates on Thursday nights and many weekends, thrived on the business strategy debates, and parlayed his wit into the role of his section's MC. Every Friday, he presided over an awards ceremony he had initiated at his section pizza party. He gave out what he called the Top Ten "Master of the Obvious" awards for classmates who said, well, the most obvious things as they vied for good grades in classroom participation. He had a way of poking fun at people without humiliating them. The highlight was his presentation of the Kiss-Ass of the Week award, which he even gave to himself once.[3]

For his part, John hadn't quite figured out what to do next, except that he knew he needed to begin to pay off $140,000 in education debt he had amassed in one undergraduate and two graduate schools. He had decided to start postgraduate life in the highest paying job he could get—as a management consultant—and begin paying off the massive loans. He hoped he and Aileen would have more children. They had arrived at business school in 1995 with only year-old John Jr., but John came home from a study group one night a year later to find the kitchen light on and a pregnancy test with two pink bars highlighted on the counter. Aileen emerged from the bedroom, a shy smile on her face.

When the baby was born—a beautiful, healthy girl—John had been delighted to see that she looked so much like him and his Italian relatives. "My Italian princess," John cooed at the puffy, red-faced baby with a mop of dark hair. John Jr., blue eyed and blond, resembled his late father's Irish-American side.

Onstage, John's speech had turned passionate. Gone were the one-liners as he urged his classmates to use the power of their business degrees in the service of others. "By virtue of our Harvard MBAs and our own talents and ambition, many of us will achieve greatness," he said. "Use it to combat disease, to fight racism, to promote the entrepreneurial spirit in your own countries, and use it especially in our position as global business leaders, to ensure the prosperity and survival not just of capitalism around the world but of 'democratic capitalism.'"

Evoking the words of a former president, John said, "As John Kennedy said, 'When one man is enslaved, all cannot truly be free.'"

Barbara thought proudly that the hours her son had spent practicing his grammar school presentations in front of the mirror in his bedroom were helping him now. He'd filled the bookshelves in their split-level ranch with the speeches of Martin Luther King Jr., Robert Kennedy, President John F. Kennedy, and other great orators. He had memorized passages from Kennedy's inaugural speech, Abraham Lincoln's second inaugural address, and Dr. King's "I Have A Dream" speech.

Today, John looked on top of the world. With his straight nose, high cheekbones, and dazzling smile, he looked to Barbara like a movie star. He carried his muscular frame like a soldier, commanding the attention of those around him despite his short stature. "He has the wife, the kids, the education, the motivation, the personality, the looks—he has it all," she thought to herself. She smiled as the audience broke into enthusiastic applause and John returned to his seat onstage, smiling.

It was a Harvard tradition for graduates to bring their children onto the stage when they accepted their diplomas at the graduation ceremony the following day. John carried Megan, in a white dress and bonnet, in his left arm, and John Jr., in his double-breasted navy sport coat, in his right arm. John's name was among the first to be called, and his classmates cheered as he climbed the steps and shook the hand of Dean Kim Clark. Then he went over to Nancy Koehn, the faculty representative for his section, who was standing beside a box of teddy bears in Harvard T-shirts. She handed Megan and John Jr. each a bear, and their dad turned and smiled into the camera.

As he slowly began to climb down the steps from the stage, Megan suddenly collapsed backward, arms flailing. The crowd gasped as John lunged to his left, then let out a collective sigh of relief as he managed to grab her while still hanging on to his son and his diploma. Safely on the ground beside the stage, he handed her to Aileen, who straightened her white bonnet and bounced her until she was smiling and gurgling again.

Nobody knew it then, but it was the first sign that something was wrong with his little girl.

2. Trouble

In early November, John and Aileen buckled the children into their car seats and pulled out of their driveway in Walnut Creek, California, heading to the pediatrician's office. They'd moved here the summer after John's graduation from Harvard so he could take a job at a financial consulting firm, Marakon Associates, in San Francisco. About twenty miles east of San Francisco, Walnut Creek was picturesque and lively, with tree-lined streets downtown and a fancy outdoor mall with a Nordstrom and Baby Gap.

For John, work was grueling. At Harvard, he'd avoided spreadsheets, nudging case studies heavy on analytics on others in his study group. He'd known Marakon would require financial analysis, but he'd taken the job anyway, convinced he could figure out anything if he had to. The job offered the largest signing bonus of any of the companies recruiting at Harvard Business School that year—$60,000, plus the $90,000 base salary. He and Aileen had charged much of their living expenses during business school on their credit cards. They now owed $40,000 to credit card companies, in addition to John's $140,000 in student loans. John planned to stay at Marakon for a year or two and pay off a big chunk of his debts. Ever an optimist, John was even more so now that he had a Harvard Business School degree. The financial security that neither he nor anyone in his family had ever known now seemed within reach.

The couple had rented a tan, four-bedroom ranch with a large backyard fenced in by rose-covered trellises. The yard looked up at the tree-lined Mount Diablo only a few miles away. At night, they could hear coyotes howling in the distance on the mountain.

Aileen had discovered she was pregnant with their third child a week after John's graduation, and she was growing heavier and more tired. She adored children, and she and John had dreamed of having five—just not quite so quickly. But Aileen was as casual about taking her birth control pills as she was about picking up and moving across the country, and both Megan and this latest pregnancy were not planned. The new baby was due in four months, in early March.

Little John Jr. and Megan were challenging in different ways. John Jr. never stopped moving. Megan was calmer, but it seemed she had inherited her father's stubbornness. If she wanted a toy just out of reach, she screamed until someone (usually Aileen) got up and brought it to her. At the time, the family joked that Megan had inherited John's Type A personality. The big yard and warm weather helped keep the kids busy. When John Jr. came home from the Pied Piper preschool, Aileen put both children in the backyard, Megan in her walker and little John in his mini toy car. He would eventually tire of the car, and then Aileen would use the overgrown vegetable garden for entertainment. She'd pile rotten tomatoes into the back of the toy car, and she and her son took turns pitching them over the backyard fence.

Almost every day, Aileen took the children to the shopping mall. Shopping was entertainment for Aileen, and it showed in her children's neat, fresh appearances. She grazed, buying only a well-chosen thing or two at a time, comparison shopping with a vengeance to stay within budget. Her children were almost always the best dressed. She had waited until the embroidered Mermaid denim jackets at the Gap were on sale before pouncing. Now Megan wore the jacket every day over her floral dresses. Like his dad, little John dressed in a uniform of khakis and blue sweaters. With every hair combed into place, the son looked almost comically like his father, save for the difference in coloring. After the mall, they'd often head over to the neighborhood park, where the sandbox kept the little boy entertained for hours, and Aileen could push Megan on the swings. Every once in a while, Aileen would sink into the grass and sit still for a minute or two, thinking that as much as this life was tiring, it brimmed with beauty and possibility.

Walnut Creek even had its own fall festival, for which John had made a special effort to be home for the weekend. He'd danced in the parade, holding Megan, wearing an ivory sweater with bright, embroidered flowers over her first pair of blue jeans, waving and shouting with laughter. They put their son on any ride he was not scared to try, some beyond his years.

In their first couple of weeks in Walnut Creek, Aileen and John had taken the children for the obligatory trip to a young pediatrician in town named Dr. Montgomery Kong. The children had been healthy. Megan had had her share of colds and bronchitis in her first few months of life, but the California weather seemed to suit her. She hadn't been sick since they'd moved in August. The couple had told Kong that they were a little worried that John Jr., two and a half, wasn't yet talking, and Megan, eight months old, didn't crawl or pull up. The doctor had seen no reason for concern, but he told them to come back if the children didn't make progress in a few months.

Now it was November, and Megan still wasn't crawling and John Jr. still wasn't talking. Suppressing her worry, Aileen made another appointment.

Perched side by side in only their diapers, John Jr. and Megan sat on the padded exam table in Dr. Kong's bright, cheerful office. John stood in front of the table so that Aileen, now five months pregnant, could rest in a corner chair.[1]

John looked at his watch. They'd been waiting fifteen minutes in the exam room, and Aileen looked pale and drained. He looked in mock disapproval at his children, his hands locked firmly on his hips. "If there were two things I thought my children would be good at it would be public speaking," he said, shaking his head at his son, "and upper body strength," tapping his daughter on the head. "You two are very disappointing." He winked broadly at Aileen. At thirty, John kept his muscular bearing by doing push-ups and pull-ups every morning before work. Hearing the grunting, Aileen, who rarely exercised for two consecutive days, would roll over in bed, shake her head, and mumble, "Why?" before slipping back to sleep. Now she giggled, and the children grinned up at him.

Kong walked in just then, catching the end of the family joke and joining in the laughter. He was a tall man with a genial manner. He listened as John and Aileen took turns explaining their concerns. "I can't understand one thing he's saying," John said, "and he's going to be three next month."

Kong looked in the boy's ears and throat for any signs of infection. He took his temperature, and found it to be normal. "Does your son understand what you're saying?"

"He understands everything," Aileen replied. "And he *says* a lot of things. We just have no idea—well, no idea what they *mean*."

"He's probably just a delayed speaker," Kong reassured them, "but I'll write you a referral for speech therapy. Let's try that first and see if it works."

Then the doctor turned to Megan. "And she's still not crawling yet?"

"She's reaching for everything she can, but she's not even trying to crawl," John said.

Kong laid Megan on her back, and pulled and pushed on her arms and legs as he did the basic pediatric exam. He didn't seem to find anything wrong. "Just to be sure, I'm going to give you a referral to a neurologist," he said. "He gave them a name and number, and told them to call and make an appointment."

Satisfied that their concerns were being addressed, John and Aileen thanked him, dressed the children, and drove home.

Aileen, not given to worry, focused on the tasks at hand—taking John Jr. to preschool and to his weekly therapist appointments, Megan in tow. John presumed that Megan was just a late walker, much as John Jr. had been, but despite his optimistic nature, he found his mind continually returning to the question of what was wrong with his little boy. What if he had a serious speech problem? As a two-year-old, John himself had been an able speaker, his mother told him. He used to sit gaily by her side as she drove their old Chevrolet Impala, asking about so many things that her exasperation once got the better of her, and she'd stopped the car to demand, "Why do you ask so many questions?" Coached by his police officer dad, he could recite by memory the Miranda warnings at age two. "You have the right to remain silent," he would tell his mother. For a child of his to have serious trouble speaking would be crushing.

The next month, John took a few days off around the holidays, and for the first time since he and Aileen had met as teenagers in high school, they prepared for Christmas without any in-laws. John paid particular attention to his son, taking him out to collect firewood and reading to him nightly. Then one evening, after reading the boy a Dr. Seuss story in bed, John turned to him with a warm smile and said, "You're my buddy."

Little John Jr. turned to his father, pulled out his pacifier, and said, "Buddy." John read several more words before realizing he had just heard his son say his first word.

"Aileen, Aileen," he shouted. She rushed in from the other room, carrying Megan. At his father's prodding, the little boy looked at his mom, spread his lips into a four-toothed grin, and repeated "buddy" proudly.

The speech therapy had helped. The boy was finally beginning to talk. It was two days before Christmas, a wonderful present for the family.

Everything was fixable, as John had always thought. If his son could repeat one word, the little boy would eventually be able to talk normally. Megan, too, would probably start crawling any time now. A new baby was on its way. Everything would be fine.

John took a dollar bill out of his wallet, wrote the word "buddy" on it, and taped it up on the wall in his son's room. On important occasions, John's maternal grandparents had always given him money with written words on the bills commemorating the event. John still had the $10 bill his grandfather had given them for their wedding, inscribed with the words "Congratulations on John and Aileen's wedding." Aileen never understood the tradition. "It must be some Italian thing," she laughed, shaking her head in bemusement.

That holiday season also brought Megan's appointment with the pediatric neurologist at Oakland Children's Hospital and Research Center, a half-hour away. In the exam room, Dr. Daniel Birnbaum, a slight, balding man with a quiet manner, listened as they described Megan's inability to crawl or stand. He looked down at the chart they had filled out in the waiting room. "She's eleven months old?" he asked. They nodded.[2]

Birnbaum put the little girl on her back. He began to poke and prod at Megan, testing her reflexes and contorting her limbs. He bent her legs and let go of them. They immediately fell to either side of her pelvis, lying flush with the table. He frowned and made a note in his records.

"See the way her legs rest in frog position," he said. "That could indicate a myopathy."

John and Aileen looked at each other, unsure what he meant, but certain that such an authoritative and medical sounding word was not good. "That just means there could be something wrong," he said. His tone was reassuring, but still Aileen shivered slightly. "It could be something minor. We'll need to do a blood test." As Aileen held Megan on her lap, a nurse stuck her arm several times with a needle, searching for a vein, drawing wails along with the blood.

A few days later, the nurse left a message on their answering machine. Her voice was studiedly neutral, conveying nothing except the need for them to return the call. With Aileen standing beside him, John dialed the hospital. The nurse said Megan's blood test had shown a high level of a certain enzyme, which suggested a potential problem. The doctor wanted to schedule a muscle biopsy, which, to their horror, the Crowleys learned was an operation performed under anesthesia in which a surgeon would make an incision in Megan's leg and cut out a small piece of muscle.

"What was wrong with her blood test?" John asked.

"Megan had an elevated level of CPK," the nurse said. It was yet another medical term John didn't understand. He knew there was a reason he had hated all those science classes at the Naval Academy.

"What's that?" he asked. There was an awful sinking feeling in his stomach as the unfamiliar medical words began to come out of the cream-colored earpiece.

"CPK is short for creatinine phosphokinase," the nurse said. "It's an enzyme normally found inside muscle cells. The large amount of it in her blood tells us her muscles are weak and something is wrong. Something is causing the fibers in her muscle to break down. We need to find out what it is."

"What could that be?" John asked.

"There are several possibilities," the nurse said crisply, her voice insistently professional, "but we won't know for sure until we do the biopsy. Would February 12 work for you?"

"But what are the possibilities?" John persisted, pressing for answers like the trial lawyer he had been before business school.

"You really don't need to think about the possibilities yet," the nurse said. "There's no way of knowing."

"But the biopsy is a long way away," John said, his voice pleading. "You have to give us *some* idea."

The nurse hesitated, then said, "It could be something like muscular dystrophy, or something else . . ." Her voice trailed off.

John said February 12 would be fine for the biopsy, hung up, and looked at Aileen. "She says Megan could have muscular dystrophy. Do you know what that is?"

Aileen shook her head slowly, her auburn hair sliding over her cheekbones, which were blanched white with anxiety. Like John, she had heard of the disease, but she didn't exactly know what it meant. To her, it sounded like the name of the disease for which people sold shamrocks for a dollar at the convenience store. Maybe it was the one for which firemen collected money in buckets at traffic intersections. Or was it the disease that Jerry Lewis raised money for in telethons?

Megan began to cry in the other room, startling them out of their tense silence. Aileen went to get her from her afternoon nap, burying the terrifying questions in the comfort of routine.

That night, Aileen put Megan to bed with her usual tenderness: sitting in the red upholstered chair in her bedroom, rocking her, gently feeding her the evening bottle, and singing her Barney songs.

John, however, couldn't stop wondering about muscular dystrophy. The next morning, he drove to the Barnes & Noble in downtown Walnut Creek and bought four books on the disease. He spent the next day paging through them nervously, learning about the different types of muscular dystrophies. The most common, Duchenne muscular dystrophy, usually began to affect boys at about five years old, weakening their muscles steadily so that they couldn't walk and eventually died. He looked in horror at a picture of a girl—who, with her dark hair and pale complexion, bore an awful similarity to Megan—walking with braces on her legs, a crutch under each arm. Nobody in his family had a physical handicap. It was unimaginable to think of his daughter needing crutches. How would she be able to play soccer, as he'd always imagined, or have her first awkward school dance with a boy?

For days, the books sat in a pile on his nightstand. He saw Aileen touch them once. She picked up the top book, looked at the cover picture of the girl with crutches, and slammed it back down, murmuring, "No."

Eventually, he slid the books under his bed and out of sight.

*   *   *

On March 6, under the cloud of Megan's uncertain prognosis, John and Aileen drove to John Muir Medical Center in Walnut Creek for the birth of their third child. Megan had had her muscle biopsy, but the results were still not in. Aileen's parents, Marty and Kathy Holleran, had flown out from New Jersey and were taking care of John Jr. and Megan.

Aileen's scheduled C-section, her third, went so smoothly that her doctor and John engaged in a lively speculation of the baby's fatherhood in the operating room. "We got a moose here," said the doctor, a handsome man only a few years older than John, lifting out the nearly ten pound baby boy.[3]

"What a big guy—just like his daddy!" replied John, who at five foot six was about the same height as Aileen, but had never minded a good laugh about his stature.

"Yeah, his *real* daddy must be a big man," the doctor retorted. As John laughed, Aileen's exasperated voice rang out from behind what he had taken to sarcastically calling the "batting cage," the screen that shielded the surgery from her view. "Would you two *mind?!*"

That evening, Dr. Kong showed up at the hospital for the routine pediatric exam of the new baby they had named Patrick. No doctor had examined their other two children so closely. Kong seemed to spend forever scrutinizing every part of the five-hour-old baby boy. Finally, after an interminable twenty minutes, Kong handed Patrick to Aileen and said, "He looks great." Aileen, smiling and relieved, cooed to Patrick as she let him nurse again. The doctor washed his hands and stepped out of the room, John following behind him.

"Dr. Kong, have you heard anything about Megan's biopsy?" John asked in a hushed voice once they were out of Aileen's earshot.

"I've heard some preliminary results," Kong said, looking down. "But nothing for sure right now. It's all very preliminary. Dr. Birnbaum will be calling you next week to discuss them."

Patting John on the arm, Kong walked hurriedly away from him down the long corridor. John stared after him long after he'd turned the corner. Finally, he stepped back into the flower-filled room where Aileen was still nursing their new baby.

3. Diagnosis

Only a week later, John and Aileen arrived in the pediatric neurology wing on the first floor of the Children's Hospital and Research Center. The waiting room that had been crowded on their last visit was empty. Aileen, two days out of the hospital, had insisted on accompanying John despite her mother's urging that she stay home and rest. John was the more emotional one, and Aileen didn't want him to be alone when he heard Megan's biopsy results. They left the two older children at home with Aileen's mother, and brought only baby Patrick so Aileen could nurse him if he woke up.

John carried Patrick in his car seat as they approached the reception desk to check in. This time, there was no wait. They were immediately ushered into a small back room, furnished with a small desk, an exam table, and three plush chairs lined up against the wall. A grim-faced woman sat in one chair, a box of tissues resting in the seat next to her.

Dr. Birnbaum stood up from behind the desk and introduced them to the seated woman.[1]

"This is Jill Cooper. She's a social worker," he said in his quiet voice. Foreboding struck John like a slap in the face, and he actually flinched. *How bad must things be for a social worker to have been called? Megan must have a disease. It's got to be her muscles. My God, will she never walk? Will she use crutches? Maybe she'll be confined to a wheelchair for the rest of her life.* He forced himself to stop. He would wait for the doctor's assessment before speculating any further.

He and Aileen sat in the two open seats beside the social worker. John pushed Patrick in his car seat under the table—still, thankfully, asleep.

"How is Megan doing?" Birnbaum asked as he sat back down.

"She's doing well, thank you," John said. "She's still not crawling forward, but I think she crawled backward a little bit the other day. It's taken some time but I think she's finally making progress."

"Good, good. Well—I know you're anxious, so let me tell you about the biopsy," the doctor said. Then he paused and took a deep breath. "The lab tests found Megan's muscle fibers full of something called glycogen. They found a lot of it. We think Megan has a lysosomal storage disorder called Pompe disease."

"Is it serious?" Aileen asked, leaning forward in her seat, lines forming around her mouth as her face tensed.

"Yes, I'm afraid it's very serious," Birnbaum said. "This is a bad diagnosis. Pompe disease is a progressive disorder. It makes the muscles weaker and weaker."

John and Aileen looked at one another, saying nothing. Muscular dystrophy had been a mystery to them when the nurse mentioned it as a possibility over the phone, but at least they'd heard of it.

"What causes this disease?" John asked at last.

Birnbaum picked up a big hardcover book from the desk and opened it to a page he had marked with a yellow sticky. He began to read aloud, sometimes breaking away from the book to explain. John noticed his hands were trembling.

"Pompe disease is an inherited genetic disorder. It is caused by a defective or missing enzyme," he said. "Without this enzyme, our bodies cannot break down a very important carbohydrate or sugar called glycogen. Our bodies make energy at the cellular level by breaking down glycogen. In Pompe patients, this stuff, this sticky glycogen, builds up in the muscles. Patients get weaker and weaker. There are forty-eight other similar diseases, each of them caused by a different defective or missing enzyme that is needed to break down an important substance in our bodies. Luckily, all of these diseases are extremely rare. Pompe affects only one in forty thousand people, so your daughter's case is actually the first one I've ever seen.

There are three different forms of the disease: infant, juvenile, and adult onset, with the infant type being the most severe."[2]

Birnbaum closed the book and put it down on the table. John and Aileen had followed most of what he was saying, but not all. He had held on to the worst part to share last.

"It's a fatal disease," he said softly, looking first at John, then at Aileen, then averting his glance from them entirely. "Most kids with the infant form of the disease don't live to be two. I'm very sorry."

Dropping her head into her hands, Aileen began to cry. The social worker handed them tissues. John blew his nose and reached over to put his arm around Aileen.

"Are there any treatments?" he asked, his voice shaking.

Birnbaum hunched over his desk and shook his head. "I went onto Medline—the most powerful medical research database there is—and I couldn't find anything."

John's eyes fell on Patrick, still peacefully asleep in his car seat under the table. "Is there a chance he has it too?" he asked slowly, finding himself unable to look away from the soft curves of Patrick's gently sleeping face.

"Yes," the doctor was saying. "If the parents both have a certain genetic mutation, which you apparently do, there is a 25 percent chance each child might have it."

"Oh, God," John said. Aileen cried even harder.

Birnbaum finally brought his gaze back to them, meeting John's eyes. John could see the regret in them, but also hopelessness. "I'm so sorry," he repeated, his hands curling helplessly across the desk in front of him.

The doctor recommended they see another neurologist for a second opinion, and gave them the name and contact information of a Dr. Miller. Then he and the social worker stood up. Birnbaum said they would both be happy to answer other questions the couple might have later, and that they should call any time.

Driving home on Route 24 East, John's mind raced uncontrollably. "The little men are at work in your head again," Aileen would often say at night when he couldn't sleep because he was thinking too hard. He remembered the crushing pain and loneliness he'd felt in the weeks after his father's death, and the ache that came back each time he saw a father and son together. But even that early loss had not prepared him for this. One—possibly all—of his children had a fatal disease for which there was no treatment, let alone cure.

Outside, it was still windy and dark. He resolved that when they got home, he would call Aileen's dad, Marty, and ask him to fly back out to California. Marty would help them figure out what to do. He was the go-to guy in Aileen's family; every family had one. Marty's mother had died when he was nineteen, and his father was so depressed that Marty was left caring for his two younger siblings. From then on, anybody in the extended family who needed anything would call on Marty. He had become a father figure to John, too, when he and Aileen began dating in high school. Yes, that was it. Marty would know what to do.

For a moment, John was comforted. Then he winced at the thought of having to actually tell Marty such terrible news. How would he tell his friends? His mother?

"What if the doctor is wrong?" he blurted to Aileen.

"Let's just not go there right now," she said. She had stopped crying and was staring fixedly out the window at the gray clouds whipping by.

Understanding, John turned on the radio. He liked to talk out his worries, but Aileen preferred silence or diversion. Natalie Merchant's song "Wonder" was playing. It was a popular song, and he'd heard the song before, but today, for the first time, he listened to the words. A high voice, filled with joy and optimism, sang about the gifts of a child and knowing she would thrive despite the visits of many doctors. "With love, with patience, and with faith, she'll make her way," Merchant sang. His heart lurched, and tears spilled onto his cheeks.

"Oh, John," Aileen said, looking at him at last. "Why don't you pull over, honey, or you're going to have an accident."

John kept driving. "I just want to get home and hug Megan," he said.

4. Hope

For all of his thirty-two years, John had met any blow he was dealt with the same steadily determined response—to try to fix it. He had tried to fix his father's death for his mother by becoming her confidant, her financial adviser—the perfect son. When his grandfather lost his health insurance, John, still in law school, had fixed that, finding him a new plan and paying for it by adding several thousand dollars more to his student loans. Since childhood, his family's finances had been shaky, and he was fixing that with his Harvard MBA and the highest-paying job he could find.

Now, as he absorbed Dr. Birnbaum's diagnosis—that his precious Megan had a deadly disease for which there was no treatment—all John could think about was what he could do to find one.

That night, after Aileen fell asleep with Patrick close by in his blue plaid bassinet, John sat down at the sofa table that served as a desk in their bedroom and turned on the computer he had bought and linked to the Internet just a week earlier. He typed "Pompe disease" into the window of a search engine, and with the click of a button, entered a new world of disease and drug discovery—one that he would not leave for the next nine years.

Pompe disease, he learned, had been discovered in 1932 by Dutch pathologist J.C. Pompe. Dr. Pompe had performed an autopsy on a seven-month-old baby who had died of heart problems, and had discovered that the tissue was overflowing with a thick, sticky substance called glycogen.

He was the first to make the connection between the glycogen oozing out of the baby's muscle cells and the symptoms of the disease—the enlarged heart and weakening of the muscles that eventually led to death.[1]

But World War II halted Dr. Pompe's work. He had joined the Dutch resistance, and the Nazis found a secret radio transmitter in his lab. He was arrested and murdered. Over the next two decades, doctors and scientists began to recognize and report more patients with what came to be called Pompe disease. Many of those diagnosed with infantile Pompe displayed symptoms similar to Megan's—the early signs of weakness in their legs that fell into the signature Pompe "frog" position when set on a flat surface. While the disease was degenerative and the patients steadily grew weaker, Pompe seemed to affect some muscle groups more and earlier than others. Along with the legs, the facial muscles tended to rapidly weaken, as did their hearts and lungs, but patients usually retained strength in their arms for longer. In 1963, the Belgian scientist Henri Hers discovered the enzyme acid alpha-glucosidase was deficient in patients with Pompe disease.[2] In the 1960s and 1970s, researchers in Europe and the United States began to discover the more than forty other similar diseases, each caused by a defect in an enzyme that processed waste material within the region of the cell called the lysosome, which functioned like a garbage disposal. This enzyme defect led to the buildup of the waste material it was in charge of breaking down.

By the 1980s, scientists had developed a new technology to decode genetic material, and they were trying to make laboratory versions of genes and other proteins. This set off a race among the handful of scientists working on Pompe disease to describe the genetic composition of the gene encoding the enzyme deficient in patients. If they knew the genetic code of the enzyme, acid alpha-glucosidase, scientists believed they could produce an artificial version in the lab and infuse it into patients who couldn't make it properly. Finally, they would be able to offer patients some hope.

In 1986, Dr. Rochelle Hirschhorn, a professor of medicine at NYU Medical Center, published a portion of the gene. The Dutch researcher, Dr. Arnold Reuser, followed two years later with a description of the entire gene. Hirschhorn came back to expand on Reuser's work and correct parts of the gene he had described incorrectly.[3] Reuser and others began to look for a way of producing large enough amounts of the enzyme to treat Pompe patients.

Reading this, John's hopes rose for an instant. Then, as he clicked on links to further articles, his heart fell again.

Making biological matter for medicinal purposes, he found, was challenging and expensive. Reuser spent several years trying in vain to find a company willing to invest the millions of dollars required to produce the enzyme for a disease with five thousand patients, at best. The financial incentive didn't seem to match the enormity of the up-front investment needed—and John, with his Harvard business degree, could understand the awful logic of the financial decision. Reuser collaborated for a time with a physician-scientist of Taiwanese origin, Dr. Y.T. Chen, at Duke University Medical Center in the United States, who was also interested in making an enzyme replacement therapy for Pompe disease.

Then, in the early 1990s, Genzyme Corporation, a tiny U.S. biotechnology firm, proved it was possible to develop an enzyme replacement therapy for a disease affecting only a few thousand people and make a profit. Genzyme brought to market an enzyme treatment for Gaucher disease, a related disorder that was caused by a defect in the lysosomal enzyme responsible for processing fats, or lipids. Genzyme grew rapidly into a profitable business, even though its therapy treated an estimated four thousand people by charging each patient a staggering average cost of $200,000 a year.

Encouraged by the success of the Gaucher disease drug, Reuser and Chen approached Genzyme separately and tried to interest the company in investing in a Pompe treatment. But the company was still small at the time, and senior management felt they couldn't take the risk.[4] The two researchers eventually found other corporate sponsors. Reuser teamed up in 1993 with a Dutch company, Pharming, which specialized in altering the genes of animals so that they produced milk containing human forms of enzymes needed for therapeutic uses. The company bred rabbits in which one gene had been added, so that the milk they made contained a human form of the acid alpha-glucosidase enzyme. The enzyme was purified out of the milk of hundreds of these transgenic rabbits.

At around the same time, Chen teamed up with a Taiwanese company called Synpac Pharmaceuticals. He made acid alpha-glucosidase in giant, stainless steel containers similar to those used to produce beer. This was fast becoming the standard method for making biotechnology products. Manufacturers filled the containers, called bioreactors, with cells taken from the ovaries of Chinese hamsters—known in science lingo as CHO cells—which had been genetically altered to produce human versions of acid alpha-glucosidase.

Nearly three hours had passed when John found a link on the Internet to a press release from Duke University. Issued on February 14, Valentine's Day—barely a month earlier—the press release announced that Chen planned to test his experimental enzyme in babies as part of an early clinical trial. The release said Chen had tested his experimental enzyme in Japanese quails afflicted with Pompe disease who were so weak they hadn't been able to flip over or fly. "The high dose GAA treatment improved muscle strength so much that both birds could right themselves when flipped on their backs. One bird could even fly a short distance," John read to himself. Based on the results, Chen was working with the U.S. Food and Drug Administration to begin a clinical trial, and "within this year, Chen and his colleagues expect to treat children born with the rare and always fatal Pompe disease."[5]

With a few more clicks, John read that Pharming, the company allied with Reuser, was also preparing to launch a clinical trial of its enzyme in four babies with Pompe disease. These developments were so new that even Dr. Birnbaum had been unaware of them.

John pressed the print button and leaned back in his chair, closing his eyes and breathing deeply. He had spent the afternoon after Birnbaum's diagnosis driving alone around Walnut Creek in his rented green Pontiac Bonneville, crying and praying. "Please God, just let Megan live until her second birthday," he had begged. For all of John's belief in his own powers of will, he was also deeply religious. Raised in the Catholic church, he had been not only an altar boy, but a family friend of the parish priest, who often ate dinner with his family. During stressful times in his life, John often attended Mass every day.

The evening after Megan's diagnosis, John had driven to San Francisco Airport to pick up Aileen's dad, who had flown cross-country as soon as he heard the news. "I don't know how, but we're going to figure this out,

John," Marty had said gruffly, staring straight ahead as they drove home. He still seemed to be stunned by Megan's diagnosis. John had said nothing in response, eyes trained on the blackness of the road ahead. He wanted to say something to Marty, to comfort his father-in-law or allow the older man to comfort him, but he could find no words to reach out through the gloom.

Now, here it was. Something real, a triumphant flash of scientific discovery to brighten the doctor's dire prognosis. He stared at the printer as it churned out word after word, page following page of information on Pompe disease, and hope flooded into his chest, his heart, his soul. He wanted to share the news.

"Aileen," he whispered, looking into the dark corner where his wife lay sleeping in bed. She didn't stir, but Patrick began to cry in the bassinet beside her. Aileen sat up with a start and blindly groped for the baby. John picked up the pile of papers from the printer and walked over to the side of the bed, reading from the press release announcing Duke University's clinical trial.

"Look. Wake up and look at this. This is amazing. It says that there are some doctors at Duke who are working on Pompe."

Aileen, still half-asleep and nursing Patrick, just stared at John, struggling to comprehend. In his excitement, John went on, "And there's more. It says a Dr. Chen at Duke is working on a treatment for Pompe. He has an enzyme already created in his lab. He gave it to some Japanese quails with Pompe, and it *worked*."

Aileen cut in. "He gave this enzyme to *what?*"

"To quails—you know, birds," John responded.

"Yes, John. Thank you. I think I know what a quail is," she said grumpily, lapsing into a sort of mock-snappiness. "But what does that have to do with Megan's disease?"

"It *means*, smartass, that some bird that somehow has the same disease and the same missing enzyme as our daughter, got this enzyme—and it made the bird stronger. Look here, it says the birds actually flew." He stabbed a finger at the printed paragraph, and waved the papers elatedly in the air. "Can you believe it, the goddamn bird flew!"

Aileen asked cautiously, "What does this mean?"

John looked her in the eye, brushed his newborn son's hair, and said slowly, "It means hope, Aileen. It means hope."

"See here, listen," he said, reading from the press release. " 'Based on these results, we believe this enzyme is a promising therapy for the human form of Pompe disease. Dr. Chen said he will initially attempt to treat only a small number of children. If it is successful, children will need a supply of the enzyme for their whole lives.' "[6]

Aileen, sitting up straight, lifted Patrick over a shoulder to burp him and told John to slow down. Understanding flashed across her face as she listened, and her eyes brightened. Her husband was telling her there was a way to lift the death sentence on their precious Megan. Aileen gently lay Patrick back in his bassinet and stood up shakily, sliding her arms around John and squeezing tightly.

"What do we do now?" Aileen asked, excited but uncertain. She knew John would have the answer. Like her dad, he always seemed to know what to do, to take charge, to make things happen.

"We call Duke," he whispered as they held one another. They stood together for a long time until Patrick's fussing grew into a full-scale wail. Aileen sighed, sat back down, and began to nurse their son from the other side, and John went back to the desk to study the printouts. It was a pattern that had become a foundation in their lives: she nursed the children with patience and love; he began to think and to plan.

That weekend, John went to Kinkos and put together a dozen booklets with tan covers that read "Summary of Medical Records of Megan Kathryn Crowley." He stayed awake until early Monday morning so he could call Dr. Reuser, the Dutch scientist at Erasmus University whose work concentrated on extracting the enzyme from rabbit's milk, when he might be arriving at work at 9 A.M. in Rotterdam.

"I am calling from the United States of America to talk to Dr. Arnold Reuser," John said, speaking slowly and loudly.

"Oh, you want Arnie," said a voice in fluent English. "Hold on."

Within a minute, Reuser, warm and sympathetic, was saying that yes, he did work with Pharming, but he was a research scientist and didn't treat patients. He advised John to take his daughter to see a Dr. Alfred Slonim at North Shore University Hospital in Manhasset, a suburb of New York City.

"Dr. Slonim is an expert at treating the disease, and he is also working with us to plan a clinical trial of our enzyme treatment in the United States," Reuser said. Companies, it turned out, collaborated with doctors not only for their expertise, but also for easier access to patients for clinical trials.

Two weeks later, on April 1, John, Aileen, and Megan pulled up at the Inn at Great Neck, a new five-story brick hotel a few miles from North Shore University Hospital. It wasn't where you would expect to bring your child to be examined by a physician, but Slonim's nurse had told them that he was having meetings there that day. Also attending would be a Dutch physician who was an expert in treating Pompe and business officials from Pharming to plan the clinical trial in the United States. Based on John's description of his daughter's symptoms, the nurse said Slonim suspected Megan might have an unusual form of Pompe disease—and one in which he had a particular interest. His Dutch visitors had never seen a patient with that variation, and he wanted to show them one. John had happened to call at the right time.[7]

Luck and good instincts had led Slonim into an area of study that would eventually make him an expert on Pompe disease. An orthodox Jew, he had grown up in Melbourne, Australia, and spent his first years in medicine as a pediatrician in Israel. In 1974, he came to the United States to take a postdoctoral position in endocrinology at Vanderbilt University. One of his first patients there was a sixteen-year-old girl who suffered from a disease similar to Pompe. The girl had developed severe hypoglycemia, or low blood sugar. There was no treatment for the disease, so Slonim had tried the next best thing—experimenting with the girl's diet. On Slonim's low-carbohydrate diet, supplemented by tube feedings of formula at night, the girl was able to go to school for the first time.

Word of the "miracle" spread, and soon families of children with that disease and related disorders, including Pompe disease, began to call. The doctor's diet-and-exercise program seemed to slow the progression of a range of related disorders.

Several hundred patients were born with Pompe each year in the United States, but many died as infants, before their parents even knew what was wrong with them. Even if the babies were diagnosed, doctors usually sent them home with no hope because medical textbooks listed no treatment. Slonim's patients found him through word of mouth or the Internet, which had just begun to become a mainstream resource. He had treated about thirty patients with Pompe before John called.

With Megan in a stroller, John and Aileen rode the elevator to the second floor of the Inn at Great Neck. John led the way down the hallway to the conference room, and Aileen followed, her knuckles white on the handles of the stroller. John knocked on a green door, and they entered the room to see six people sitting around a long, dark table covered with papers. A broad-shouldered, balding man who looked to be in his sixties rushed toward them, hand outstretched.

"I'm Alf Slonim," he said, with a big smile and a pronounced Australian accent. He shook hands vigorously with John and Aileen, then immediately dropped into a crouch in front of Megan's stroller.

"Hello, little girl!" he boomed, his face only about six inches from hers. Then, in a quieter tone, he muttered to himself, "Yes, lovely, beautiful little girl. Just beautiful."

Megan, in her pink windbreaker and matching bow, leaned forward in her stroller, staring at him.

"What a pretty pink bow, little girl," he continued, again speaking to Megan. "You certainly took a long trip to come see me." Then he glanced to the side and said wryly, "Your daddy was most persistent with my nurse, making sure you got here," drawing a laugh from John and chuckles from several of the seated men.

"What's your name, little girl?" he asked, his accent making the word *name* rhyme with *thyme*.

Megan looked up at Aileen and grunted, wanting her mother to answer the question.

"This is Megan, Dr. Slonim," Aileen said, unclenching her jaw into a nervous smile.

Slonim's age, his gentle manner, and his kind face reminded John of his mother's father, his grandpa, the man who had helped raise him when his father died. The two were inseparable for most of John's childhood, and had remained close until Frank Valentino's death two years earlier. Instinctively, John felt that this Dr. Slonim was a good man, someone he could trust. He seemed familiar even though they had only just met.

John looked over at the conference table, curious about the identity of the others in the room.

"This is a good time to break," the man at the head of the table was saying to the others. He was tall and heavyset, with a full head of brown hair and a Texas drawl. "Randall House," he said, coming around the table to shake hands with John and Aileen, his gold Rolex glinting in the overhead lights. "You talked to my wife on the phone several weeks ago."[8]

John recognized the name. He had found Mr. House's phone number on the Internet the night after Megan's diagnosis. He'd read that Randall and his wife Marylyn had founded an advocacy group, the Acid Maltase Deficiency Association (AMDA) three years earlier, when their daughter was diagnosed with Pompe (also known as acid maltase deficiency in its adult form). Tiffany, now fifteen, had what was then known as the juvenile form of the disease. It was less severe than the infantile type, but she, too, wasn't expected to live into adulthood. Patients with the infantile form made virtually no enzyme correctly, but those with the juvenile and adult forms actually made between 1 and 40 percent of active enzyme themselves. Still, it wasn't enough, and glycogen built up sufficiently by adolescence or adulthood for symptoms to develop—usually weakness in the legs and lungs. Where the hearts of infants with Pompe were severely enlarged and usually failed by age two, juveniles and adults often started off with no cardiac problems. For them, the disease progressed more slowly, but over time they too had difficulty breathing and developed cardiac problems that led to early death.

The Houses owned a successful construction business in San Antonio, and they had used their personal fortune to finance the first conference for Pompe researchers in 1996, drawing top scientists and doctors from around the world to San Antonio.

"Yes, Mr. House. It's great to meet you," John said, looking up at him eagerly. "I would very much like to be involved with your group."

"Well, we would very much like your support," House said. "But the best thing for you to do right now is to look after your daughter here."

Slonim interrupted, asking John if Mr. House and Ans van der Ploeg, a physician and Pompe expert from the Netherlands, could remain in the room while he examined Megan. John and Aileen nodded.

"Do you mind?" he asked Aileen, reaching down to lift Megan out of the stroller.

"No—please," Aileen said, stepping back. Megan didn't resist as the doctor placed her in the middle of the conference table, surrounded by piles of papers. As Slonim and John pushed the papers to either end of the table, Aileen undressed her daughter. John glanced at the papers he was stacking. "Pharming Study Draft Protocol," he read on the cover of a document, eyes widening.

"Megan, can you lift your arms, please?" Slonim asked.

Megan, stripped down to her diaper, raised her arms, looking over at her mother and father.

"She's extraordinarily compliant," Slonim said to them.

"Yes, Doctor, she likes to show off how smart she is," John said with a laugh.

"Just like Daddy," Aileen tweaked him, relaxed enough now not to miss the opportunity to make fun of her husband.

"Ouch, Aileen," John said, wincing and chuckling. He winked at Megan. "But Mommy is right, isn't she, Megs?"

"Very good," Slonim said to Megan as she nodded in agreement with her father. "You are one smart little girl. Now, can you roll over?" he asked. Aileen put Megan on her stomach. Megan promptly flipped over onto her back.

The doctor pulled a stethoscope out of his briefcase, put it in his ears, and listened to Megan's lungs and heart, frowning slightly. She flinched at the coldness of the metal and looked up at her mother inquiringly. Slonim felt her stomach with gently splayed fingers. "Her liver is enlarged, as we would expect," he said, and made a note on a chart on the table.

"Let's move to the floor now," he said. "Let's see if she can crawl."

Murmuring encouragement in Megan's ear, Aileen gently lowered her onto the carpet. John set his daughter's Winnie the Pooh stuffed toy a few feet away. He held his breath, watching, as Megan rose slightly on all fours and pushed with her arms, sliding back a little. Her legs didn't move at all, and she began to cry.

"Oh, Megan," John said, picking her up and hugging her. "She can't crawl," he said, looking up at Slonim.

Aileen unclipped the Pooh pacifier that hung from Megan's jacket and popped it into her mouth, shushing her. There was nothing she could do about her daughter's wrenching weakness, but at least she could allow her maternal instincts to meet an immediate need.

"Is she able to swallow food?" the doctor asked.

Aileen nodded.

"Can I see her x-rays?" he said. John handed him the x-rays taken in California two weeks earlier.

Slonim beckoned to van der Ploeg and House to come over and look over his shoulder. "Notice on the outside that she's reasonably strong. But notice here the profound enlargement of the heart," he said in a low voice, his forefinger tracing the shape on the transparency. "It's lying on the lungs, which could very soon cause significant respiratory issues."

He pulled out chairs for John and Aileen. They sat down, Aileen dressing Megan on her lap as John questioned the doctor.

"Dr. Slonim, it's still so hard for us to believe Megan is sick. She looks so normal. Tell me, if you hadn't been told she had Pompe, would you have known just by looking at her?"

"John, I've got to tell you, she looks good," Slonim replied. "But there are the telltale signs for those of us who know. See how her face is a little bit flat and how her mouth is almost always open a little. And I bet you she doesn't smile much, if at all. This is all because her muscle tone is weak. And do you see how you can always see a little bit of her tongue when her mouth is open? All of our Pompe children look like this."

John stared silently at Megan, shaking his head, as Aileen pinned the pink bow back in her hair. Suddenly, everything about the way his daughter looked began to make sense. "We always wondered why she looked so serious and never seemed to smile," John said. "I've always called her our 'Serious Little Italian Princess.'"

"I used to say, 'Why won't you smile? I know you're happy,'" Aileen chimed in, kissing Megan's cheek. "To think it was just that she couldn't, at least not without a lot of effort."

"But here's the really good news," Slonim interjected. "I think there's a reasonable chance she doesn't have the classical form of Pompe or she wouldn't be this strong. I think she's one of those rare kids who have a hybrid form, between the classical and juvenile form. I'm calling it nonclassical infantile. I know that's a lot of words, but what it means is that you may have a little more time. Not much, but a little bit. With the right diet and nutrition, she could maintain her strength for some time. Many of these children live to be maybe five years old."

"That's very good news, Doctor," John said, elated to be told there were years—not just months—for Megan to get on one of those experimental medicines that might save her. Aileen nodded beside him.

"But even though your daughter is strong, she's susceptible to getting sick fast. She may get very sick in the next year. You need to get her as strong as you can.

"Look, it's very important that Megan receive adequate nutrition," he continued. "We should talk about having an operation performed on Megan to insert a tube in her stomach for supplemental feedings. It's called a gastrostomy. I recommend you do it as soon as possible."

The smiles disappeared from John's and Aileen's faces as they waited in silence for him to explain. They had been feeling relief to hear the doctor confirm his hunch that Megan had a less severe form of the disease. Time had never seemed so valuable, and he had just given them several more years with their daughter, but now he was suggesting something terribly invasive for a baby girl who had nothing visibly wrong with her. The only people they had heard of with stomach tubes were in comas in the intensive care unit.

"Trust me, she's not going to get any stronger," Slonim said kindly, reading accurately into their silence. "She's only going to get weaker over the next year. As her muscles weaken, she's not going to be able to swallow enough calories. You need to do everything you can to keep her strong so that she can survive respiratory infections that can take a heavy toll on children with the disease. And this is the first thing I would do.

"Look, John, I know it sounds drastic, but I strongly recommend it," the doctor continued. "I have a patient in upstate New York whose disease was rapidly progressive. We put a stomach tube in for feedings, and he's now much stronger because of it. Please—trust me."

The couple nodded somberly. Slonim seemed so knowledgeable and caring that they didn't doubt his words.

"When do we get it done? Where do we go?" Aileen asked, swallowing rapidly.

"You need to go see a gastroenterologist," he said. "I know a good one in New Jersey that I'll send you to. You'll be in good hands with him."

"What about your clinical trial, Doctor?" John asked, pointing at the documents on the table. "Could Megan be in your study?"

"It's too early to enroll patients," Slonim said, standing up. "There are still some technical issues we need to work through." He looked from the pile of papers on the table to Randall House and van der Ploeg, who stood together in the far corner. "We're still working out the design for the trial. We hope to get started this summer," he said. His smile filled John and Aileen with hope.

"And let me tell you this," he continued, his eyes resting on Megan, sitting quietly in Aileen's lap with her pacifier in her mouth. "If your daughter was going to have Pompe, this is a good time to be born with it."

5. God Doesn't Give You More Than You Can Handle

SPRING–SUMMER 1998

WALNUT CREEK, CALIFORNIA; RUMSON, NEW JERSEY

John and Aileen stood beside Megan's crib at home in Walnut Creek, watching their daughter sleep. Her room was small and cozy, painted a soft pink. The crib stood against the right wall, the sheets printed with pastel animal figures to match the mobile that swung lightly overhead. Megan lay on her left side, as always, breathing steadily.

"She looks so peaceful," John said, patting his daughter's back tenderly. "Other than the metal pole, you would never know she's sick."

They had arrived home from the doctors' visits out east and Easter with Aileen's parents, and within hours, a medical supply truck had driven up to drop off the IV pole that would hang Megan's feeding bag attached to her gastrostomy tube. She was still eating normally, but the supplemental feedings through the IV were supposed to make her stronger—or at least keep her from getting much weaker if she didn't get enough nutrition by mouth. They had taken Dr. Slonim's advice and had had a gastrostomy performed on Megan while they were still in New Jersey. Since then, a plastic bag of creamy formula had hung on the pole beside her bed every night, draining through a quarter-inch tube into the gastrostomy—the little hole in her stomach made by the surgeon, which closed with a stopper during the day.

"Let's go make some dinner," Aileen said, tugging John toward the door. Patrick and John Jr. were asleep in their rooms farther down the hall.

In the kitchen, Aileen boiled a pot of water and opened a box of pasta.

"It's cheap, easy, and delicious," she said with a laugh. John uncorked a bottle of red wine and poured himself a glass.

Both the kitchen and the dining room opened into the family room, and as John took a first sip, he stared at the spot on the carpet where only months earlier a fresh pine Christmas tree had stood.

"I can't believe we only have six or twelve more months before Megan gets really sick. It just doesn't make any damned sense," he said.

"You're right—she looks terrific. Beautiful and terrific," Aileen said quietly. She walked over and poured herself a glass of wine.

"Are you sure you want to drink that? You're still breast-feeding."

"It'll help Patrick sleep a little better," she said with a grin. "He's Irish. He can take it."

John relished the evenings when the children were asleep and he had Aileen to himself. There was so much on his mind that he couldn't express during the day when they were juggling the care of three children aged three and under.

"You know, she *is* weak compared to the other kids. Look at Patrick. He's not even two months old and he's stronger than she is. Something is wrong, that's for sure."

"Patrick is really strong," Aileen agreed noncommittally, her eyes fixed on the pasta as she drained it and divided it into two bowls. She wished John would talk about something besides Megan's health. She couldn't think about it all the time or she would drown in sorrow and fear. But John had been an endless talker and planner since the night she'd met him in 1984 at a friend's Halloween party. He was a senior in high school, dressed as a priest for the party. She, a junior, was too cool to wear a costume. "You never take a crap without coming up with a new plan," she would often tease in later years. She'd chosen Trinity College in Washington, D.C., in part so she could be close to John, who was at the Naval Academy in nearby Annapolis at the time. They'd both known they would marry, and she wasn't altogether surprised when John proposed to her several years later on the steps of the Lincoln Memorial, the night before he graduated from Georgetown University. John had worked in the men's department at

Bloomingdale's over the holidays, one of many part-time jobs he'd taken to save for the two-carat diamond he pulled out of his pants pocket. She watched that same diamond sparkle on her finger as she set the used pasta pot on the stove to clean later.

"You know, this winter we'll take Megan somewhere warm so we avoid the cold season. We've got to protect her until we're sure the medicine is here," he said, standing beside her now.

"John, I'm not going to shelter these kids," Aileen said, her tone gently challenging as she poured a jar of marinara sauce over each of the bowls. "Think about the other two. What kind of life is it for them with a sister who's locked in so she doesn't get a cold? That's no way for them to live."

"Well, I'm sure the medicine will be here before the winter anyway," John replied, sidestepping an argument. In the fifteen years they'd known each other, they had almost never fought, in part because Aileen was easygoing and avoided conflict, but also because John gave in on the areas that were considered her domain—the children, the home, their social life. "It may only be another month or two before she's in the clinical trial anyway. . . ." he said, his voice trailing off.

"Yeah, we'll see," Aileen said, carrying the bowls of pasta over to the kitchen table. "Let's sit down and eat and talk about something fun. What are we going to do this weekend?"

"You know, I think we need to go back to Duke and Long Island again soon," John continued, so preoccupied that he missed Aileen's obvious effort at diversion. "I want to make sure we're in their face—the squeaky wheel gets the grease. We need to be on the doctors' minds when they're deciding who gets in the clinical trials. People tell you things when you're in their physical presence that they won't tell you over the phone. Aileen, I think we should move back east."

"What about your job?" she asked, dropping her fork with a clatter, looking at him in shock. "We just moved out here eight months ago."

"I can commute back and forth."

"You know it's going to be hard going back and forth. I'm sure we can find good doctors out here," she said, leaning forward, eyes searching his face—now flushed red with intensity and emotion. Just how far along was he in this thinking? Once John embraced an idea, she knew it was almost impossible to change his mind.

"Maybe *good*, but I don't have time for *good*. I want the best for Megan," he said, a tremor in his voice. He reached across the table to hold Aileen's hand.

John's emotion moved Aileen, and her eyes filled with tears. Taking a deep breath, she squeezed John's hand and said, "Honey, I love you. Of course I want the best for Megan. Tell me what you think we should do."

"I think we need to move back east," he said, biting his lower lip in an effort to compose himself.

"Okay, then," she said. She straightened her shoulders and wiped her eyes with her napkin. "Let's just do it."

By the end of May, Aileen had flown east with the children and settled into her parents' brick five-bedroom house in Rumson, New Jersey. Even after their children were grown and had their own homes, Aileen's parents still bought big houses—the family was all to them. Most of the paintings on the walls were gilded portraits of their children and grandchildren. They wanted enough space so their three children—Aileen was the middle one, the only daughter—could all come and fit comfortably with their spouses and children on the holidays. Even with Aileen and the three kids, the Rumson house didn't seem overcrowded.

At her parents' house, Aileen could finally get some rest. Someone was always visiting and willing to lend a hand. Even better, poor John Jr.—who, as the oldest and healthiest, hadn't been getting as much attention as he would like—suddenly had four adults to fuss over him. Her brother, Marty Jr., lived outside Philadelphia, and showed up on many weekends to take little John out to McDonald's. Her dad spent hours lounging on the back deck with the boy, emptying the hot tub and letting him fill it up again with the garden hose. Some weekends, the whole family headed to the beach. On other Saturday afternoons, they invited friends and family over for barbecues. Aileen's parents were always ready to host a party, and Aileen, who was as extroverted and social as they were, enjoyed the distraction of the constant stream of people. Most of the time, she could pretend everything was okay.

John came only on weekends at first, spending his weeknights in their house in California, which was empty save for the master bedroom furniture and his clothes. But within a month or two, lonely and exhausted, he had persuaded his consulting firm to let him work out of its company's Stamford, Connecticut, office. That way, he could live with the family at Aileen's parents' house. He still had a long commute—two hours each way—but at least he wasn't flying across the country each week. He began looking in the employment section of the newspaper for jobs with shorter hours and offices closer to Rumson. He had never considered a job with a drug company, but the newspapers were full of advertisements for positions in the area; New Jersey was often referred to as the pharmaceutical capital of the world. Aileen's Aunt Sandra, who worked as a senior human re-sources executive at Bristol-Myers Squibb Company, got him an interview at the big drug-making company. Soon he had a second interview set up.[1]

At play dates and in the park, Aileen remembered Dr. Birnbaum's warning that each child stood a 25 percent chance of having Pompe dis-ease, and she constantly compared Patrick with other babies. Her stocky, blue-eyed baby looked easily stronger than babies a few months older. He nursed vigorously. He was able to put some weight on his chunky legs. She told herself that she didn't need to worry about this infant who looked and felt like a little wrestler.

In July, John scheduled follow-up visits with Dr. Slonim and Dr. Chen, whom they had seen after the appointment with Slonim on their first trip east following Megan's diagnosis. John told Aileen they needed to find out what was going on with the trials and make sure Megan was included. "We need to send the message that we're willing to be anywhere and every-where at a moment's notice," John insisted.

This time, their first visit was with Dr. Chen at Duke University Med-ical Center. Moving had depleted their bank account, and the best airline price John could find to Raleigh-Durham Airport was $800 a ticket. So in-stead of flying, they packed their Ford Expedition for the six-hour drive to North Carolina. They left little John at home and brought Patrick along so that Aileen could keep nursing him and her mother wouldn't have to take care of two kids.

It was a long, hot drive. They drove past the brick buildings of the U.S. Marine Corp base in Quantico, Virginia. John, seeing Patrick awake in the backseat, began to tell him about it.

"You know, Patrick, you're going to grow up to be big and strong like

Daddy and his daddy," he said. "Grandpa was a tough Marine. He was with the Second Force Recon. You know what that is, Patrick?"

"Sure he does, John. All four-month-olds know that," Aileen said, rolling her eyes.

"He's listening to me, Aileen," John said. "Look back there—I can see how his head is positioned. I can tell he's listening."

Patrick, his car seat facing the rear, was quiet. He had a habit of staring with his piercing blue eyes at whoever was talking, seeming to comprehend. John was sure he was listening now with the same infantile intensity, even though he couldn't see his daddy. Megan, beside him, was asleep in her forward-facing car seat, head flopped down on her chest, hands and arms outstretched.

"The Second Force Recon are the elite of the Marines, Patrick. They're the Special Forces. Your grandpa got a lot of bad guys. Your daddy used to wear a uniform and march around, too. I spent a week here at Quantico with the Marines one summer many years ago, shooting machine guns and jumping out of helicopters, when I was at the Naval Academy."

John fell silent then, as he always did when he talked about the Naval Academy. In part because his father had been a Marine, he often wished he'd stayed at the Academy instead of transferring to Georgetown after a year and a half. He had grown frustrated with the heavy load of math and science courses, and discouraged over being scheduled for a second tour at sea, this time over Christmas. John remembered the rush he used to feel at lunchtime as he raced from his room in Bancroft Hall, his forefinger feeling for the corner of his belt to make sure it was in line with his shirt, into the massive courtyard where five thousand plebes and upperclassmen stood at attention for their three-minute inspection. He had been a model midshipman.

"Patrick, you know, a life in the military may be more meaningful than anything else for you," he said after a time. "It may be more meaningful than anything your daddy can do with his Harvard MBA."

"Oh, John," Aileen said, rubbing his shoulder. She, more than almost anyone else, knew how much he'd struggled over his decision to leave the Academy. Even though John's father had died when John was in second grade, he had instilled in his son the belief that part of a truly rewarding life involved serving your country in the military. John wanted to impart the same deep sense of respect in his children for those who had sacrificed in America's wars. Maybe his sons would carry on the military tradition that had somehow skipped a generation.

"In twenty-one years, Patrick, you will be Second Lieutenant Patrick Francis Crowley, an officer of the Marines," John said grandly. "Then you'll make your daddy and grandpa very proud."

They arrived on the first Thursday of the month, which was clinic day for Dr. Chen. The large waiting room was full of children with genetic disorders, the doctor's specialty. Aileen and John stood in line to check in, parking the double stroller so that it faced them, Megan in front, Patrick behind her. Aileen turned around and saw a brown-haired boy in a stroller behind them who looked eerily familiar. His face was a little flat and almost entirely expressionless. His mouth didn't close completely and his tongue protruded a little. She looked up at the parents and saw that they were staring at Megan with the same look of recognition. It was the first time John and Aileen had seen another child with Pompe disease.

"We're here to see Dr. Chen," Aileen said, smiling at the couple.

"You're seeing Dr. Chen? So are we," said the boy's mother. "I'm Debbie Walter. This here is my husband Bo, and this is our Joseph." She smiled down at her son. She said they had come up from Pinson, Alabama, for three-year-old Joseph to be examined.

Aileen and John checked in, and then waited by the counter while the Walters finished. The couples walked together to the waiting area.

"When was Joseph diagnosed?" Aileen asked.

"A year ago," said Mrs. Walter. "It's been really hard on us because our eldest son was killed in a car accident a couple of years ago."

Aileen was stunned, and her eyes glazed over. "Oh my, I am so sorry," she whispered. John shook his head and said he was sorry too. All it took was one conversation with someone in a worse position to help you stop feeling bad for yourself.

"Is that your younger one?" Mrs. Walter asked, trying to see behind Megan in her denim Mermaid jacket, her Winnie the Pooh pacifier in her mouth.

"Yes, that's Patrick back there. Our poor little redheaded 'stepchild,'" Aileen said, joking about how often her easygoing baby was forgotten.

"He's so quiet and such a good baby. We also have an older boy, John, who's home with Nana—that's my mother."

"How are the other two doing?" Mrs. Walter asked. "Any symptoms of—?"

"They're both fine," Aileen said quickly.

"That's good, because we've talked on the phone to other families with the disease. Sometimes the siblings have it too," Mrs. Walter said.

"Megan Crowley," the receptionist called out. The couples exchanged phone numbers and promised to talk by phone in a few days.

Dr. Chen was as warm and deliberate in his exam as he had been on their last visit. He checked Megan's gastrostomy and did what they now knew was the routine Pompe exam. He asked Megan to raise her hands. He put her on her stomach and she flipped over. She did everything he asked eagerly, eyes watching him. She didn't seem measurably weaker. He made a few notes and was ready to say good-bye when his eyes fell on Patrick, who was sitting in Aileen's lap.

"How's the little boy?" he asked.

"He's very strong," John said.

"He eats very well, and look at his legs," Aileen said, pulling up one of his pant legs to reveal a fat calf.

"While he's here, if it's okay, I'd like to do a blood test to rule out Pompe disease," Chen said.

"I don't think it's necessary, Doctor," John said, remembering how Megan had shrieked when she'd had blood taken. "Patrick's so strong and so healthy—he's very different from Megan, who was always weak."

"Let's test him, just for peace of mind," Chen said, gently but firmly.

Aileen nodded, and John relented. She held Patrick as a nurse drew blood. John turned the conversation to the main reason he'd brought Megan back for a checkup.

"So Doctor, how is the clinical study looking?" John asked.

The doctor frowned, and he shook his head.

"The CHO had a bad run," he said.

"What's that?" John asked, wondering if the doctor was using a Chinese word. Chen spoke with a strong Chinese accent.

"These are the cells that we grow the enzyme in," Chen said. "They are originally taken from Chinese hamsters' ovaries, so we call them CHO for short. Unfortunately, we're having lots of trouble with them."

John pressed for more details and found Chen to be a patient explainer of science. He told John that the enzyme was made in giant bioreactors by the CHO cells. John remembered reading about this on the Internet the night after Megan's diagnosis, but he hadn't understood how the process worked. These cells acted like little factories, churning out the missing Pompe enzyme, acid alpha-glucosidase. The process had been used for about a decade, since scientists had discovered that cells culled from the ovaries of this breed of hamsters not only multiplied quickly in a test tube, but also produced enzymes and other kinds of proteins that seemed to work effectively in humans.

Chen told John the manufacturing process was still very tricky—as much an art as a science. The cells had to be grown carefully in a sterile environment. The smallest mistake could contaminate the product and force scientists to begin the three-month-long process of producing protein all over again.

"That's what had happened to the company in California making enzyme for us," Chen said. "Bacteria got inside; maybe from the air handling, maybe from not being cleaned right. It happens all the time." He cleared his throat and shrugged. "Either way, unfortunately, we can't start without that enzyme. We won't be going into trials anytime soon."

Aileen looked down, quiet. The thought that things could go wrong when famous doctors at big-name hospitals were working on something had never occurred to her.

Two days later, the phone rang at Aileen's parents' house. It was Dr. Chen. Aileen, biting her lip, her face pale, stepped into her father's study to take the call. Like the rest of her parents' house, the walls of her father's study were crowded with gold-framed family pictures. Aside from the big wooden desk in the center and a few books on the shelves, the rest of the study was all snapshots of the children and grandchildren.

As she picked up the phone, Aileen noticed her mother standing outside the door. Needing privacy, she felt the urge to hang up the phone and call the doctor back, but she knew she needed to know what the doctor had to say even more urgently.

Chen greeted Aileen in a quiet, concerned voice. He asked how the children were doing. "Fine, Dr. Chen," she replied. Then, without fanfare, he told her he regretted to report that Patrick's blood test had come back showing a high level of the same enzyme Megan's did—CPK, or creatinine phosphokinase.

"But, Mrs. Crowley, I don't want you to think too much until we do another blood test," he continued. He didn't have enough blood from the sample taken to be certain the results were accurate. He asked Aileen to take Patrick to a clinic nearby to have a second blood sample taken and sent to Duke for a confirmatory test.

"I'm really sorry to bring this bad and confusing news," he said.

Aileen didn't ask a single question. She thanked him, hung up, and put her head on the desk. Behind her, she felt her mother stoop to put her arms around her and hug her tightly, but Aileen pushed her away in defiant disbelief. How could this be happening? Chen had said the results weren't reliable, but she knew that was just to cushion the blow. She knew they were. Her son Patrick had Pompe disease, too.

John was at his desk at Marakon in Stamford, Connecticut, when the phone rang.

"You're not going to believe this," Aileen said. It was how she began many conversations, prefacing what she had to say with a question or a dare for him to guess what the news might be. Her voice, normally so cheerful and sweet, sounded distant and rough, almost angry.

"Dr. Chen just called," she said. "They got the bloodwork on Patrick. It looks like he has it too."

John sat at his desk for a few minutes after hanging up. Everything had stopped. Everything had changed. He needed time—time to help his family. No more late nights at work. No more getting phone calls at his office two hours away from home. He picked up the phone and called the senior partner. They exchanged small talk, but John got quickly to the point. "For family reasons, I've decided Marakon is not the best place for me."

"I understand," came the measured response. John had told this partner and others about Megan's dire prognosis to get the transfer to the Stamford office. "I'm disappointed, but I understand your family situation. When do you plan on leaving?"

"Two weeks," John said without apology. He thought about telling this man the crushing news he'd just heard about Patrick, but he couldn't.

Driving home that night, John remembered his mother saying, "God doesn't give you more than you can handle." Well, she couldn't have been more wrong. She'd told him many times that because he'd experienced such a terrible loss as a child with the death of his father, he could count on the rest of his life being easy. It was unexplainable and inconceivable, John thought, that a loving God could ask any man, any family, to bear this death sentence that had just been handed down on a second child.

He walked in the front door and found Patrick alone in the living room on his mechanical swing. John pressed the stop button, picked up the baby, and held him high over his head. The baby opened his mouth and smiled, a fishing line of drool bobbing in the air above John's face.

"You, little buddy, are not going to get sick," John whispered. "No way you get sick."

6. The Road to Power and Influence

During the summer of 1998, with Megan and Patrick strong, playful, and looking to everyone else like perfectly healthy kids, John and Aileen could consciously ignore the disease. There was so much to do. John focused on his job search, and, after a series of interviews, accepted a $120,000-a-year position as a director at Bristol-Myers. He was thrilled with the salary and the expectation of working eight to ten hours each day, seemingly a vacation compared to the demands of consulting. He liked the idea of running a business group, and the job at Bristol-Myers put him in a lead role in marketing neuroscience drugs. He and Aileen began to look at houses for sale close to Bristol-Myers's headquarters in Princeton.

Aileen spent almost every minute of the day feeding, bathing, and playing with the children. She would leave one kid at home with her mom and take the other two to the neighborhood pool or the park, making sure they all got a chance to get out of the house each day. It was little John Jr., now three years old, who took most of her energy. He was unfocused and hyperactive. She couldn't put a bowl of Cheerios in front of him and expect him to eat three consecutive spoonfuls. No sooner did she turn around to get a cup of juice than he had jumped up and was halfway up the stairs to his bedroom. If she left him alone in the bath for five seconds to get an extra towel out of the closet, she'd find him running through the house naked and wet. She wondered aloud to her mother how she had managed to take care of him and the two younger ones on her own before they left Walnut Creek, and told John she didn't know how she was going to handle all three when they eventually moved out of her parents' house. He took her worry as a call to action and immediately filled out an application for an au pair in a program he had seen advertised.

At night, John continued to search for information on Pompe disease in his father-in-law's silent study, with only the silver-blue glow of the screen lighting his way. He reached into the dark portals of the Internet for any new hope. He regularly checked Randall House's patient group website, which seemed to be updated frequently with news of the Pompe world.

One night, John found a new press release on the site. It was two pages long and announced a partnership between Pharming and Genzyme, the Cambridge, Massachusetts, company that sold a drug for the related Gaucher disease and was one of the most successful biotechnology firms in the world. Henri Termeer, the chief executive, was quoted as saying, "We are very excited about working with Pharming to develop this potentially lifesaving treatment." The release also said that Pharming would be starting a clinical trial later that year.

The name Genzyme sounded familiar to John, and he realized that it was because the company had had a palatial brick manufacturing plant across the street from his Harvard dorm. Through Genzyme's website, he found that it employed five thousand people and had a stock market value of about $2 billion.

"It can only be good news if a big company is interested in Pompe disease," he said aloud in the dark room. He saw the deal as an endorsement of Pharming's experimental Pompe medicine and a sign of hope for his children.

If Megan's and Patrick's lives were to be saved, they needed to get into the clinical trial that the press release spoke about. On the Harvard Business School website, he searched for fellow graduates working at Genzyme or Pharming, hoping for an opportunity to leverage his membership in the Ivy League elite to help his children. The network of graduates extended into almost every major corporation. Sure enough, he found fifteen graduates at Genzyme, but didn't recognize any of the names. Pharming, far smaller with just about a hundred employees, had none.

John remembered that when he met Dr. Slonim in that hotel conference room, he had been introduced to a Pharming executive named Gerben Moolhuizen, and he had saved the man's business card. John fished it out of his briefcase now, wondering if Moolhuizen was senior enough to be making decisions on whom to include in Pharming's upcoming clinical trial. Megan and Patrick had to be in that trial. He needed to push their case with whoever was in charge at Pharming, even if that meant going to the Netherlands—a place he had never been to, much less thought about.

At his desk at work the next day, John called Slonim and asked what he thought of the idea of traveling to the Netherlands. "Sure, John, I think you should go over and see what's going on for yourself," Slonim said. "You never know what can come out of a trip. I went there myself last year, and look at the result—I'm going to be running Pharming's trials in the United States."

John hung up and pulled out a legal pad and began to draft a letter in longhand. "We met at the Inn at Great Neck where Dr. Slonim was examining my daughter, Megan," he wrote. "I have since learned that my son Patrick also has Pompe disease, and I would like to learn as much as possible about the treatments being developed. I am interested in traveling to the Netherlands next week to visit with you and tour your facilities." He put the pen down. This company was probably flooded with letters like his from desperate parents seeking to cozy up to company officials and get their child in the next trial. He needed to do something to distinguish himself.

Then he thought of Randall at the head of the conference table, with Moolhuizen and Slonim designing the clinical trial. What separated Randall from John and every other parent? The answer was obvious—Randall was the head of a patient group. He was a wealthy person who had personally funded a research conference for scientists working on Pompe disease.

Money, John thought. It always came down to money.

He picked up the pen, drew a line through the page he had written and flipped it over, beginning anew. "I am chairman of the recently formed Children's Pompe Foundation," he wrote. "Our goal is to raise $1 million over the next several months. . . . I would like to learn more about your technology and planned clinical trials and discuss with you in detail the various ways in which the Children's Pompe Foundation may advance the efforts of your company."

It really wasn't a lie, he told himself. He and his father-in-law had talked late one night over a bottle of wine about starting their own foundation to raise money for the disease. They'd even downloaded the requisite tax form from the Internet. He intended to start a foundation, and he would. He stared at a picture on his desk that Aileen had framed for him of the three children: Megan looking like Pebbles from the Flintstones, her hair in a ponytail on top of her head; chubby Patrick, his eyes wide and angelic; and John Jr. with his huge, manic grin. John had never known that he could love anything so much as he loved his children—as he *had* loved them since the day they were born. How far would he go to save them?

He stood up, tentatively, to take the letter to his secretary to type— and then a troubling thought pushed him back into his seat. Was it really right to be claiming to be head of a foundation that didn't yet exist? Was that how he, John Crowley, son of a cop, formerly a star student at the Naval Academy, a lawyer by training, an executive at a big drug company, should comport himself?

And then he realized that he really didn't care whether he was being completely forthright with Pharming. This was not about making sure you obeyed the rules so you advanced up the ranks at the Naval Academy. Slonim had painted a grim picture of how weak and sick the children would get over the next year unless there was some intervention. Nobody else was going to make sure Megan and Patrick were chosen when the clinical trial was ready to start. There was no one else to count on, no one who would save his kids. And without that experimental medicine, his children would die.

John walked briskly to his secretary's desk and handed her the letter. In a few minutes, she was back, sliding the typewritten draft in front of him. John read it over and jotted a few corrections. "Here's the phone number in the Netherlands—please fax this right away," he told her.

The very next day, Moolhuizen was on the phone suggesting dates for a trip. John's instinct had been correct. Drug companies pay attention to patient groups. They can help companies by paying for vital research, influencing politicians, and prevailing upon the FDA to approve a drug more quickly.

Before John left for the Netherlands, there was one more phone call he had to make: to the House family.

It wouldn't be an easy conversation. John knew that Randall felt his own foundation, AMDA, was doing everything possible to further research on Pompe. What he didn't know was that Randall was very close to getting his own daughter, Tiffany, a place in Pharming's upcoming trial. Having spent three years courting Pharming's senior management, Randall was loath to let this brash new kid—in some ways, he thought, a younger version of himself—stride in and endanger all he'd done to save Tiffany.[1]

Now, on the phone, John described his plans for the Children's Pompe Foundation—for all intents and purposes a competing organization. Even though he knew Randall would be unenthusiastic, he hadn't anticipated the depth of his antipathy toward the idea.[2]

"It's not a smart idea, and I don't like it at all," the older man responded. The AMDA was already leading the charge; for another organization to come along now would just muddy the waters—and possibly divert funding and attention away from the AMDA. "What you're suggesting is a waste of time and money," Randall told John, his voice cold. "It's best just to take care of your kids."

"We don't want to compete with you," John said, trying to assure him that they wouldn't be working at cross-purposes. "We just want to raise money from our family and friends, and if our family is in the forefront, we can do a better job of that."

"I think it's a bad idea," Randall repeated in a clipped tone.

After a few more back and forths, it became clear that neither man was going to bring the other around. "Well, Randall, I'm sorry you feel this way," John said politely but defiantly as he brought the conversation to a close. "We each have to make our own choices, do what's best for our families, and starting a foundation is what's best for Megan and Patrick. So that's what I'm going to do."

John hung up, wondering if he'd made the right choice.

*   *   *

A week later, John flew to Amsterdam. Aside from his travels in the Navy, he had made only one trip out of the country—a week's vacation in Italy, given to them by Aileen's parents right after he graduated from law school. It had been easy to get around because he spoke some Italian, but he had never been to a country where he didn't speak the language.

To his relief, virtually everyone in Holland spoke English. Pharming sent a small Mercedes to his hotel to pick him up. As a lover of cars, John was impressed—until he noticed that every cab they passed was also a Mercedes. The driver headed out into the countryside on an hour-long drive south past farms, each with a windmill and carpets of farmland.

Then the car pulled into the driveway of a concrete building with a small sign bearing Pharming's name.

"I'm so sorry to hear about Patrick," said Moolhuizen, a tall, bespectacled man about John's age, as they sat down in his office. He said Pharming planned to file paperwork within the next month seeking government approval to start clinical trials in Europe and the United States. The preclinical trials, done in animals, had already been completed.[3]

"The results are brilliant," he said, handing John two eight-by-eleven glossy white pictures showing microscopic photographs of tissue samples stained purple and dark pink.

"This first picture is the muscle fibers of a mouse with Pompe disease before receiving Pharming's treatment enzyme," he explained. "The big purple pools that fill most of the page are glycogen that has overrun the muscle. In the second picture, after the mouse has been treated with our enzyme, see how the purple pools have receded into small circles."

John, looking from one picture to the next, saw that the smaller purple pools had been replaced with reddish strands. "Those are healthy muscle fibers," Moolhuizen said, pointing at the ribbon-like swirls.

John looked up from the pictures, smiling. "When do you think you'll be starting clinical trials?"

"If all goes well, very soon," Moolhuizen said. "We are planning to begin in the next few months. We have only a small amount of enzyme, so the first patients to be treated will be babies under a year old who need less of the enzyme. We want to treat everyone, but we just don't have enough of the enzyme."

John's smile disappeared as he absorbed what Moolhuizen had just said. If the trial was only for babies younger than a year old, that meant that Megan, now one and a half, would not qualify to participate.

Before he could protest, Moolhuizen was telling him the two test tubes held upright in a small wooden stand on his desk were samples of the company's enzyme treatment.

"Take a look," he said, handing one of the tubes to John.

The phone rang, and Moolhuizen picked it up, swiveling his chair away. John held the test tube, staring at the clear liquid in the bottom, overwhelmed at the thought that he was holding the substance that would save his children's lives.

He looked up at Moolhuizen, who was still engrossed in his telephone conversation. Suddenly, the impulse to slide the test tube casually into his pocket overwhelmed him. If he stuffed one in his pocket, would Moolhuizen notice? Or maybe he should take both—one for Megan and one for Patick. The room seemed suddenly too hot, and his tie and jacket too tight.

But almost immediately, reason returned to him, and he remembered reading that the enzyme wasn't a one-shot cure. Patients needed to be given the enzyme in infusions every few weeks, probably for a lifetime. He might be able to steal a couple of vials, but where would he get the next dose? He reached over and stuck the test tube back in the holder.

As Moolhuizen finished his conversation and put the phone down, John's mind took another leap. What if the foundation he was going to start paid for a clinical trial in older children, like Megan, with the non-classical form of the disease? That would ensure that there was a trial for Megan to get treatment.

"At the foundation, we're close to raising a million dollars for research," he said. The words slipped out of him without hesitation. "We'd be willing to help fund a clinical trial in children with the nonclassical form, children who are a little bit older." He hadn't, of course, raised a cent yet. But as with his letter telling Moolhuizen about the new foundation, John felt no guilt as he described the results of fund-raising he hadn't yet done. He was certain now that he'd said the words that he would go home and begin fund-raising, although he wasn't sure how he would raise a million bucks—it seemed like an enormous, almost mythic amount of money. But he pushed the thought to the back of his mind; he would figure that out later.

"I'll talk to my people here about that," Moolhuizen replied, his eyes lighting up.

Later that afternoon, a car drove Moolhuizen and John south toward Geel, Belgium, where Pharming was building a new manufacturing plant to make the Pompe enzyme. After a long drive, they pulled up to an industrial park where Pharming occupied the second floor of a sleek building. Moolhuizen led John inside to a sterile changing area, and helped him pull on a white cotton jumpsuit, booties, and a shower cap. Moolhuizen covered himself in the same getup. It was the kind of gear that brought to mind the sterile laboratories in movies where lifesaving medicines and vaccines were made—laboratories just like the one he stood in now. Finally, John thought, he was entering the world where his children's medicine was being created, and becoming an insider like Randall House.

Moolhuizen led him through one fluorescent-lit room after another, filled with metal tables covered with laboratory equipment. Then the two men entered a room with a freezer. Moolhuizen opened it and pointed to a block of frozen milk about the size of John's microwave oven at home. Moolhuizen said it was taken from the thousands of rabbits that his company milked every Monday. It would be thawed and purified to remove the acid alpha-glucosidase enzyme.

"The bodies of animals and humans work using the same system of chemical messengers, called enzymes," Moolhuizen explained. "But you can't treat humans missing the acid alpha-glucosidase enzyme simply by removing it from rabbits and injecting it into humans."

The rabbit enzyme, Moolhuizen continued, was different enough that the human body would identify it as a foreign substance and mount an immune response. So in each of the rabbits, scientists had added the human gene responsible for making acid alpha-glucosidase, so that the rabbits made predominantly human acid alpha-glucosidase. He said Pharming would have preferred to make the enzyme in cows because they're easier to milk, but they also take longer to mature. The scientists chose rabbits because they mature and multiply so quickly.

In another room, Moolhuizen showed John a big, winding glass-and-metal apparatus that he said was the purification system where the rabbit milk was slowly heated and evaporated so that only the enzyme remained. The process, from milking to purifying out the enzyme, took three days.

After they had changed back out of their white jumpsuits, Moolhuizen led John outside through a muddy field to a fifty-thousand-square-foot concrete slab surrounded by construction trailers. Standing in the middle of the slab, gesturing to one side, he said that half of the building would be used to house ten thousand rabbits. The other side would hold the laboratories, freezers, and purification equipment. Within six months, he said, the building would be finished and, soon after, Pharming would have enough enzyme to supply the world's Pompe patients.

Moolhuizen led John into one of the construction trailers to meet his boss, Rein Strijker, managing director of Pharming's Belgium operations. Strijker, wearing a dark suit and red tie, sat at a chair in front of a long, gleaming wooden conference table. After the introductions and handshakes, he leaned his chair back and asked, "So, Mr. Crowley, how can I be of assistance?"

"I understand Pharming intends to begin a clinical trial soon but only in infants," John said eagerly. "I run a family foundation and I am willing to fund a trial in older children with the nonclassical form of the disease."

Strijker sat up in his seat and said, "That would be of interest to us. How much money have you raised so far?"

"I have commitments for several hundred thousand dollars," John said, nodding rapidly, hoping he sounded convincing. "Within six months, I expect to have a lot more. My target is $1 million."

Strijker sat back and said, "Well, that's very interesting, John. Let's speak again when you reach your target."[4]

7. Megan

John was back at his desk at Bristol-Myers in the early evening of Monday, September 14, when Aileen called. Megan was breathing heavily, and a pediatrician had said she should go to the emergency room. John promised to meet her there.

He had returned from the Netherlands to a hectic schedule at Bristol-Myers. He was absorbing volumes of information on a group of antibiotics, antianxiety medicines, and antidepressants, which he played a major role in marketing. He had flown to San Diego for a meeting of the company's regional marketing directors, where he proposed a standardized way to write their business plans for next year. The directors, most much older than he and with a lot more experience in the pharmaceutical industry, received his proposal with skepticism. But his boss, Brian Markison, had embraced the plan and put John in charge of implementing it. It was the most immersed in work that John had felt in a long time. It would be a challenge getting all of those sales and marketing directors to change the way they operated. The deadline was a little tight, but not overwhelming—just enough to get his adrenaline going. By September 30, he needed to pull all of the regional plans together into a single comprehensive proposal for the pharmaceutical business.[1]

John climbed into his old Volvo sedan and drove east on Route 195 toward Monmouth Medical Center. It would take an hour to get there in this old car that couldn't drive over sixty miles an hour without rattling. Megan had had a cold all weekend, but it hadn't seemed like anything serious. Was their pediatrician overreacting?

As John rolled down the window, he remembered that he hadn't yet filled out the forms to start the Children's Pompe Foundation. Besides his job, he'd been absorbed in the paperwork involved with buying the house he and Aileen had finally settled on, a four-bedroom colonial on a cul-de-sac in a new development in Pennington, a town adjacent to Princeton. He couldn't afford to delay any longer with the foundation papers. As had happened today, a health problem could erupt with Megan at any time. He needed to get his foundation going so Megan could get into a clinical trial before she got really sick. As soon as he got home tonight, he vowed, he would get the forms finished.

He found Megan on an exam table in the emergency room, a big blue bow in her hair. She saw her dad and began to cry, pointing at her left big toe, to which a clip had been attached for measuring the level of oxygen in her blood. It pinched and she wanted it off. A doctor came in and read the oxygen level. He said it was 20 percent below normal. He carried an x-ray in one hand that he clipped onto a fluorescent-lit screen in the corner. "Your daughter has pneumonia," he said, pointing to a darkish area in the picture of her lungs.

John and Aileen looked across the room at one another. They knew pneumonia was dangerous for any child, and it could only be worse for a child with a muscle-weakening disease. "As a precautionary measure, I would recommend we admit her," the doctor said.

Within hours, Megan was settled into a room on the pediatric floor. A small tube under her nose brought a steady stream of oxygen, easing her breathing. Under her blue pajamas, three heart monitors were taped to her chest. A nurse had attached an IV tube to the top of her left hand. After screaming with each stab of the needle, she was now calmly sitting up in bed watching Barney on TV.

That night, and for the next three nights, Aileen slept on the pull-out chair in Megan's room. By Thursday, three days after she was admitted, Megan seemed better, and her doctor suggested discharging her with a tank of oxygen to support her breathing for another couple of days. But by 5 P.M., the hospital still didn't have the insurance company's approval to pay for the oxygen tank for home use, and her doctor delayed releasing her for another day. John volunteered to spend Friday night at the hospital.

Megan fell asleep early that evening, and John settled into the chair to read. He was in the middle of a Tom Clancy book—*Executive Orders*—about a terrorist crashing a jetliner into the Capitol and killing the president. John carried a book with him wherever he went, mostly action novels, war stories, or history. In a few minutes, he grew too tired to read further. He switched on the TV to watch *20/20*, and then drifted off to sleep.

All through the night, beeping awakened him. Every time Megan moved, the heart monitor seemed to go off. At about 4:30 A.M., he heard beeping again, and then louder alarms. He sat up and looked in Megan's direction. She was half-seated, her arms waving. John jumped up to her bedside and saw she had vomited and was choking. On the monitors, the numbers showed that her heart rate was racing and her oxygen saturation plunging. He tried in vain to find the call button, and then ran into the dark hallway, shouting, "Help, help! Is anyone there? Please help!"

Megan's room was in the middle of the pediatric floor, about six doors down from the nursing station. In a few seconds, a nurse came into the room, looked at Megan—now unconscious—and ran back into the hallway screaming, "Somebody help! I need help!"

Several other nurses, an intern, and the pediatric resident appeared in quick succession. The resident, a slight Asian-American woman, stuck a finger into Megan's throat, trying to clear her airway, but the little girl still didn't breathe. The resident put a mask over Megan's face and began to squeeze the Ambu bag (a self-reinflating bag used during resuscitation), to force air into the little girl's lungs.

"Let's get her to the PICU," she snapped. The medical team and John pushed Megan's bed down the hallway as the resident ran beside the bed, squeezing the Ambu bag continuously to keep her breathing. The wheels screeched loudly, drawing black marks all the way down the hallway from Megan's room to the pediatric intensive care unit. In their haste, the team had forgotten to unlock the wheels. Megan remained unconscious, her face gray and her lips blue.

The PICU was a big room with a central nursing station and two beds on each side. It was empty. A nurse lifted Megan onto the first bed on the right, and the resident directed the other nurses to give her one shot after another. On the heart monitor, John could see that Megan's heart was racing and slowing and racing and slowing.

"Call Dr. Hofley," the resident said to one of the nurses as she continued to pump the Ambu.

John wanted to call Aileen, but he didn't dare leave Megan's bedside. For the next half hour, the nurses and resident struggled to stabilize Megan's heart and breathing. John stood a few feet back from Megan's bed, silently praying that she wouldn't die. He thought about how she had been fine the four nights Aileen stayed with her. Would Aileen blame him for not being attentive enough to prevent this from happening on the one night he was in charge? How could this even be happening when the hospital had been ready to discharge her the day before?

Finally, Dr. Marc Hofley appeared at the bedside. "Tell me what's going on," he said with quiet authority. The faces of the resident and nurses instantly calmed. Hofley was a pediatrician with specialty training in pediatric critical care medicine, and he oversaw the children's intensive care units at the hospital. With short brown hair and small square glasses, he looked to be John's age and stood not an inch taller, but the respect he commanded was evident from the second he walked into the room.[2]

"We need to intubate her," he said, indicating that they needed to put a breathing tube down Megan's throat. The resident and nurses had tried unsuccessfully to intubate Megan several times before he arrived.

Then Hofley noticed John standing in the corner and came over to him. "I'm going to need to ask you to leave while we intubate her and put in some special lines," he said kindly. John nodded, feeling relief that a doctor who seemed so capable had arrived. He desperately wanted to call Aileen.

From the pay phone outside the PICU, John telephoned Aileen's parents' house. Aileen's dad, Marty, who was preparing to go golfing, picked up.

"Dad, we've got a real problem here," John said, his voice strained. He told Marty what had happened. "I don't know if she's going to make it," John finished. Marty didn't ask any questions. He would wake Aileen and drive her over, he said.

John positioned himself outside the doors of the PICU, peeking in the small window. Megan, still surrounded by nurses, remained on the bed, naked and unconscious, a tube or monitor attached to every limb. "Please, please, Megan, don't die," he said softly. "C'mon, Megs, don't let go." He felt dizzy and nauseous, and realized he was sweating. He took off his sweater and set it on a chair, and began to pace up and down the corridor, empty except for him.

When he looked in the window again, the nurses were still rushing around Megan. He noticed that she filled only the top quarter of the bed. Was she in pain? Was she suffering? It was unbearable to think of anything hurting his tiny daughter. "Dear God, please don't let her suffer," he began to pray, his nose pressed against the window. He remembered the certainty with which Dr. Slonim had described how quickly she would weaken over the next year. Maybe it was better that she should die now rather than endure more suffering.

It was the hardest thing he'd ever said, but he forced the words through his numbed lips: "God, please don't let her suffer anymore. If death is inevitable, let it come."

With a start, he realized he couldn't see Megan any longer. He was crying so hard the window had fogged. He wiped the window with a handkerchief and began pacing the corridor again.

Even if death was best for Megan, how would Aileen ever endure the loss? As husband and father, as the parent who was *there*, he'd have to be the one to tell her. What could he say that wouldn't break her already battered heart? Should he say, "Honey, Megan died this morning—there was nothing you, or anyone, could have done"? Just thinking the words made him ache with misery. Maybe he would say, "Honey, Megan loved you very much, and you did everything you could, and now she's at peace." Would he even be able to get a single word out when he saw Aileen's face?

From his years as a devout Catholic, John looked in his heart for what he could hang on to now. He'd been an altar boy. He still had the second grade CCD book he'd used in preparing for First Communion the year his dad had died. He'd kept his religious faith in the face of that monumental loss—or perhaps because of it.

John had continued going to Mass each day as a freshman at Georgetown. At Harvard, he continued to attend daily, finding in the ceremony of

Mass that sense of peace and space for reflection that was absent in the rush of life. These days, he'd been stopping at St. Paul's Church in Princeton at 6:45 each morning on his way to work. The priest there, Monsignor, Nolan, had lost his wife and newborn child years earlier during childbirth, and John felt he could relate to personal loss.

What would happen to Megan if she died? Mass or no Mass, John had to admit he didn't really know if there was a heaven—but he believed. He believed because he wanted to believe, and because he was certain there was a force at work in the world, something bigger and better than ourselves.

"God chose you for a reason," many people would later say as they tried to understand how John and Aileen ended up with two children with such a dreadful disease. John would nod agreeably, but in truth, he didn't believe God had had that strong a hand in causing the children's sickness. He'd read somewhere that nature wasn't cruel, just brutally random, and he believed there was truth in that statement. Religion was about how you lived that life you'd been randomly given. It was, he believed, about choosing to do things that are good, even when life delivers the worst.

When Aileen arrived, Hofley and his team were still struggling to keep Megan alive. Hofley came out of the emergency room and asked Aileen and John to wait down the hall in the room where Megan had spent the past few days.

"The next couple of hours are critical," the doctor said tensely. "You need to be prepared that there's a good chance Megan may not live through the morning."

Aileen sat nervously between her father and John, unsure how she was supposed to prepare. Her eyes were red-rimmed, but dry. She didn't know what to think. She didn't even want to think. She found herself just waiting for something to happen. Hofley appeared every so often over the next few hours to tell them he was still working on Megan and that she remained unstable.

John excused himself and went back to the pay phone. He wanted to tell his mother and his brother Joe what was going on. He reached Joe at the police station in Baltimore where he worked. As he began to talk, he began to cry. He couldn't stop. Joe, accustomed to being the one supported by his older brother, struggled to find words of comfort. "I'm so sorry, John. I'm so sorry," he repeated.

At about noon, Hofley showed up again. This time, the lines around his mouth had smoothed and the intensity in his soft voice had been replaced by resignation, as if he had endured a long battle that had ended. John was just not sure *how* it had ended. He wanted to ask, but he was afraid to know the answer, so he waited, holding his breath, for what the doctor would say.

"I know this has been a long, difficult few hours," Hofley said when he finally spoke. "And I am very pleased to be telling you that your daughter is now stable. Come, I'll take you to visit her. I've given her a drug to temporarily paralyze her because when she regained consciousness, she started pulling at the breathing tubes and resisting the breathing support.

"Your daughter is some little fighter," he added softly, shaking his head and looking from John to Aileen. "I wish she would just close her eyes and rest, but she's determined to stay awake."

As they entered the PICU, John and Aileen saw Megan lying on her back, her eyes open, scanning the room. Her eyes settled on them and immediately filled with tears. Aileen rushed over to kiss her.

John, still incredulous that Megan had lived through the morning, rubbed her matted hair gently. "All right, kid," he said, staring gravely into her big dark eyes. "If you want to fight, we'll fight, too."

For the next few weeks, Megan battled what Dr. Hofley diagnosed as a staph infection that she must have picked up since being admitted to the hospital. The infection had turned into sepsis, a condition that is often fatal because the organs in the body shut down. Hospital rules prohibited people from sleeping in the intensive care unit, so there was no pull-out chair for John and Aileen to sleep on. The nurses urged John and Aileen to consider taking a room at the Ronald McDonald House nearby, but they couldn't fathom leaving a two-year-old alone anywhere, let alone one who was critically ill. They took turns all night in the straight-backed chair beside her bed.

Aileen became expert at watching the numbers on the monitors carefully so that she picked up immediately if Megan's fever was up or her heart rate falling or her oxygen saturation low. Megan's heart stopped beating three times during those early weeks. Each time, as doctors and nurses scrambled around her, Aileen, calm and dry-eyed, held Megan's hand, adjusted her tubes, and made recommendations. John handed out copies of the Duke and Pharming press releases about the clinical trials to make sure Dr. Hofley and the intensive care nurses knew there was hope for Megan, reason to fight to save her despite her dire prognosis.

Many times, Aileen's parents felt like they'd walked into a scene out of *ER*—one in which their daughter was playing a leading role. Marty Holleran had always known his daughter was firmly grounded, big hearted, and kind. But he couldn't think of what in her life experience had prepared her for this. Her life thus far had been utterly carefree, except, perhaps, for the stress of her family's frequent moves as her father advanced up the career ladder first in the U.S. Army and then at General Electric Corporation. But even those moves never seemed to bother her. She had maintained a steady B average and a throng of friends in every school. Until now, Marty had been certain that his daughter's adult life would be an extension of her easy, joyful childhood.

After about three weeks, Megan's condition improved enough that John felt comfortable returning to work full time. His boss and colleagues at Bristol-Myers were so supportive that they'd already finished and filed his business plans for him so that he met the September 30 deadline. During those early days and nights beside Megan's hospital bed, he'd completed the paperwork to start his Pompe foundation and mailed it to the Internal Revenue Service. He even called the IRS and spoke to a worker, telling her about Megan's illness and how he needed the foundation to raise money to help her. The worker said she would push to get the papers approved quickly.

John also began to recruit members for his new foundation, cold calling down the list he'd gotten from Slonim of children with the same non-classical form of Pompe disease as Megan and Patrick. One of the first people he reached was Greg Assink, the branch manager of an equipment rental company outside of Grand Rapids, Michigan.

"Hey, Greg, Dr. Slonim told me about you. My name is John Crowley and I'm a father of two children with Pompe disease, the same nonclassical form as your Kelsey, I understand," John began.[3]

"We're in the same boat, then," Greg responded with sympathy. "I have two children with serious disabilities, too. My two-year-old boy is autistic, and then we have five-year-old Kelsey who has Pompe. I am so happy you reached out to us. How are you and your wife coping, John?"

"We're okay, but there are days, you know. It hasn't been easy, Greg," John said, amazed, for the second time in his life, at how easy it was to talk to complete strangers who shared the same terrible experience of knowing they could lose their child any day. The first time John had known that ease was when he met the Walter family at Dr. Chen's office. Today, as then, the words just tumbled out, and John shared things he hadn't said even to some of his closest friends. "We almost lost our little Megan, who is two years old. She's still in the hospital, in the intensive care unit. Our youngest, Patrick, is only one year old and he's still strong, but he has it too. Megan's nearly dying has convinced me that we can't afford to wait, Greg. Time's the real enemy. All of us parents of children with Pompe disease need to band together. All of the clinical trials are being done on infants. If we want to save our kids, we've got to drive research forward for toddlers and older kids."

"How are you going to do that?" Greg asked.

"I'm a director, soon to be vice president at Bristol-Myers," John said, proud to be able to use his latest promotion to gain credibility. "We're not personally wealthy, not even close, but we *are* well connected. I went to Notre Dame Law School and Harvard Business School; my father-in-law was a vice president at GE. We're starting up an organization, the Children's Pompe Foundation, to raise money for research and clinical trials for children with Megan and Kelsey's form of the disease. We intend to use every connection we have to raise money to start clinical trials for children with the nonclassical form of Pompe."

"We've been giving to the AMDA," Greg said. "Our church and our family have all been giving to the AMDA," Randall's organization.

"The AMDA does wonderful work," John said, not missing a beat. "They've done a great job funding research. But I think there's room for more than one organization, and for an organization like ours with a specific purpose."

"That's true," Greg said, liking the enthusiasm he heard on the other end of the line.

"Give it some thought, Greg," John said. "We're only doing this because we're running out of time. If we wait around and let trials go forward only in infants, it will be too late for Megan and Patrick and Kelsey and all the other children like them by the time the companies are ready to treat them."

"John, I feel like we're the same kind of person," Greg said. "We're both Type A personalities." Then he laughed. "Well, if I'm a Type A, it sounds like you're a Type Triple A. I would like to work with you. Let me talk to my wife and see what she thinks."

A few days later, Greg called John back. He told John that after their last conversation, he'd spoken seriously with his wife. Their children's illnesses had made them intensely religious, and they'd prayed that night for guidance. Greg discussed John with the group of six men in his Bible study group, and even called Slonim to ask what he knew of John Crowley.

"My family and my church all feel that we should work with you," Greg said. "You have all of our support."

In between the phone calls to families, John also called a moving company and arranged for the boxes and furniture he and Aileen had stored in her parents' basement to be transported to their new house. They had been planning to move into the house in late September, a few days after Megan was admitted to the hospital. Of course, they'd had to postpone.

John Jr.'s new preschool, Hopewell Presbyterian, had started three days a week and was a few blocks away from the new house. John settled into a routine of camping out in the new house in sleeping bags with his namesake son, surrounded by their unopened boxes, on the nights before he had preschool. Then John would drive to work, and afterward he'd show up at the hospital for several hours.

Some nights he stayed at the hospital so he and Aileen could take turns at Megan's bedside—one of them sleeping in the waiting area while the other sat in the intensive care unit. On other nights, John would go home to his in-laws' house to try to get a decent night's sleep. The au pair program they had applied to had sent over a young German woman named Anne, and she was also staying at Aileen's parents' house. Aileen's mother and Anne were managing the care of Patrick and little John. Aileen, meanwhile, had spent forty-two nights in a row at the hospital.

* * *

One night, John told Aileen he had a surprise. He left the hospital and returned to Megan's bedside a short while later with an Italian take-out dinner and bottle of Chianti, already uncorked and hidden in a brown bag.
Megan had fallen asleep, and Aileen sat in her usual perch in one of the
two straight-backed chairs by her bed. With a sly smile, John poured the
contents of the brown bag into a Styrofoam cup and handed it to Aileen.
Then, filling a cup for himself, he sat in the chair beside her and pushed it
until it was flush with her seat.

They sat together, drinking the Chianti a little too quickly, joking
about whether the nurses at the other end of the room had figured out
their ruse. Before long, the bottle was empty. John, stealing a quick look in
the nurses' direction, wrapped both arms around Aileen and pulled her toward him, kissing her passionately. "Honey, you are so beautiful," he whispered, when he finally drew a few inches away from her face.

Aileen rolled her eyes, running one hand through her hair, and giggled, "I can't remember the last time I put on makeup. I look like a sight."

"You're always ravishing," he protested, kissing her fingers, her chin,
and her forehead. Then, looking intensely into her eyes, he said, "I'm so
sorry this has been so difficult. I never knew you could be so strong."

"You know I love you," Aileen whispered, smiling.

"Do you remember the first time we kissed?" he asked.

"Of course I do," she said. "On the couch in your mom's house watching the end of *The Spy Who Loved Me*. The song "Nobody Does It Better"
came on and you kissed me for about ten seconds and looked at me and
said, 'That was nice.'"

John let out a little laugh. "The nurses are probably watching us but
pretending they don't notice," he joked.

"They probably feel sorry for us," she chortled softly. "I don't care
anymore anyway. I just miss you, John."

Whispering in Aileen's ear that he had another surprise, John led her
outside the intensive care unit and down a corridor. Suddenly, he pushed
open a door on the right side and yanked her inside. Aileen found herself
standing inside a cleaning closet with a wall of wet hanging mops on each
side. "I scoped this out on my way in this evening," her husband was whispering excitedly. "It's been four weeks since we made love. I couldn't wait
one more day." Aileen silenced him with her lips, reaching for the blissful

mix of love and comfort and pleasure that she had only ever known through him. Sandwiched between the walls of mops, they made love that night with a tenderness they hadn't known before, their passion heightened by the pain of shared suffering.

When they returned to the intensive care unit, they found it as quiet as when they left it. Megan was still asleep and the nurses continued to talk among themselves, their eyes trained on the monitors at the command center. Aileen, blushing, her hair tangled, sat back in the chair, and John covered her with a blanket, tucking it in around her. He kissed her cheek and straightened the crooked parting in her hair. Then he walked down the hallway, his hands in his pockets, smiling, heading for the waiting room for a few hours of sleep.

Since the night when she choked and nearly died, Megan had been on a ventilator almost constantly. John told Dr. Hofley that to qualify for the first clinical trial, Megan needed to be able to breathe on her own. "I don't know if she can do it, but we'll try," Hofley said. He tried to wean her off the ventilator several times, but she was unable to breathe on her own and once went into cardiac arrest.

"Her muscles aren't strong enough to breathe anymore," Hofley said after the last frightening try. "She needs a tracheotomy."

Reluctantly, John and Aileen agreed. Aileen asked if Dr. Michael Tavill, an ear, nose, and throat specialist they knew and trusted, who had treated the children before, could perform the surgery. Hofley made the arrangements, and a day later, John and Aileen accompanied Megan, sitting up in a blue hospital gown on the surgery gurney, to the edge of the operating room and kissed her good-bye. Tavill wheeled her into the operating room and performed the half-hour surgery, cutting an incision in her throat through which a breathing tube was connected so that she could use a ventilator permanently. At the age of two, Megan would never again breathe on her own unless a treatment was developed to reverse the disease.

As they sat together outside the operating room, leaning forward in the straight-backed metal chairs, Aileen asked the question she had been suppressing since she'd realized the tracheotomy was inevitable.

"John, does this mean she'll never get in the clinical trial?"

"Along with her not being a baby, this will make it harder to get her in the trial," John admitted, sounding tired. Then he straightened, and conviction filled his voice. "But I sure as hell am going to find a way."

Finally, after Megan had been at the hospital for six weeks, Hofley said he was ready to release her. In the short term, Megan couldn't even go home unless her parents learned not only how to operate the ventilator but also how to replace the tracheotomy, the tube connecting the machine to her throat. At home, they would have some nursing help, but they needed to be able to care for Megan themselves because the nurses wouldn't be there around the clock.

Dr. Hofley decided to release Megan to a nursing home for children on ventilators called the Children's Specialized Rehabilitation Hospital. In Mountainside, New Jersey, the center housed some children temporarily while their parents learned how to take care of them; others lived there permanently. The director recommended a three-week stay to train parents, but John and Aileen insisted they could learn everything in a week. They were desperate to get Megan home.

In the meantime, Aileen's relatives, eager to do something to help besides bring food and toys to the hospital, volunteered to get their new house ready for them. Aunt Sandra, the one who worked at Bristol-Myers, her sister Marsha, their husbands, Jim and Jay, and another cousin, Beverley, spent a weekend unpacking all the boxes and setting up all the furniture. They joked that they were Mennonites doing a barn raising, and got so caught up in the spirit that they even put clothes in the closets, pictures on the walls, books in the shelves, and mums out front on the doorsteps.

No sooner did Aileen and John arrive at the rehabilitation hospital with Megan than they started feeling less sorry for her. Many of the children had no visitors, and they cried and reached out to John and Aileen. Aileen didn't let herself go over—she knew it would be impossible to extricate herself. But John missed the lesson on how to bathe Megan without getting her breathing tubes wet because he was holding the child in the next bed, who screamed every time he was put down.

At the rehab hospital, the day of the test of their medical skills arrived. John had volunteered to go first. A nurse pulled apart the Velcro strap that held Megan's tracheotomy in place so that it fell out of her throat. John's job was to show he could put it back in. Megan began crying and pushing at the tube. Without it, she couldn't breathe. John grabbed her hands with one of his while he tried to push the tube back in with his other hand. He struggled, unable to slide the tube in, watching Megan's face grow pale and more frantic. He looked helplessly at the nurse.

"I can do it," Aileen said, jumping up. "Megan, honey, Mommy's going to put it right back in." She took the tube from John's hand and gently slid it into the opening in Megan's neck. On the next try, John, too, was able to get the tube back in. The nurse looked at both of them, trying to decide if what she had seen was enough to save the child's life the next time the tube came out. Finally, she nodded and scrawled her signature on the form indicating that the Crowleys were capable of keeping Megan alive.

Now, finally, they were ready to take Megan home.

8. The Conference

FALL 1998
PENNINGTON, NEW JERSEY; BETHESDA, MARYLAND

Life had changed dramatically. John and Aileen's new home was like a hospital. Nurses and therapists came and went all day and night through the unlocked front door. The keys to their house got lost, and they didn't even bother replacing them. Meanwhile, John spent every evening either on the Internet or phoning the IRS to get his foundation papers approved.

Day and night, the whooshing of Megan's ventilator filled the house. It pumped twenty-two breaths a minute into her weak lungs, swishing louder or softer, faster or slower, depending on the settings. The alarm sounded dozens of times each day, signaling that Megan's airflow might be disrupted from a tangle or disconnection in the long plastic tube that connected her tracheotomy to her ventilator. If she arched her back or made some sudden movement, the tracheotomy tube would pop out of her neck and Aileen or John would race over to thread it back in. If she pulled on the tubing that connected the tracheotomy to the ventilator, or if John Jr. tripped over it, one end or the other would come unplugged. The worst were the mucus plugs that built up every so often in the tracheotomy tube, blocking her airflow, presenting an immediate, life-threatening emergency.

At first, both John and Aileen would both sprint to Megan's side when a beep sounded, but they soon learned to wait until six or eight beeps had elapsed and jump in only if it was apparent the nurse couldn't immediately find the problem and correct it. For her part, Megan grew accustomed to at least one crisis with her breathing every day. Her solemn dark eyes trained on the face of John or Aileen, she remained calm unless she detected concern—a raised voice, a frown—as they tried to correct the problem. Then the little girl would panic and grab and push at her tracheotomy, making it much harder to thread back into her neck. But after a burst of crying as soon as her airflow was restored, Megan would begin another game of Barbies.

In November, John learned that sixty-five Pompe disease researchers and doctors from around the world were planning to gather at the National Institutes of Health (NIH) in Bethesda, Maryland, for a conference. Randall and Marylyn House and their Acid Maltase Deficiency Association were organizing and cosponsoring the third annual meeting of Pompe researchers. Concerned about the lack of communication and cooperation among researchers working on the disease, the couple had sponsored the first Pompe disease meeting in their hometown of San Antonio two years earlier. At the Hyatt hotel downtown, about 30 scientists working on Pompe and related disorders met for the first time. They had been competing with one another on scientific milestones for years but had never had occasion to gather and share information. Marylyn presented a detailed case study—the best researchers would later say that they had ever heard—of a juvenile with Pompe: her own daughter, Tiffany. With the smiley, pony-tailed thirteen-year-old, her spine already so deeply curved with scoliosis that she had trouble walking, a poignant presence at the meeting, the researchers felt inspired to work collaboratively, with patients in mind rather than research papers. They went home to their labs and began to exchange ideas, DNA samples, and mice. For the next decade, Pompe researchers would talk about that first meeting as a life-changing, work-altering experience, and credit the Houses for bringing them together.[1]

Looking for any new source of information and hope, John called Dr. Slonim on the phone and asked how he could get himself invited to Randall's next meeting. By now, Slonim had grown fond of John. He had come to relish his frequent phone calls, enjoying his sense of humor and appreciating his urgency. "It's important for John to get involved not just for his children's sake, but also for himself," he had told his nurse Linda. Slonim encouraged John to attend the meeting and told him to call Randall to get his name added to the list of invitees.

John hung up and immediately dialed Randall at his office. He knew Randall hadn't liked his plan to start his own foundation, but he hoped he had moved past that.[2]

"Hello, John, how are you?" Randall said, warmly.

"Fine, Randall," John said, feeling encouraged.

"How are Megan and Patrick?" Randall asked.

"Well, quite frankly, Randall, things could be better. We've had a pretty rough time," John said. "Megan got pneumonia and then a staph infection in the hospital. She was in the hospital for six weeks, but we finally have her home."

"I'm terribly sorry to hear that," Randall said, and John believed him. Randall was one of the few people in the world who knew the terror of living every day under the threat of losing your child. He took a deep breath and plunged into his request.

"Hey, Randall, I heard about your research meeting coming up in Bethesda and I wondered if I could attend."

"Well now, John, the meeting is only for scientists," Randall said, the warmth gone. "We're not inviting any parents."

"But I need to meet these doctors," John pushed. "I need to tell them about Megan and Patrick's cases. I need to find out about any new research going on. I'm running out of time."

"If we invite you, other parents will want to come," Randall said. "They would interrupt the flow of scientific discussion. The goal of this meeting is to promote understanding and cooperation among the scientists to get a cure for this disease as quickly as possible. This is not a parents' meeting."

"What do you mean, Randall? I have to be there," John pressed, his tone pleading.

"And what I'm saying is you cannot be at this conference," Randall said firmly, bringing the conversation to a quick close.

John sat at his desk, shocked. He called back Slonim and told him what had happened. Slonim phoned Dr. Paul Plotz, a scientist at the National Institutes of Health, which was cosponsoring the meeting, and told him about John's desire to attend. Plotz said nobody could be barred from a meeting at the NIH—least of all a parent—and he agreed to telephone Randall and tell him so.[3]

A few days later, the phone rang at John's office. Marylyn House was on the phone with her lawyer.[4]

"Just know you may come to the conference, but you are not welcome," she said, fuming. "It's not me and my husband who don't want you there, it's the doctors. We're so close to getting a treatment. If you get involved, you're going to screw it all up.

"We're going to set the ground rules, though, and they're going to be very strict. You have to sit in the back row, you can't talk or ask questions, you're not even to talk to doctors during breaks."

Then the lawyer told John he would need to sign a confidentiality disclosure agreeing not to reveal any scientific secrets he learned.

"That's fine," John said. He hated Marylyn's angry, lecturing tone, which made him feel like a child, but he knew he had won this round. He would sign whatever paper they put in front of him. In the years ahead, it would prove to be a crucial victory.

On December 2, John checked into the Hyatt in Bethesda, Maryland. He had arranged to have a drink that night with Gerben Moolhuizen, the Pompe disease coordinator at Pharming with whom he had spent the day in the Netherlands a few months earlier. They met at the hotel bar.[5]

Moolhuizen, ever gracious, asked John how his children were doing. John told Moolhuizen about Megan's health scares that fall.

"What about the boy?" Moolhuizen asked.

"Patrick is still healthy, but I see some signs of weakening. We all wish we weren't noticing it, but the little guy is starting to have a bit of trouble swallowing and will probably need a gastrostomy."

The two men ordered a round of beers. As they took their first sips, John looked directly into Moolhuizen's eyes and made his first direct plea on his children's behalf.

"Gerben, I need to get this drug to my kids really soon," he said.

"John, I'm trying," Moolhuizen said, "but production is very, very tough. It's not as simple as we thought to get this enzyme out of the rabbits."

"How are the clinical trials coming?" John asked.

"We plan to start very soon the trial in Europe in infants," Moolhuizen said.

"What about the U.S. trial?" John prodded.

"That may be some time," Moolhuizen said, looking down. He said that Pharming's new production plant in Geel, Belgium, would need to pass an FDA inspection before the enzyme treatment could be infused into patients in the United States. And even if Pharming got the go-ahead from the FDA, the company wouldn't be able to produce enough drug for a second trial for some time.

"What about Genzyme?" John asked. Surely Pharming's partner, with its deep pockets and manufacturing expertise, could solve these problems.

"The partnership isn't going well," Moolhuizen said. "Genzyme is not able to help us with the problems with the rabbits." They were difficult to milk, and the milk contained less and less enzyme as they aged, he said. It was proving hard to get enough enzyme from the herd of rabbits to treat more than a handful of people.

John took a swig of beer, letting the disappointment sink in. After reading about the Genzyme partnership, visiting the Netherlands, and touring Pharming's production facilities, he had come to see the company's clinical trials as a life raft for his children. Now, in a moment of candor, Moolhuizen was pulling it away from him. John could raise all the money in the world to fund a clinical trial, but if the companies couldn't make enough of the drug, he was nowhere.[6]

The campus of NIH buildings was so vast that it took John an hour and a half the next morning to find the right meeting hall. When he arrived, the meeting was already under way in a building called the Cloister, a former abbey. John walked through a long lecture hall with vaulted ceilings, and into an adjoining room where about sixty people sat listening intently. He saw the back of Dr. Slonim's balding head in one of the rear seats and slid into a vacant chair beside him. Slonim reached his right arm over and patted the younger man on the back, as if sensing John's frustration at being so late and his awkwardness at having forced his way into the meeting. At the podium, a scientist John didn't recognize was talking about experiments in his lab.[7]

John sat quietly, trying to follow. He soon realized he didn't understand anything the man was saying. He tried to remember when he had taken his last biology class. It was in tenth grade at Bergen Catholic High School and was taught by the school's assistant wrestling coach. He'd have to learn a lot more science if he was going to run a research foundation.

As the day progressed, speaker after speaker whose names he knew only from the Internet rose to talk about their work. It was the ultimate crash course in the molecular biology of Pompe disease. Arnold Reuser, the pioneering Dutch scientist who had worked on Pompe disease for most of his life, came to the podium. Wiry, with frizzy white hair and a flair for the dramatic, Reuser put up one slide after another that looked similar to the ones John had seen in the Netherlands a few months earlier—mouse tissue replete with big purple pools of glycogen and only a few red strands of surviving muscle fiber, and subsequent slides showing a dramatic shrinking of the purple areas after treatment.[8]

"Look how much our enzyme has reduced the glycogen pools," Reuser said. "This is very exciting data for everyone in this field."

John liked Reuser's passion and optimism.

Dr. Chen, his children's own doctor, a soft-spoken presenter, described his experiments giving the enzyme he had grown in CHO cells to Japanese quails, one of the few species of animals known to naturally develop Pompe disease. He showed photographs of the quails that could only hop around before being treated, and the one that was flying after a few weeks of injections with his enzyme. One day, John thought, these doctors and scientists would be making presentations showing slides of Megan and Patrick's muscle tissues cleared of glycogen after receiving the treatment enzyme. Instead of quails flying, the videos would show his children walking.[9]

Dr. Frank Martiniuk, a research associate at New York University, advocated gene therapy as the solution. He reported using a "gene gun" to insert the gene that codes for the Pompe enzyme into mice. The muscle cells that received the gene began to produce the Pompe enzyme, acid alpha-glucosidase. The big challenge was figuring out how to get the gene into all the muscle cells of the body.[10]

The final presentation the next day unsettled him. A surly, white-bearded researcher suggested that neither Chen's nor Reuser's enzymes would work. The physician-researcher's name was Dr. William Canfield and he was a biochemist from the University of Oklahoma.[11]

"It's not enough to make the enzyme correctly," Canfield said. "For the enzyme to be taken up properly, you need the correct glycosylation."

John had never heard the word, and he didn't think anyone else at the conference had used it.

"What's glycosylation?" John asked Slonim in a whisper.

"He's talking about the importance of carbohydrate and phosphate structures attached to the enzyme, where everyone else at the meeting has been focused on the enzyme alone," Slonim whispered in reply.

Canfield said neither the enzyme made in CHO cells nor rabbit milk had the right attachments of carbohydrates and phosphates to be transported to the lysosomes of muscle cells, where they were needed. He had spent a decade in his lab figuring out how to make the right attachments, and he believed he had finally worked it out.

John noticed researchers associated with Pharming and Duke shaking their heads in disagreement in the rows ahead of him. They were mostly molecular biologists, and most of them didn't know Canfield, a biochemist. And they clearly did not agree with him. John found himself wanting to dismiss Canfield, too.

"Is this guy for real?" John whispered, hoping Slonim would have something derogatory to say about this researcher's negative pronouncements. Everything Canfield was saying implied that Pharming and Genzyme's treatments were never going to be effective.

"Nina and Paul think he's onto something," Slonim said, using the first names of the NIH researchers, Dr. Nina Raben and Dr. Paul Plotz. "They invited him to attend."

John said nothing. If Canfield was right, hope was even further off than it had seemed before.

When the speakers were finished, John saw Canfield standing uncertainly amid a group of scientists in the back of the room. As he had done repeatedly over the two-day meeting, Dr. Slonim ushered John over and introduced him as the head of the newly formed Children's Pompe Foundation. The two men shook hands.[12]

Randall stepped up to the podium to invite the researchers to be his guests for dinner. He had arranged for a bus to pick up everyone outside the Hyatt at 7 P.M. and take them to a French restaurant called La Miche, where he had made reservations.

John, standing quietly beside Slonim as he chatted with the other scientists, knew that the invitation probably didn't apply to him. But if he could somehow push his way into the event, he thought, he would have a chance to get to know a few more researchers. Perhaps he would even talk further with Randall and mend relations.

Back at the hotel, John dressed for dinner, putting a blue blazer over khakis and a blue dress shirt. As he waited in the lobby, he could see Randall outside, beside a school bus. The researchers had formed a line to get on the bus. John waited inside until most of the group had climbed past Randall before appearing at the end of the line.

"Hi Randall," he said as his turn came, smiling and extending a hand.[13]

"Oh, no, you're not coming to this dinner," Randall said, shaking his head, crossing his arms, and standing in the entrance. "It's my party and you're not invited."

John looked up at Randall. At over six feet, his gold Rolex on his arm, he was everything John wasn't—big, rich, and experienced in the business and Pompe worlds. He couldn't help the wave of embarrassment that washed over him, feeling indescribably small and poor and young.

"That's fine, Randall," John said, turning to leave. "That's fine."

The bus with all the other conference attendees pulled out of the driveway. John rode the elevator upstairs, staring at his shoes. As he waited for his bow-tie pasta in marinara sauce to be delivered to his room, he sat on the bed, his head in his hands, thinking of his mother. Even as she'd quoted President Kennedy and other men she admired for advocating for justice and equal opportunity, she had always added her own dose of realism, telling him you were nowhere in the world without money.

His mother was right, he thought. Money brought power—the power to include or exclude others. Grabbing the remote control from the side table, he hurled it across the room, where it ricocheted off the wall and knocked the top of the ice bucket onto the floor. Swearing, he picked up the remote and clicked on the television set, remembering a quote he'd read somewhere and saying it out loud, in an admonishing tone: "Life isn't fair—get used to it."

9. The Marriage

It was 1 A.M. when John finished writing a letter to the Harvard Business School classmates who were in his same Section J, asking each of them for a $500 donation to his new foundation. He e-mailed drafts to his three close friends and study group mates at Harvard who had offered to send it to members of their sections. He was counting on the generosity and means of the legendary Harvard old boy's network to get his nascent organization off to a start.

He turned off the computer in his study, climbed up the stairs, and took a left into Megan's bedroom for the final check he made every night. In the pale yellow glow of the nightlight, he saw her sleeping on her left side, her favorite stuffed dog, Pinky, in her arms. "Goodnight, Megs," he whispered, kissing her cheek. She stirred and opened her eyes, lifting her right arm and raising her pinky finger, pointer, and thumb in the air, the middle finger and ring fingers down—sign language for "I love you." A tutor had been teaching her sign language, and she communicated using a combination of spoken words and signs.

John smiled, bent over, and kissed her one more time, and then looked over at the night nurse, a big woman, who sat at the desk in the corner, her head in her hands. He did a double-take, realizing the nurse was asleep.

"Excuse me," he said, tapping her lightly on her shoulder.

She jerked awake, looked up at him with bloodshot eyes and mumbled an apology. "So tired. Bad night, bad night last night with the children."

She stood up from the chair unsteadily and took a few steps toward him. He recognized the smell on her breath with a shock.

"You're drunk," John said.

"No, I'm not," she said, stepping backward.

"Yes, you are. I can smell the alcohol," John said, incredulous. "Get out. Get the hell out of this house."

He watched her leave, then stomped down the hallway to his bedroom and stood beside Aileen, who was sleeping.[1]

"Aileen, you'll never believe it," he said. "The nurse the agency sent tonight is drunk."

"What?" she said, sleepily.

"The goddamn nurse is drunk. I can smell it on her breath."

"She's not drunk. She's just weird and tired. They're all weird and tired. At least she's awake," Aileen said, waving him away. "Go to bed, honey."

"Aileen, don't you have any standards at all?" he said, anger building. "The nurse was slurring her words. I told her to leave."

"Jesus, John," Aileen said, sitting up in bed, fully awake. "Now what are we going to do?"

"How can you allow someone like that to take care of Megan?" he exploded.

"You're screaming, John. Calm down," she said in a loud, angry whisper. "You're going to wake the kids. And I wish you'd stop blaming me. You've fired ten nurses in ten weeks."

"We need to get better nurses," he said through clenched teeth. "I'm going to call the nursing agency tomorrow and tell them to stop sending us this crap."

"We've both called the friggin' nursing agency ten times to complain that the nurses suck," Aileen said, exasperation flooding her voice. "There's a friggin' nursing shortage, John. I'm just grateful when someone shows up to help."

"We can't have people like that taking care of Megan and Patrick," John said, with a sharp intake of breath, trying to calm himself.

"They've got nobody else to send," Aileen said. "I need the extra pair of hands to play with Megan while I feed Patrick. I never leave Megan alone with any of the bad nurses, so don't give *me* crap."

Staring at Aileen coldly, John shook his head and said, "I'll sleep in Megan's room for the first half of the night. You can do the second shift." He rummaged in his closet for his sleeping bag, grabbed his pillow from the bed and stomped down the corridor toward Megan's bedroom.

Aileen heard a car starting up outside. She stood at the window, watching as the nurse's old Buick Skylark lurched out of the driveway.

The next morning, as John left for work at 6:45, he reminded Aileen to call the nursing agency to complain about the drunken nurse and ask for a replacement. "I'll handle it," she said, not looking up as she tied John Jr.'s shoes.

This morning, Aileen drove John Jr. to Hopewell Presbyterian Elementary School instead of letting their au pair take him as she did most mornings. John's teacher had asked Aileen to come in to talk to her about her son. Their best nurse was on duty today, so Aileen left Megan at home.

The teacher, a gentle soul, smiled ruefully as she told Aileen about the trouble with her son. He was a sweet boy, she said, but he couldn't follow instructions. With eighteen students and only one assistant, she needed her students to be able to perform simple consecutive tasks. "I can't ask your son to put on an apron, sit down, and paint without him getting lost somewhere along the way," she said. He needed a teacher by his side to participate in any activity.

"I'm sorry—I'll work with him at home," Aileen said grimly. "It's been a difficult year and he hasn't always gotten enough attention. His sister has been very sick." The teacher nodded sympathetically, having heard about Megan being in the hospital during the first few weeks little John was in school.

As she drove home, Aileen allowed herself to cry, having fought hard not to let the tears flow in school. She knew John Jr. had trouble focusing, but she had hoped the problem would somehow disappear when he was at school. She just couldn't face another problem. Over the past eleven months, the children's illness had begun to eat at their marriage. John thought Aileen was lazy; she felt unappreciated. The night before, battling over the nurses, had made both of them wonder if their marriage would survive.

At home, Aileen found Megan and Patrick on the couch in the den, side by side, watching Barney on TV. The nurse sat in between them and their au pair was in the kitchen making macaroni and cheese. "Hi, honey," Aileen greeted each of them brightly, crouching in front of the couch and kissing each child.

"And whose birthday is it tomorrow?" she asked. Megan looked at Patrick, who pointed at himself.

"And how old are you going to be?" she asked.

Patrick smiled up at her and raised one finger.

"That's right, honey," she told him. "What a big boy you're going to be!"

In the kitchen, Aileen swung into action. She dialed her mother to ask her to pick up a birthday cake for Patrick at the bakery near her house, which was famous for excellent desserts. She took a tube of chocolate chip cookie dough out of the refrigerator and divided it into bowls.

"Who wants to make cookies?" she asked, returning to the den. Two pairs of eyes lit up. She lifted Megan, asking the nurse to follow with the ventilator—a big box, at fifty pounds about as heavy as a first-generation microwave oven. They put the child and the machine on the kitchen counter beside one bowl of cookie dough. Then Aileen sat Patrick beside his sister with his own bowl of dough.

The children grabbed handfuls of dough, squished them into balls, and flattened them onto the pan. Aileen dumped a bag of M&Ms on the counter for the kids to add to the mixture. Megan grabbed a handful and threw them on the floor.

"Those are for the cookies, Megan, not to throw on the floor," Aileen said sternly.

Megan reached into the bowl again and flung another handful on the floor.

"If you do that one more time, Megan, you're going in a time-out," Aileen said.

Her eyes on her mother, Megan cupped her hands, filled them to the brim with M&Ms, and threw them up in the air, where they pelted to the ground around her mother's feet.

Wordlessly, Aileen scooped up her daughter, still connected to her ventilator on the counter, and strapped her into the booster seat attached to a kitchen chair. Arms crossed, lower lip jutting outward in a pout, Megan sat in the booster, staring straight ahead while her mother and brother added the remaining M&Ms to the cookie dough. Even in punishment, Megan was defiant. She would not cry.

In the late morning, John called to check in.

"How are the troops?" he asked, sounding like his old upbeat self.

"Great. We're making cookies," Aileen said, matching his chipper tone. "You should see them licking the cookie dough off their hands."

"Have you called the nursing agency?" he asked.

"I'll call them as soon as we finish the cookies," Aileen said quickly.

"Ai-*leen*," he said, stretching her name into a long drawl of irritation. "Could you please do something? Can't I rely on you to do anything?"

"Yes, yes. Fine. I'm sorry, John. I'll do it right away," she replied, biting her lip.

Aileen hung up and helped the nurse wash off the children's hands in the kitchen sink. "Ugh—they have cookie dough in their hair and on their clothes. We're going to have to give them both baths," she sighed. Aileen led the way up the stairs with Megan, the nurse following with the ventilator. Then she made a second trip to carry Patrick. As the nurse played peekaboo with Patrick, Aileen bathed Megan, standing her in a plastic ring that attached to the bottom of the tub with suction cups. Megan splashed happily, filling and refilling her set of plastic cups. Her ventilator sat on the floor beside the tub, pumping twenty-two breaths per minute into her lungs as always, indifferent as to whether she was in time-out or in her bath.

At noon, Aileen returned to school to pick up John Jr. From his teacher's strained smile, she could tell it had been another bad day at Hopewell Elementary. She had forgotten to tell John about the teacher's complaint. She would discuss it with him tonight if she could squeeze in a conversation in between the children's bedtime and his nightly fundraising marathon on the phone and computer.

On the drive home, she and John Jr. stopped to buy party supplies at Pennington Market. She strapped him into the grocery cart and pushed him around the store gathering candles, balloons, party plates, and napkins.

"Do you know who's coming to the party tomorrow?" she asked him. He shook his head, still not a big talker.

"Nana and Poppy are coming," she said, referring to her parents. "And Barley and Big Poppy are coming"—the kids' names for John's mother and stepfather. "*And* Uncle Marty and Great Grandma and Aunt Michele. We're going to have a big party for Patrick."

John came home around six as Aileen was feeding little John and Patrick. Megan couldn't swallow food anymore, and got all her nutrition now from stomach feedings at naptime and during the night. She sat in front of the TV while Aileen spooned apple sauce into the mouths of other two.

"How are Archie and Edith?" John asked, looking over at Megan in her usual spot on the couch and Patrick in his booster seat in the kitchen.

"We're not Archie and Edith," Megan said in her muffled voice, dark eyes looking at her father, adamant.

"Now I get it," he said, chuckling. "You're Frick and Frack."

She shook her head, shouting, "Uh-uh." Patrick smiled, revealing a mouth full of applesauce, and waved his favorite Barney spoon at his dad.

"How could I forget?" he asked. "Gertrude and Stanley. You're Gertrude and you're Stanley."

"He's Stanley," Megan said. "I'm the Little Mermaid. I'm a princess."

Then Megan remembered her project that day. "Daddy, come here," she said. "Look." She pointed to the plate of M&M cookies wrapped in plastic on the kitchen counter.

"Megan, did you make those for me?" he asked.

"No," she said.

"Who did you make those for?" John asked.

She pointed at herself.

"You can have one—just one," she said.

"That's my girl," John laughed. "She's always thinking about Number One."

"Megan had her first time-out today," Aileen chimed in from the kitchen chair, still feeding the boys.

"No," Megan shouted.

"Should I tell Daddy what you did?" Aileen asked.

"No," Megan shouted again, this time waving her arms.

"All right, I won't," Aileen said. "All I'll say is that because of Megan, we nearly didn't have enough M&Ms to make those cookies."

The evening passed in bedtime stories for the children. John read Megan her new favorite book, *The Little Mermaid*; Aileen read a Barney board book to Patrick while John Jr. watched TV. Then she put her oldest boy to bed, reading him an extra story. Somehow, she told herself, she had to find the time and energy to give her eldest son more attention.

As she and John sat down to eat the take-out pasta dinner he had picked up on the way home, he asked, "Did you call the nursing agency?"

"Oh no, honey. I was so busy," she said, picking up her fork. "I'm sorry. I'll call tomorrow."

"Aileen," he barked, slamming his fork and knife down on the table. "Can't you do one damn thing? Come *on*. I'm working all freakin' day. I'm up half the night fund-raising for the foundation. Can't you at least manage the nurses?"

"Well, it's your fault if you work so hard. Don't blame me, John," she said, her temper flaring at last. "Things were really busy around here. You try taking care of three children in diapers. And what's the point of even calling the nursing agency to complain? It's not like the nursing agency has any better frigging nurses to give us. How many different ways do you need them to say the same thing—they *don't have* any other nurses."

There was a tense moment while they stared at each other, then John backed down. "Well, do we at least have a nurse tonight?" he asked, his tone pointedly helpful.

"We don't have anyone tonight because you fired her, John," Aileen said, coldly.

They ate the rest of the meal in silence.

Patrick woke up with a bad cold on his birthday. His eyes were red and listless. Aileen and John were both tired from having split the night shift for two consecutive nights, sleeping on the floor in Megan's room. Aileen dressed Patrick in a new blue and green striped one-piece outfit and carried him downstairs where Megan sat on her daddy's lap, John Jr. beside them.

"Happy birthday, baby Patrick!" John Jr. shouted. Patrick smiled, showing his new front tooth. Megan held up both arms and waved for Aileen to bring her baby brother over. She kissed him on his cheek and said, "Happy birthday."

An hour later, the relatives began to arrive. Aileen's parents were first, followed by her brother Marty. Soon John's side of the family had joined in—his mother, grandmother, stepfather, stepbrother Jason, and Aunt Michele.

Patrick, tired from his cold, fussed for much of the party. But when he saw the cake, the white icing top decorated with red, blue, and green balloons, he squealed and clapped. As the relatives sang "Happy Birthday," Patrick grinned and blew out his candle.

John looked at Patrick's cherubic face—at his brown eyes, which had changed in the past few months from their original blue, at the wisps of light brown hair around his face—and wondered how long they had before he got really sick. He looked at Aileen's smiling face, makeup disguising her exhaustion, leading everyone in "Happy Birthday" a second time so Megan had a chance to blow out the candle, too. Aileen had such a beautiful soprano voice, he thought. She had been the leader of her college choir, and everyone who heard her thought she could have a career as a professional singer. But she refused to even consider the idea. "I just want to be a mom," she had said then, shaking her head, and repeated many times since.

John Jr. began to cry, protesting that he needed a chance to blow out the candle, too. Aileen, giggling, lit the candle a third time and made everyone sing the whole thing one more time. Looking at her, John knew that in this moment, the children's disease didn't figure in her consciousness at all. She was happy just being with her kids, surrounded by her family. John wished he could let go of Megan and Patrick's prognosis and enjoy the good days as much as she did, but he felt weighted down. He couldn't stop thinking for even an instant that they would die before age five unless a new treatment intervened.

Now it was present time. Patrick, on Aileen's lap, helped tear open the wrapping paper. Out came a stuffed Barney that sang, "I love you, you love me," when its tummy was pressed, a Barney puzzle, and a pile of Barney books. Megan grabbed the singing Barney from Patrick, shouting, "Mine!" Aileen gently unclasped her fingers and handed it back to the birthday boy.

The little girl fell into a full-fledged tantrum, the alarms on her ventilator shrieking as her crying disrupted the airflow. "*Mine!*" she screamed.

"Megan, let's take a special walk," John said, standing up immediately. Carrying Megan in one arm and her ventilator in the other, he took her into his study and sat her on his lap. Megan stopped crying and reached for the two closest framed pictures, handing them to her dad. She liked hearing him tell stories about the people in the pictures that filled the tables and walls.

"This is my dad wearing his Marine uniform," John said. "You know, Megs, when you grow up, you can be a Marine like your grandpa. And you and I both know you'd be tougher than any boy Marine," he chuckled, thinking about how she refused to die that morning at Monmouth Medical Center six months ago. Megan looked up at him, nodding seriously, believing with all her heart that one day she would be the bravest girl Marine ever, and then pointed to the next picture.

Two days later, Patrick's cold went into his chest. Aileen could hear him wheezing. Dr. Hofley told her to bring the baby to Monmouth Medical Center, where he had cared for Megan when she nearly died the previous fall. A blood test showed that Patrick had respiratory syncytial virus (RSV), a common but potentially dangerous condition for young children. With Aileen by his side, Patrick spent a week in the hospital, his bed covered with a plastic tent pumped with an antibiotic mist. Unwilling to trust Megan's medical care to any of the nurses, John stayed home from work.

Patrick returned home, the virus overcome, but he was back in the hospital within two weeks, again laboring to breathe. This time, Hofley diagnosed him with pneumonia, admitted him into intensive care, and recommended that he also have a tracheotomy to insert a breathing tube in his throat. On Saint Patrick's Day, a surgeon performed the operation.

Patrick had been in the hospital for only a few days when John called Aileen at the hospital to tell her Megan was wheezing, too. A nurse had showed up to take care of Megan, but he didn't trust her in an emergency.

"I can't do this without you," he admitted.

Aileen told him to bring Megan to the hospital.

John settled Megan in her car seat in the back of their Ford Expedition, her ventilator and an oxygen tank at her feet. He told the nurse to sit in the middle seat and strapped John Jr. into his car seat on the other side. Then he sped down Interstate 195 toward the hospital.

"I'm hungry, Daddy," John Jr. squealed after they'd been driving only a few minutes. John looked at the clock on the dashboard and realized it was 4 P.M. and he hadn't fed his son anything after his morning Cheerios.

John remembered the Burger King at the next exit. "We'll get off at the next Burger King and get you whatever you want," John said, patting the little boy's knee. As he swerved into the restaurant parking lot, Megan's ventilator beeper went off. The nurse checked the tubing connections and found them solid, but the beeper continued to shriek. "I think there's something wrong with the machine," she said nervously. Megan began to cry and grab at the tubing.

"Attach the Ambu bag," John shouted, anxious. The nurse unzipped the emergency bag they always carried in the car and attached it to the tube from Megan's tracheotomy. She squeezed the bag to drive air into Megan's lungs, the backup system for just such a situation in which the ventilator failed. Megan continued to cry and flail.

"Here, give it to me," John said, not trusting this nurse to bag Megan properly. Squeezing the Ambu with his right hand, he used the other to steer the car up to the drive-through window. John Jr., fearing his plans would be interrupted yet again by one of his sister's medical meltdowns, screamed, "I'm hungry." John shouted out the order over the cries of both children—"Two cheeseburgers, two large chicken nuggets, two Diet Cokes, and a milk!"—still pumping the Ambu desperately.

Moments later, the attendant handed John the food, looked dazedly at the mayhem erupting in the car, and escaped behind the drive-through window with a bang.

Forty-five minutes later, they arrived at Monmouth Medical Center. Megan was wheeled into the hospital, looking painfully small to her dad as she sat upright on the adult-sized stretcher, her stuffed dog Pinky in her arms, her ventilator in front of her. An attendant walked beside the stretcher, squeezing the Ambu bag. John followed, holding little John's hand, feeling nauseous. He was out of breath and more scared than he cared to admit from that harrowing car ride.

"I don't know how Mommy does this every day, John," he said, more to himself than to his son, needing someone to talk to. He couldn't imagine how Aileen faced day after day of caring for the children, knowing a life-threatening emergency was certain to erupt at some time, at which point their lives would rest on the quickness and correctness of her response. He shuddered, remembering the night Megan almost died in the hospital—and how terrified and helpless he had felt. Thank goodness Megan would be getting into a clinical trial and receiving a treatment soon. This family could not live under the threat of this disease for much longer.

"Hi, Megan," a trio of nurses called as she was wheeled into the children's intensive care unit, empty except for Patrick in the bed at the far end. Megan waved, and John thought that she looked happy to be back in the unit where she'd stayed for so long the previous fall.

It turned out that both children had pneumonia. As the days dragged on, Aileen felt an overwhelming sense of frustration. She had mastered the medical stuff. She could read the monitors and summon nurses—and Dr. Hofley, if she saw cause for worry. It was keeping a two-year-old and a one-year-old entertained in bed in the same room for two straight weeks that challenged and exhausted her. She put on one Barney movie after another for Patrick, but even he was getting tired of them. Megan had assembled the ballerina puzzle a dozen times a day since she got there. More than anything in the world, Aileen longed to be home.

One afternoon, as she sat between the children's beds, watching them nap, the intensive care unit quiet except for the Darth Vader–like breathing of the children's ventilators, she suddenly recalled the words of a fortune-teller who had read her palm on the boardwalk in Atlantic City years ago. She had been an eighth grader staying at a beach house nearby with her parents. She'd sat on the floor of the fortune-teller's storefront booth, holding out her palm as the woman made her predictions: "You're going to get married when you're twenty-two years old to someone whose initials are either J.O. or J.C.," the old woman had said, squinting at the lines on Aileen's hand. "You'll have three children. The middle one will be a girl," as Aileen nodded happily. "And, oh my, young lady, I can see it here, you are going to be a nurse." The last part had jerked Aileen out of her fantasy world and she had shaken her head.

"It's all right except for the nursing stuff," she had laughed, telling the fortune-teller that she was either going to be a teacher or own her own clothing store.

When Aileen met John, she had remembered to tell him about the J.C. initials and the three kids, but she had forgotten all about the nursing prediction—until now. She was not a nurse in name, but she spent most of her days attending to her children's medical needs. Tears slid down her cheeks as she thought of how different her life was from how she had envisioned it. She had given birth to three beautiful children, but on most days she felt more like their nurse than their mother.

John arrived with John Jr. to find Aileen pale and subdued. He kissed her and asked, "Are you all right?"

"I'm fine," she said, turning her face from his.

John didn't press, a little annoyed at her curtness. With the two youngest out of the house, he felt more rested, he realized, feeling suddenly guilty. Home had been peaceful these past few days without the stream of nurses, the ventilator, and the two sick kids—and, he thought privately, without Aileen.

It was early April when John and Aileen brought Megan and Patrick home from the hospital.

Soon after, Aileen asked her best day nurse if she would stay for the night. She hoped that would ease the tension with John over the nurses that was spilling over into their marriage. As usual, he was up writing letters thanking the Harvard classmates whose donations—$50,000 thus far—had been flowing in. His close friends, Sherm Baldwin, John Gordon, and Mike Ostergard, and the Section J president, Dave Hughes, had each called dozens of classmates to solicit donations to reinforce the plea in John's letter. The famed networking opportunities of Ivy League schools were already paying off. He had made abiding friendships with people who had money to give or the wherewithal to raise it.

From his study, John heard Megan's ventilator beeper go off. He paused, waiting for the nurse to find and fix the problem. As it beeped for the eighth time, he ran up the stairs and into her room, tripping over something on his way to the machine. The beeping had also awakened Aileen, who charged into the room a moment behind him and saw immediately that Megan, in her sleep, had pulled on the tube connecting her tracheotomy to her ventilator. It had disconnected, cutting off her airflow. Megan, in her Barbie Princess nightgown, was crying, her lips turning blue, eyes wide and tearful with terror.

Aileen crouched beside the ventilator and quickly attached the tube that had come disconnected. John picked up Megan and put her in his lap. "Everything's all right, honey," he said, holding her tightly. She began to cry loudly as her airflow was restored.

"Where's the nurse?" Aileen asked. Looking around, they saw that the "thing" John had tripped on when he ran into the room *was* the nurse! She was asleep on the floor—and still hadn't woken up. Aileen reached down and shook the woman awake. John pressed his lips together tightly, but didn't say anything while they resettled Megan and made sure the nurse was alertly standing guard over her.

Once they were back in their room, however, his temper exploded. "How can you allow someone like that to take care of Megan?" he shouted.

"She's our best day nurse! She's just tired," Aileen said.

"Don't you have any standards at *all*?" John said, not for the first time. "You're willing to settle on any nurse, however incompetent, who walks through the door!"

"Nobody's as perfect as you are, John," she replied bitterly.

"I'm going to fire her right now," he said. His voice was hoarse with anger. "It's not like she just fell asleep. She made a little bed for herself on the floor and stretched out. Megan could have *died*."

"John, she's our best nurse. Please don't fire her. Just having a body to help carry things or, God, just to have somebody to play frigging Barbies with Megan is better than having nobody. Just let her stay for the night. We won't have her on the night shift again. I promise," Aileen pleaded.

John relented, but neither he nor Aileen slept that night. They tossed, listening for the beeping of the ventilator. And all night John fumed to himself. He had had it. He had just *had* it. Where would this family be if not for him? The nurse Aileen had seemed so satisfied with had fallen asleep. He wished he had a wife who would share the burden of organizing and planning their lives. It wasn't fair for John Jr. to have handicapped siblings. He needed some brothers and sisters who could run around with him. He and Aileen wouldn't have more kids. They couldn't risk bringing another child into the world with Pompe disease. He remembered how peaceful the house had been when Aileen and the kids were at the hospital. Maybe he and Aileen should live separately. He would buy the house next door and share the care of the children.

Across the bed, Aileen lay on her side, facing away from John, her back a stiff line against the bedsheets. She thought that she had never seen John so angry and out of control. She couldn't remember one argument they had had before the kids were sick. On the rare occasion when he had lost his temper, it was only for a second—and never at her. And he would always pull back with the same discipline with which he managed every aspect of his life, from exercise to work to juggling credit card payments. But now his temper flared almost daily.

Well, so what if he was angry? She was pretty angry herself. As if her days at home with three children—two on ventilators—weren't hard enough, she now had a husband who was constantly criticizing her. She didn't think the nurses were great, either, but it wasn't her fault. There was no way to change the nursing shortage in the country, and she never left the children home alone with the bad ones. Angry tears trickled down her face and into the flannel of the bedsheets.

A few nights later, some friends from high school invited John to go out in Manhattan. It had been at least a year since he had gone out with friends. He called Aileen and told her he would be home late. "That's fine," she said. He took the train from the Princeton station into Manhattan.

John and his friends went from bar to bar that night, getting more and more drunk. At about 2 A.M., he called Aileen again, this time to say he was spending the night at his best friend from high school's apartment in the city. In all the years they had been together, he had never gone out with friends and not come home. She slammed down the phone, feeling more alone than she had in her whole life.

John arrived home the next morning, hungover and tired, to find Aileen cold and strained. She didn't bring up the past evening until that night, when the children were asleep and her bedroom door was closed. Then she rounded on him with the full force of months of pent-up fury.

"Where were you last night, asshole?" she demanded.

"I do everything around here," John retorted, unapologetic. "I deserved a night off. Why can't you help more anyway?"

"*Help* more?" Aileen retorted. "Nobody can take care of these kids like I can. I'm doing my part—I'm taking care of these very sick kids. It's no picnic, John. Why don't *you* try staying home with them all day?"

They stood at the foot of the bed, glaring at each other, until John sat down heavily, his shoulders slumped. After a sharp intake of breath, he spoke again. "I don't think our marriage is working anymore. Maybe we should think about living separately."

Aileen, lips pressed tightly together, picked up a magazine and lay down on her side of the bed. "Do what you want, John," she said tightly. "If you don't want to be in this marriage any more, the kids and I can go live with my parents."

"No—I don't want that," he said, horrified at the idea of Aileen and the kids moving in with her parents.

"Well, what *do* you want?" she asked with feigned disinterest, eyes still trained on the magazine in front of her.

"I don't know," he said helplessly. He shuffled out of the bedroom and slept on the couch downstairs.

The next night, John and Aileen, who a year earlier had almost never argued, found themselves fighting again. It started with John paying bills downstairs in his study, stressed out as usual about covering the credit card bills and extra medical bills along with everything else that went with having a house and three children. He showed up in their bedroom as Aileen lay watching TV, complaining that she spent too much money on kids' clothes. "Do you really have to buy something at Baby Gap or Target every week?" he said. Within minutes, the argument had spiraled outward to include the future of their marriage.

"What is going *on* with you?" Aileen finally asked, her voice rising in frustration and despair. "What do you want from me? Just tell me what you want."

"A divorce," he thought to himself, but he couldn't bring himself to say those words. They stared at one another in hostile silence until he broke away from her gaze, saying nothing.

"Well, when you decide what you want, you just let me know," she said, raising the volume on the television set with the remote control and looking past him. The sight of her withdrawing from a fight—yet again—infuriated him.

"Fine. I'm going to leave," he declared.

"Okay," she replied, her jaw clenched, staring at the TV. "When are you coming back?"

"I don't know."

"If that's what you feel you need to do, go right ahead," Aileen shot back. She knew her frosty, dispassionate tone frustrated her husband more than any display of anger—he didn't know how to fight with someone who wouldn't engage, and more than anything, he hated to be ignored. She needed John more than ever, but her anger wouldn't allow her to make any overture for him to stay. "I'll be waiting for you when you get back," she said flatly. "I'm not interested in a divorce, but if that's what you need, you let me know."

John dug a backpack out of the closet, shoved a few changes of clothes inside, and walked toward the door. He desperately wanted Aileen to jump up, wrap her arms around him, and say she loved him and that everything would be all right—he desperately wanted her to beg him to stay. At the door, he hesitated once more, glancing back into the room.

She didn't take her eyes off the television set.

Alone in his car, John sped north on Interstate 95, his mind racing. New York flew by, then Connecticut. He didn't know where he was heading. He would just drive and it would come to him. It was liberating to be out of the house and away from all the demands. Tonight, there would be no beeping. There would be no writer's block over fund-raising letters. There would be no peeking around the corner at inept nurses. No arguments with Aileen. Tonight, he was free.

A couple of hours later, he passed a sign saying "Welcome to Massachusetts." Shocked that he had driven so far, he pulled off at the next exit and into a parking lot. He had no idea where he was going, and he needed to think. As he shut off the engine, he realized he was behind an old New

England church. Without another thought, he closed his eyes, bowed his head, and folded his hands together, just as his mother had taught him to do as a little boy; just as he still did at Mass every day.

"Please, dear God, show me the way forward," he begged aloud. "Is it really part of your plan for me to be so miserable? What if the clinical trials never happen and the children get sicker? I don't think I can do this. Please, God, show me what to do."

As he sat there in the darkness, his mind began to quiet, a calm descending and soothing. One by one, the troubles and sorrows clamoring for his attention gentled and stilled and finally faded into a blessed silence. He unclenched his folded hands and laid them on the steering wheel, savoring the astonishing peace that came from simply letting his tired mind drift, emptied and light.

For a long while his mind remained serenely blank, and then he thought of Ed Devinney, his roommate from his U.S. Naval Academy days and still his best friend. Now he knew who would help him find his way, and he wondered why he hadn't called him earlier. He picked up his cell phone and dialed him.

Ed was asleep in bed in Norfolk, Virginia, when the phone rang. By now he knew that calls late at night from John could only mean trouble. "What's wrong?" he asked, sleepiness draining from his voice.[2]

"I just left Aileen," John said simply, with his newfound calm. "I just couldn't take it anymore."

"Where are you?"

"Somewhere in Massachusetts. I don't know, Ed. I just don't know what to do. . . ."

Ed had tried to advise John during another painful crossroads in his life—and he was unhappily aware of John's marital troubles today. At the Naval Academy, the pair had clicked immediately with a shared sense of humor and daring. As the son of a sailor who had fought in the Korean War, Ed had grown up knowing he wanted to be a naval officer. He was a calmer person than John, but equally ambitious—a quiet leader to John's more outgoing nature. They'd spent every Saturday of their first year as "plebes," or freshmen, escaping from campus together in the backseat of Aileen's car. Plebes were forbidden from straying more than ten miles from the Academy grounds, consorting with females, or drinking alcohol.

To be caught doing any one of these things was to lose all privileges for the rest of the year. Together, John and Ed had broken the three cardinal rules of plebe life almost every weekend.

Ed had been a part of John and Aileen's relationship almost from the beginning. Every Saturday morning, the two roommates had ambled down an alley on the edge of campus, trying to look like they were taking a casual stroll. Aileen was always parked in the alley, waiting eagerly. When they were certain nobody was watching, John and Ed raced to her car, leaped in the backseat, and ducked as she sped the thirty miles to Washington. To make sure the plebes didn't stray far, the Navy required that they report back on campus at 5 P.M. and again at midnight. That meant Aileen had to ferry the two young men back to Annapolis two times every Saturday, often racing at twice the speed limit to get them there on time.

The fun ended the summer after their first year, when they were required to spend twenty-eight days at sea. That tour of duty soured John on the Navy. Ed spent his days mostly in port in Hawaii, but John's ship tossed in storms in the Mediterranean and chased Russian submarines around the North Atlantic. He was sick almost the entire time, and the only land they saw was the Straits of Gibraltar. When they finally returned to port, his mother took one look at him and rushed him to the emergency room. He had been fighting mono his entire time at sea and had lost nearly twenty pounds. He wasn't able to return to the ship for the final day that remained to reach the targeted twenty-eight days of duty.

According to the Navy rules, he was a day short, so he was told he'd be sent back on the water for another cruise over the Christmas holidays. Every college kid longs for the holidays, but with nowhere near the desperation of a first-year military officer whose free time is intensely restricted. John was crushed and dismayed by the unfairness of it all. Many of his classmates had had easy tours of duty, carousing in ports, while he stayed at sea the whole time—sick, no less, and performing his duties flawlessly. Did he really want a life controlled by superior officers enforcing seemingly inflexible rules? It wasn't like he was enjoying the academics either. He didn't like the heavy load of science and engineering courses. His eyesight had deteriorated, so he couldn't even become an F-14 fighter pilot as he'd always wanted. He began to think about going back to Georgetown, where he had spent his first year before enrolling at the Academy. Georgetown had told him he could return any time.

Ed was heartbroken at the thought of seeing John leave. But he tried to be unbiased during the long walks they took by the docks, week after week, John dwelling on the same question of whether to stay or go.

"John, is this all about the cruise, or is there some other reason why you want to leave?" Ed would ask.

"I just can't get over how unfair it is," John would growl.

"Think about the investment you've made here. You're so good." John was on the Commandant's List, the top third of the class academically, and ranked second in the brigade of midshipman in leadership.

"Is it worth giving all of this up?" Ed pressed.

John's mother begged him to stay at the Academy, but Aileen didn't offer any direction. She privately thought the Academy was too constraining, but she believed it was a decision only he should make. She thought there were already too many people trying to influence him, and told him she'd be happy whichever road he took.

It was an agonizing decision—one that took months to reach, but in the end, John decided to go back to Georgetown. Ed remembered every detail of the hundred-yard walk from John's room to the parking lot that day in November 1987: the cold chill of the wind slipping into the neck of his uniform, the sound of their shoes against the gravel, the look of agony on John's face. Aileen hung back to let the two friends have a final few moments together. At the curb, John had put down his bag and looked around at the buzz of Academy life. Ed saw hesitation rise up for a second and felt a surge of hope. But as quickly as the indecision arose, it passed, and John was reaching up to give Ed a hug. The two men and Aileen stood together for a long minute, arms locked, crying. Then John picked up his bag and walked to the car, leaving Ed and the Navy behind.

Ed, absorbed in the Navy, had missed John and Aileen's wedding because his ship was in the Persian Gulf. But he visited as often as he could; he thought of them as family. He stayed in their big suburban home near Indianapolis when John was a young lawyer and John Jr. had just been born. He showed up at their two-bedroom apartment at Harvard soon after Megan's birth. In Ed's eyes, John and Aileen had always been the ideal couple.

Just recently, Ed had spent several days with them in their new home in New Jersey and was devastated to see what had happened to them. One minute he was downstairs hearing John complain about Aileen and saying he wanted out of this marriage. The next minute, he was upstairs saying goodnight to the children, and Aileen, holding Patrick in her lap, was beseeching him to intervene on her behalf. "Ed, you've got to tell John. You've got to set him straight. Don't let him leave us." She and John had each been on the phone with him again several times after that visit to talk.

And now, here was John again, still in agony, having apparently taken the first step toward leaving Aileen and his kids.

"I just don't think Aileen and I are right for each other," John was saying. "We got married so young. We never dated anyone else, at least not seriously. I don't know if I love her anymore. I'm just not happy with my life. This is not the life I want."

"Are you sure it's Aileen that's the issue?" Ed asked quietly.

"I feel like I'm doing everything. I'm trying to figure out the nursing, I'm trying to start a foundation, I'm calling doctors, and I'm holding down a full-time job," John replied, his calm giving way to a torrent of anger and frustration. "I can't even rely on Aileen to manage the nurses. I can't rely on Aileen for anything."

"John, I know you're feeling a lot of pressure. I know this has been a very tough time," Ed interjected soothingly, listening but carefully refraining from trying to convince John one way or another.

"I can't even talk to Aileen anymore. We're in different worlds. She's walking around planning birthday parties and pretending everything's fine. She doesn't want to think about what's ahead," John said.

"I think Aileen wants me to leave," he added, his voice hushing slightly. "I don't think I'm the right guy for her. I work all the time. I'm no fun anymore. She'd be happier with some big Irish guy who'll watch TV with her at night—someone who wouldn't put so much pressure on her."

Ed thought of Aileen on his last visit—pale and desperate, begging him to make John stay—and couldn't stop himself from correcting his friend. "John, I know Aileen doesn't want you to leave," he said, reassuring but firm. "I know Aileen needs you and the kids need you. I can't even imagine what they'd do without you. Whatever issues you and Aileen have with each other, the children are the most important thing right now. You and Aileen aren't going to resolve your issues right away. Maybe you should just set aside your issues with each other and keep the focus on the kids."

John hung up and sat silently in the parking lot for another hour. He knew what Ed wanted him to do, but he didn't know what he, John Crowley, wanted to do.

Well, that wasn't entirely true. He did know: he wanted to escape from a life with two sick children and nurses and a wife who seemed in denial that everything was terrible.

But was it the *right* thing to do?

John listened to the cars swooshing by on the road behind him. He looked up through the front window and watched the full moon beaming down on his face. It bathed the white church in a luminous, tranquil light.

Moments later, the car's engine revved up and it accelerated out of the driveway onto the interstate—southbound, heading home.

10. Sharon

SPRING 1999
PENNINGTON, NEW JERSEY

On a Saturday morning soon after, a black limo pulled up at the end of the cul-de-sac and stopped outside the Crowley house. John and John Jr., dressed almost identically in jeans and blue "Navy" sweatshirts, were throwing a Nerf football back and forth on their front lawn. The car door opened and out stepped a short, buxom, middle-aged woman with shoulder length platinum blonde hair, dressed in bright orange from her sequined baseball cap to her knit pantsuit and her Birkenstock sandals. White gold rings glittered from every finger and rows of bracelets hung from her wrists. Walking briskly up to John, she stuck out an arm, smiled, and said, with a pronounced Arkansas drawl, "You must be John Crowley. Hi, I'm Sharon Dozier."[1]

As he nodded, slightly stunned, she breezed past him toward the front door, asking, "Where are the kids? Are they inside?" She had disappeared into the open doorway before he could answer.

John stayed outside for a little while, throwing the ball some more with his son, feeling disconcerted. He couldn't believe she had showed up for a first meeting in that getup, but he supposed he should have taken a cue from what he'd seen as her unconventionally loud, pushy tone on the telephone.

John had returned home from his agonized drive that night and slid into bed beside Aileen, determined to make things better. He vowed to stop blaming her for the children's bad nursing care and work instead to find a solution. As a first step, he persuaded Bristol-Myers to drop the agency that took as its fee part of the hourly rate that the company paid for nursing. As a self-insured company, Bristol-Myers could bend the rules in extreme circumstances, and the company agreed to allow John to serve as the nursing coordinator and use the full hourly fee to hire more qualified help. By pooling the nursing allowances for both Megan and Patrick, John calculated he could hire someone to live with them and manage the children's medical care. So he had agreed to pay a headhunter $20,000—almost all of his Bristol-Myers bonus from the previous year—to find him "the Marcus Welby of nurses," someone superbly trained but also possessed of a gentle, pleasant temperament, a grandmotherly figure who could live with them and stabilize the household.

The headhunter had found two potential candidates—both from out of state. John's first choice, a grandmother from North Carolina, had dropped out of contention after an initial phone conversation, unwilling to move to New Jersey, leaving only this Sharon to be interviewed in person. In a phone conversation, she said she didn't want to move either, but she was willing to live with them during the week if he would pay for her to fly home to New Hampshire on weekends. That sounded unworkable, but he had no other candidates, so he arranged for her to fly down for a visit.

"C'mon, let's go inside and see what's going on," he said to his son with a sigh. Their regular Saturday nurse had not shown up, so Aileen was inside attending to Megan and Patrick. Aileen had given John the go-ahead to look for a nurse manager, but with little enthusiasm. She had given up entirely on the possibility that they could find a good nurse. He dreaded her reaction to this lady, afraid she would dismiss her as a crackpot and blame him for yet another nursing problem. This day was surely headed the way of all others at home—downhill, he thought. Sharon Dozier was never going to work out.

In the den, he found Megan and Patrick sitting in their usual spots on the couch, watching TV. He walked into the adjoining kitchen where Aileen, washing dishes, rolled her eyes at him in a dry, sardonic "I told you so" kind of way.

"Nice outfit," she whispered.

"Maybe it's hunting season in New Hampshire," he quipped, relieved that at least Aileen was willing to laugh at the situation. "Where is she?"

He followed Aileen's gaze to the floor on the side of the couch closest to Megan. Sharon was crouched beside the ventilator, fiddling with the adjustments.

"Oh my God," John said, shocked.

"Hi, Mr. John," Sharon called out brightly, having heard his last loud exclamation. "I'm just showing Miss Aileen here the best settings for the kids. They were set too high."

"I told you over the phone, Sharon, about the insurance company insisting that you not touch the kids or their medical equipment because you don't have a license to practice in New Jersey," John said politely but firmly. The woman had just arrived, and she was already breaking the rules.

"I'm here all day for my interview, Mr. John. I may as well help you guys. You sure need it," she said with a big smile.

"Well, you're right about that," he said, taken aback by her confidence and total disregard for the rules. Unlike the other nurses who came in and out like the shift workers they were, Sharon was clearly ready to help. There was something refreshing about that, and he suddenly felt very grateful. She seemed to implicitly live by one of his foremost rules in life: "It's better to ask forgiveness than permission."

"You know, there's something nice about a person who isn't afraid to break the rules," John relented. "I've become pretty good myself at arguing against all the stupid rules. When Megan first came home from the hospital on a ventilator, we were told that after the first week we could only have eight hours of nursing a day. Parents are supposed to manage their child's nursing care the rest of the time. 'I'm sorry, but that's our rule,' our caseworker said. And I told her, 'Yeah, I heard about that rule. That's a very good rule. Now let me tell you why it doesn't apply to my children.' I told the caseworker that Aileen has two other children to take care of, a baby and a four-year-old in preschool. There's no way she can watch over Megan's medical needs while also attending to the other children. My company now pays for round-the-clock nursing."

"Well, you are lucky, Mr. John, that's all I'll say," Sharon said. "I know plenty of families that don't have the nursing they need."

"Lucky—that's funny, Sharon," John said, suddenly quiet. "I haven't thought of us as lucky in a long time."

All day, Sharon attended to the kids, talking nonstop at a high volume.

After she had adjusted the ventilator settings, she began to find other flaws in the children's medical care. "Miss Aileen, you shouldn't do that," she said, when she saw Aileen using the same suctioning machine to clear Megan's and Patrick's tubes. "You need to get the insurance company to pay for another one of these. You're going to give him every infection she has." At feeding time, she questioned why Aileen was giving the children so much formula. She thought they were getting too much food and it wasn't good for them. She asked to see the supply room, and Aileen led her to the corner in the basement where they kept a few extra tubes and medicines. "These are all the supplies you have?" Sharon asked, incredulous. She told Aileen that they could order extra supplies so they didn't have to keep re-ordering and run out. "I didn't know that," Aileen responded to each thing. "Nobody told me that."

"Don't feel badly, sugar," Sharon said. "Nobody ever teaches parents the rules of good nursing and the tricks about ordering supplies. They teach you how to save your children's lives, and home you go. But there's a lot more to good nursing care. It's taken me thirty-three years to learn what I have."

When it came time for the children to take their afternoon naps, Aileen told Sharon that they needed to carry the little ones and their ventilators upstairs to their beds. Aileen lifted Megan into her arms, asking Sharon to follow, lugging the ventilator and battery. Sharon had to ask Aileen to pause every few steps so she could catch her breath. Once Megan was settled, the two of them went back downstairs and repeated the routine with Patrick.

As they settled Patrick into his bed, Sharon piped up again, "Where are the emergency bags, Miss Aileen?" Aileen said they had a bag of emergency medical equipment downstairs. "You really ought to have one beside each of the kids' beds," Sharon commented.

Sharon waited by the bedroom door as Aileen kissed Patrick good-night, nuzzling the little boy under his neck. Once she closed the door behind her, she paused, her hand on the knob, and looked off into the darkness of the hallway. "You know, I'm thirty-one years old, and never in a million years did I think my life would be like this," she said, her voice thin and distant, unconsciously conveying despair.

Sharon's heart went out to the young mother. She thought of her own two adult daughters, Misty and Christy, and shook her head. Nope, neither one of them could handle a situation like this—of that Sharon was convinced. With her long auburn hair, porcelain complexion, and tired green eyes, Aileen looked both beautiful and forlorn.

"Sugar, there's no way you could know all of these things unless somebody showed you how," Sharon said, reaching up to give Aileen a hug. How in the world, she wondered, did this young mother get through one single day—let alone wake up the next morning and go through the same brutal regimen again?

All day, Sharon tried not to be critical and overbearing, but she couldn't help herself. She was bossy by nature, and she thought the children's medical care was a mess. It was exhausting attending to two children on ventilators, and nobody had told the Crowleys they could demand more equipment to make their lives easier. They ought to get a second set of ventilators and IV poles so they didn't have to lug the equipment up and down the stairs twice a day, she thought. She'd tell them that some other time.

With the sick children resting, Sharon lowered herself onto the couch in the den to rest. John and John Jr. were coming through the door again, carrying the same Nerf ball. Sharon looked at the Nerf ball with "Notre Dame" written on it and wondered if he went to that college. His sweatshirt said "Navy" on it, so she had been thinking he was in the Navy. But before she could ask, he was back out the front door. Aileen had made John Jr. lunch. She stuck him in a high chair and plopped a bowl of macaroni and cheese in front of him. Sharon stopped herself from asking what a four-and-a-half-year-old boy was doing in a high chair. Sensing Sharon's silent question, Aileen said, "I can't get him to sit still for a second. This is the only way I can get him to eat."

Sharon watched the little boy lift the fork to his mouth and set it down before he took a bite.

"How long is Sharon staying?" he asked.

"Until tomorrow, John, now eat your food," Aileen said.

The little boy picked up the fork again, but before he could put the macaroni in his mouth, he saw his father out the window in the backyard trying to fix the swing.

"Daddy, Daddy," he shouted, trying to get out of the chair. Aileen groaned, pulled a chair up to his high chair and began to feed him herself. Sharon had seen enough children with attention deficit hyperactivity disorder to diagnose one, but for the second time during her visit, she stopped herself from saying anything.

A few hours later, Megan and Patrick were awake, and Sharon got up to help Aileen give them breathing treatments—pounding on their backs, suctioning their breathing tubes, and inserting medicine in them to ease the airflow. Then Aileen and Sharon put the children and their ventilators in wheelchairs and pushed them to a nearby park. As they walked, Aileen's eyes brightened and her voice grew animated. Sharon noticed that she smiled much more often and chatted easily with the parents of neighborhood children they passed along the way. At length, she pulled up at the edge of a pond, stopping Megan's wheelchair on the muddy bank just a foot from the water's edge.

"C'mon, Sharon, let's feed the ducks," Aileen said excitedly, giggling as she whipped out a loaf of bread hidden on the little shelf under Megan's wheelchair, on top of the ventilator. Sharon stopped Patrick's wheelchair beside Megan's and joined Aileen, tearing apart slices of bread and flinging chunks into the water. Soon, a dozen ducks were quacking and feasting at their feet.

"Give me some," Megan piped up. "I want to throw it myself." Patrick sat quietly beside her, content to watch as Megan went through one slice of bread after another.

Sharon was impressed with Aileen's attitude and told her so. "You know, Miss Aileen, I'm so glad to see you take the kids out to do stuff. I've taken care of handicapped kids for the past twenty years and I've seen too many parents who won't let them go anywhere. If I take care of your kids, I need to know that I can take them out every day to the park and the beach and to movies and picnics. I'm not going to treat them like they're dying."

"I don't have a problem with that," Aileen said. "I want them to have as normal a life as possible."

She paused, and then she added, "Of course, we don't think they're going to be like this forever. We're waiting for a clinical trial to start that will get them the enzyme they're missing and make them all better."

Sharon started to ask Aileen when this trial was starting, but Patrick was now crying, pointing in the direction of home. "I think he's had enough," Aileen said. "It's all right, honey, we're going to go home now," she soothed. She started pushing Patrick's wheelchair toward the park entrance, and he quieted down.

Sharon had only touched the handles of Megan's chair to follow her mother when the little girl let out a scream of protest. "I want to stay—just five more minutes," she wailed.

"I can't, sugar, your brother is tired and we have to go home," Sharon said.

As Sharon pushed, Megan cried and twisted, tears streaming down her face. Aileen seemed unfazed, even when the beepers on the ventilator began to wail.

"I'm sorry—Megan does this every time we leave. She never wants to go home," she said apologetically.

Sharon thought Megan seemed a little spoiled, but she really liked her spunk. "It's always better when the kids want to do more than to have them sitting around refusing to go anywhere," she replied, looking at Aileen with a big smile.

They returned home, gave the children sponge baths and more medicine to help with the breathing, and read a few books before settling them in bed. By 8 P.M., the children were finally asleep. Aileen asked Sharon if she wanted a drink.

"Miss Aileen, I would love a glass of wine," Sharon said, more tired than she could ever remember feeling. Aileen sliced some cheese over a plate of chips to make nachos—dinner. John joined them, and they ate together, standing at the bar in the kitchen.

"Did Aileen tell you about the clinical trials we're waiting for?" John asked as soon as he joined them. He handed Sharon copies of the Pharming and Duke press releases. She had been curious about the experimental medicine ever since Aileen mentioned it in the park.

Sharon skimmed the documents and asked, "When do you think these trials might start?"

"We're hoping any day," John said.

"That's what they've been saying for a full year," Aileen said.

"If these doctors don't get started soon, we'll find other doctors who will," John said. "We've started a foundation of our own. We're going to raise money so we can fund the trials if nobody else will."

"Well, good luck to you, Mr. John," Sharon said. "Nothing would make me happier than to see these babies cured.

"Now, Mister John," she said, changing the subject to indulge her own curiosity. "I saw you throwing a Notre Dame Nerf ball with your son. Did you go to school there?"

"Yup. For law school."

"Wow. I ain't never met anyone who went to Notre Dame," Sharon said, playing up to him.

"Go ahead, hon. Give her the list of schools," Aileen prompted John, knowing that he was dying to list the litany of prestigious schools he had attended.

"Well, I went to Georgetown and the Naval Academy undergrad, Notre Dame for law school, and then Harvard Business School," John said.

"That's more schools than my whole family combined," Sharon said, impressed but also recognizing he liked the opportunity to show off—and giving it to him.

"Mine too," John said. "Lots of great schools. And I've got the student loans to prove it!"

"One other thing, and it's not about schools, it's about George Washington," Sharon said, looking from John to Aileen. "I saw a sign coming in from the airport about 'Washington's Crossing.' Is that the spot where George Washington crossed that river?"

"Funny you should ask, Sharon," John beamed. "Our home is just a few miles from the very spot where George Washington crossed the Delaware River from Pennsylvania into New Jersey to launch a desperate attack on the British garrison at Trenton."

Sharon had no idea what she had just done. John loved American history. He continued on for ten minutes, delivering a soliloquy about Princeton's place in American revolutionary history. "And on January 3, 1777, all of this culminated in the battle of Princeton."

When he finally stopped, Sharon, who had listened to this recitation of

American history politely if dispassionately, smiled at him and simply stated, "That's great, Mister John. Truly fascinating. But you know, a simple 'yes' or 'no' would have sufficed."

John laughed with his boyish smile, liking her wit and sarcasm. He knew he'd been had on this one.

"Now tell us about you, Sharon," he said. "How did a good Southern woman like you end up in New Hampshire?"

"My husband Eddie and I raised our girls in a small town in Arkansas, where I worked as a home care nurse taking care of handicapped children. I took care of the first baby in Arkansas ever to be sent home from a hospital on a ventilator. I even ran my own nursing agency. But then Eddie—he had managed a men's clothing store in Arkansas for twenty years, and then he got an offer to be assistant manager of a new Wal-Mart in New Hampshire for a whole lot of money. We sold the store and moved north."

"How do you like it up there?" Aileen asked.

"We love it," Sharon said. "Our girls both followed us up there with their husbands and children. We all live together in a big old house with nine bedrooms."

"Do you really think you could commute back and forth between here and New Hampshire?" Aileen asked.

"I don't see why not," Sharon said. "I drive two and a half hours each way to go to a hospital in Massachusetts where I work weekends. On weekdays I do the night shift for a child in Maine, and I work days for a family in New Hampshire. I am already what they call a traveling nurse."

By the time they went to bed, it was past midnight. They'd been talking and laughing for three hours, and the three of them had emptied two bottles of wine.

When John climbed into bed that night, Aileen said, "I like her, orange outfit or no orange outfit. That woman knows what she's doing with the kids."

"She's a wiseass," John replied. "She'll fit in with the family just fine."

It was one of the few things they had agreed on in a long time.

On Monday morning, the headhunter called to tell Sharon the Crowleys wanted to offer her the job.

"I'm fifty-four years old. Maybe I'm too old for a job like that,"

Sharon said. She'd been thinking about it the whole day. "I'm pretty much wiped out from my weekend with that family." She wasn't sure whether to accept. She had liked Aileen right off, finding her eager for help and easy to get along with, but John struck her as a bit full of himself with his Notre Dame Nerf ball, his Navy sweatshirt, and all of his colleges and degrees. She couldn't believe he'd had the audacity to deliver a lecture on American history in response to her innocent question about a road sign. But under that cocky exterior, she was certain he was just as desperate as Aileen, or he wouldn't be paying a headhunter thousands of dollars to find her.

"Why don't you at least negotiate salary and see what you think," the headhunter pressed.

"Listen, have you ever taken care of two handicapped children on vents at the same time, mister?" she retorted. "This family bought a house that isn't handicapped-accessible—they are so convinced their kids are going to get saved by a miracle medicine. And I just spent my weekend taking the kids and the equipment up and down and up and down the steps."

"Well, think about it, Sharon," the headhunter said. "All I can say is this family really liked you, and they definitely really need you."

A few days later, rested, and having gotten the go-ahead from her family, Sharon called back to say she would talk salary. If she could make the same amount of money taking care of one family, life would be easier than driving to three different homes in three different states, as she'd been doing each week. And like it or not, she knew the truth about herself—she bored easily and relished a new challenge. Those two children were going to get sicker quickly, unless they got into the clinical trial their parents kept talking about. Keeping them alive—let alone healthy and happy—would be a challenge unlike any she'd ever experienced.

So Sharon made what she thought was a fair proposal. "I need a salary of $70,000, and a travel stipend of $800 a month to help pay for the plane fare. And most important, I must have complete control over the nurses. I've been in situations in the past where nurses try to go around me and ask the family for a day off. I need total control of nursing."

The headhunter called back the same day to say the Crowleys had agreed to everything. They had just one question, he said. "Can you start in two weeks?"

11. Betting on Research

SPRING–WINTER 1999
PENNINGTON, NEW JERSEY; NEW YORK, NEW YORK; DURHAM,
NORTH CAROLINA; BOSTON, MASSACHUSETTS

With life at home stabilized, at least for now, John threw himself back to the task at hand: figuring out which scientist was most likely to succeed with a drug.

Money from family, friends, and Harvard Business School classmates had poured in—more than $60,000 in the first few months of 1999. But who to give it to? There was no one "expert" to ask. Randall was backing Pharming, but Moolhuizen, the head of the Pompe program at the Dutch company, had told John there was no plan to begin a U.S. trial soon. Chen had been delayed several times, and John couldn't pin him down in telephone conversations on the question of when his trial would start.

Slonim suggested that John meet his friend Frank Martiniuk, the research associate at New York University who had been among the presenters at Randall's research conference at the NIH. Martiniuk had worked for years under one of the prominent Pompe researchers, Rochelle Hirschhorn, and the two had only recently parted ways. Slonim considered Martiniuk to be the cowboy of the Pompe research community—brilliant but a little undisciplined.[1]

At Martiniuk's suggestion, the two men met at East Bay Diner across from Bellevue Hospital Center in Manhattan, where he had an office and lab. Tall and lean, with wavy gray hair, Martiniuk was the son of a New Jersey farmer turned truck driver. He had a hardened New Jersey accent and a down-to-earth manner. "Call me Frank," he said, smiling widely as they sat down in a small booth in the corner.[2]

John got right to the point, telling Martiniuk candidly about Megan and Patrick, the Children's Pompe Foundation, and his desire to fund researchers who could produce the fastest results. "We're looking for a scientist who can move quickly into a clinical trial," John said. "We need to beat science—and we need to beat time."

"You've found the right guy then, John," Martiniuk said, his Jersey accent lengthening the name so that it rhymed with yawn. "I've produced some enzyme in CHO cells in my lab. I've treated some mice with Pompe disease. And I have to tell you, John, the results are spectacular." His results were so new he hadn't had time to confirm them or perform the analysis to present them at Randall's conference.

"Can I see the mice?" John asked, leaning forward.

"I would be honored," Martiniuk said. "Let's call it a date. How about a week from today?"

John, Aileen, and John's mother Barbara drove in together to Bellevue Hospital for the tour. John wanted Aileen, in particular, to accompany him so she wouldn't lose hope for the children. He had noticed the distant look on her face when he was telling Sharon about the Pharming and Chen trials, and he knew the delays had dampened her faith that their children would ever get better.

Martiniuk met them at the front gates of the hospital and led them through a labyrinth of crowded corridors to an elevator that took them to the sixth floor. The group chatted nonstop with Martiniuk, discovering that they had a lot in common. He was animated, talking fast and loud, peppering almost every sentence with the words "you know." He said he lived in Union City, which Barbara rushed to tell him was only about six or seven miles from the house where John was raised and where she still lived.

"John, where'd you go to high school?" Martiniuk asked.[3]

"Bergen Catholic," John replied.

"I'm the JV basketball coach there!" Martiniuk exclaimed.

"What's a smart scientist like you doing coaching basketball?" Barbara interjected.

"I played, you know, semipro ball and I love the sport," Martiniuk said, stopping in front of a tan door with a sign that said "Radioactivity—Keep Out," which he said was his trick for keeping out unwanted visitors without having to lock the door. John thought that was very unacademic, and he liked it.

Martiniuk pushed open the door and an appalling, putrid stench emerged, offering the first clue of what lay inside. John followed him into a dark room so narrow and crammed with equipment, plants, and papers that the group had to walk single file. Old magazines, tomato plants, antique-looking bottles of chemical reagents, and a few cages of mice lined the shelves.

John turned to Aileen, who was following close behind. She raised her eyebrows skeptically and gave a slight shake of her head. John shrugged his shoulders a fraction of an inch in return. This looked nothing like the labs they had seen at Duke University or Bristol-Myers.

"This mouse has been getting enzyme for, you know, three to four weeks. Look at him go. He's like an athlete, an Olympic athlete," Martiniuk said, pointing to a sleek brown mouse in a cage. The mouse was scampering energetically through a maze of half-chewed cardboard pieces. "And see those two sick-looking mice in that cage," he continued, pointing to a cage on the shelf below with two animals with shabby, unkempt coats, awake but unmoving. "These are untreated mice with Pompe disease. Don't they look terrible?"

"Dr. Martiniuk, are you telling me that *this* healthy mouse over here looked like *those* sick ones over there before you gave them your enzyme?" Barbara asked.

"You better believe it," he said, with a wide grin. "I'll give these sick ones the enzyme tonight, and you come back here in eight weeks and they'll be just like these strong mice over here."

"Do you want to see the enzyme?" he asked, opening a seven-foot-tall refrigerator with glass doors to pull out a vial of colorless liquid.

"I make it myself," he said, "right over there." He pointed to a hood in the corner of the room. The hood contained a small glass vial with a tiny mechanical arm that was spinning the liquid inside the vial. There were scores of apparently unrelated beakers and vials under the same hood.

"If I had the resources, I could scale up production and treat patients," Martiniuk said.

"Would you be able to treat Megan and Patrick?" John asked.

"I don't see why not," Martiniuk said. "They're patients with the disease. They live close by. It wouldn't be favoritism or anything. It would make sense to put them in my clinical trial."

Barbara grew tearful and turned to Martiniuk, hugging him and saying, "You're the one who will save these babies."

Hope lifted John's spirits above the smell and chaos. "I'd like to be the fellow who helps kick-start your trial," he said, breathless. Here was the chance he'd been looking for to get personally involved in advancing research. "If we funded you, how much money would you need?" He stared at the cage with the strong brown mouse, picturing Megan and Patrick as toddlers running up and down the steps in their house. He felt the same excitement he had in the Netherlands looking at the slides in Moolhuizen's office of tissue from mice treated with enzyme, and again at Randall's meeting, watching Dr. Chen's video of the diseased quails flying.

"John, I would need, you know, a minimum of at least $180,000 for one year to hire an assistant and to buy the mice and materials," Martiniuk replied.

"What could you do in one year?" John asked.

"If all goes well, I could be ready to file an application with the FDA to treat a few patients."

"Do you really believe you could get it done?"

"We could work with a doctor at the NYU School of Medicine to treat a few patients under what is known as a physician's investigational new drug application," Martiniuk said. "It would be a very small clinical trial, a way to get some patients treated very quickly. So, yes, I believe we can get it done."

John, Aileen, and Barbara talked nonstop on the drive back home. Aileen and her mother-in-law had very different opinions on the researcher, as they did on most subjects.

"He's brilliant, absolutely brilliant," Barbara said effusively from the backseat.

"His lab didn't seem very professional," Aileen replied, frowning, from the front passenger seat. "It was so dirty. Do you think he can really make a drug for Megan and Patrick?"

"You can't really call it a lab—it's more like a garage," John laughed. "Doesn't he remind you guys of Doc Brown from *Back to the Future*? He has the same flowing wavy white hair and wild eyes and eccentric personality. He's so crazy he *has* to be brilliant."

"If we wanted to go back in time in a Delorean, that's one thing, but we're looking for a guy who can make something to save our kids," Aileen said. "I don't know about this guy."

"Aileen, I don't know whether he can do what he says he can," John said. "But he's the only guy who's willing to commit himself immediately to make an enzyme to treat Megan and Patrick. Who knows when Chen and Pharming will get going with their trials? We need a backup."

Aileen didn't reply immediately, looking out the window as they pulled onto the New Jersey Turnpike, still uncertain. In the world of science and medicine, she knew they were completely out of their league. There was no way of knowing if Martiniuk or any of these scientists were for real. "You know, you're right," she said at last. "We really don't have many other options."

"John, you give him the money as soon as you can and get him going on this," Barbara added quickly. "I just know he's our man."

John called Martiniuk the next morning and told him the foundation would award him the first research grant. Martiniuk didn't offer John any assurances, and John didn't ask for any. That very day, he wrote the largest check of his life—$60,000—counting the zeros twice to make sure he had gotten it right. He put it in the mail immediately, not wanting to waste one single day in the race to save his children's lives.

Barely a month later, in May, Dr. Chen called to tell John he had permission for the first time from the FDA to test his drug in three infants, and that he finally had enough of it to begin his clinical trial.[4]

John wasn't expecting that call. More than a year had passed since Megan was diagnosed, and Chen had been delayed so many times John had almost given up on him. John was thrilled to hear a trial was finally getting started, even though it would only include babies younger than a year old, which Chen, like the researchers at Pharming, believed was the fastest route to getting FDA approval. It was a practical approach as well. Babies also needed less of the enzyme therapy, which was extremely difficult to make and in short supply.

"If this test goes well, by the end of the year I hope to be able to treat children as old as yours," Chen said.

"Just tell me how I can help, Doctor," John told him.

"Maybe your foundation can help pay for computers and staff to manage the trial," Chen suggested.

The next week, John and his father-in-law Marty flew to North Carolina to see firsthand what was going on with the trial. A smiling Chen greeted them in the waiting room of the low-slung brick Lenox Baker Children's Hospital. He told them he would take them to see the first patient in the trial, a four-month-old-baby who had received his first infusion a few days earlier. His name was John Koncel.

John did a double-take. "I talked to the parents, Deb and Barry, a few weeks ago on the phone. They're from Chicago, right?"

"Yes, that's right. They came to see me just two weeks ago," Chen said.

"They hadn't seen you yet when they called me," John said, sounding embarrassed. "They wanted advice and I told them, 'I've been doing this for over a year and the enzyme has been a month away the whole time.' I told them their baby might have a very short life, and they might end up doing more harm than good by dragging him all around the world in search of a treatment. I can't believe how wrong I was, Doctor. If they'd listened to me, their baby wouldn't be here today in the trial."[5]

"John, it's okay. Believe me, I second-guess myself and my advice all the time," Chen said.

"C'mon, John," Marty said, patting him on the back.

"I'm never going to discourage anyone from doing everything he can to save his child, no matter how futile it seems," John said fiercely. "I remember Randall telling me something similar when we met a year ago in the hotel conference room where Dr. Slonim had examined Megan. I didn't take his advice then, and luckily the Koncels didn't take mine."

Chen led John and Marty outside to an old hospital building, up an elevator, through a set of double doors and into the second patient room on the left. The baby lay in his mother Deb's arms wearing a white one-piece. He was so thin that they could see the palpitations of his swollen heart, as it seemed to pound out of his chest. His eyes were alert, staring up at the visitors, but he didn't lift his head or turn it in their direction; his legs were motionless, his arms hung limply by his side.[6]

John and Marty stayed for only a minute before the doctor beckoned and led them back down a corridor to his office. They were silent on the walk back, struck by how weak baby John looked. Megan and Patrick, who had a less severe form of the disease, looked like prizefighters compared to this baby. John had heard and read descriptions of the "floppy" babies with the classical form of the disease, but seeing a patient was a whole different experience.

"The enzyme has not yet taken effect on baby John," Chen said. "We gave him the enzyme a few days ago. We will know in a few more weeks if it is working."

One month later, Chen called, uncharacteristically ebullient. The doctor was normally so circumspect that John had to rely on his training as a trial lawyer to pry any information out of him. Today, he overflowed. "Baby John is much stronger," he said. "The treatment is working. Do you want to come see?"

John flew down again, this time accompanied by Aileen and Dr. Slonim. Taking Aileen was part of his effort to pull her into his orbit of hope; he asked Slonim along, thinking this would give him the chance to talk with Chen and perhaps the two doctors could collaborate in the future.

Chen, beaming, led the entourage to the same room in the old hospital building. As they walked down the corridor, Chen said he had just gotten the results of the baby's echocardiogram, showing that his heart had reduced in size and had grown stronger. "Most Pompe babies die of heart failure, so a stronger heart is the most important," Chen said.

This time, baby John's room was packed. His aunt and uncle were there, talking excitedly about their plans to take him out for the day. The baby's mother sat in the same chair with baby John in her lap.[7]

Was it the same baby? He was almost unrecognizable. He was sitting up, with just a little head support from his mom. He had been so weak before that John hadn't noticed how cute he was, with his full head of blond hair and enormous blue eyes. Alert and curious, he reached his arms up to the visitors and smiled. Then, following his mother's lead, this baby who had struggled to bat a mobile before his treatment began to patty-cake.

"This is the answer," John said, tears in his eyes. Chen introduced the Koncels to the Crowleys and Slonim. John hugged Deb, the baby's mother; Barry, his father; and then the aunt and uncle, sharing in their joy. This baby's transformation meant hope for Megan and Patrick and all others with Pompe disease. There was no doubt in John's mind that Chen had in hand the miracle drug that would save his children.

Slonim crouched beside the baby, his big nose reddening like he was going to cry. He had been caring for patients for two decades with little real hope to offer. "Trust me, this is amazing," he kept saying.

Once John had finished hugging everyone, he looked for Aileen and found her standing in the doorway, a glazed look on her face. As their eyes met, he saw she was struggling with jealousy, and he recognized it as the same sentiment he had been repressing as he tried to share in the Koncels' joy. The Koncels had found in a few weeks the healing drug for their baby that John and Aileen had been seeking for more than a year.

Luck and timing had been on this family's side. Barry Koncel, an architect, and Deb, an office manager for the American Medical Association, had been referred to Chen by their baby's doctor. They had rushed baby John to Duke to be examined, and were told the same thing—that Chen was hoping to start a clinical trial soon. But where the call had not yet come for John and Aileen, the Koncels had barely returned home a week when the phone rang. It was the genetics counselor for Chen's office on the other end, saying the FDA had approved his trial. "How quickly can you come back here?" she wanted to know.

Today, as Chen led the group from the room, he told them that the hardest part for him was picking the patients to participate in his trial and be given a chance at life over others. He had one severe restriction—the company manufacturing the enzyme had produced enough so far to treat only three babies. Chen knew of four babies who were less than a year old and could still breathe on their own, two criteria for qualifying for the trial that aimed to prove the enzyme treatment could not only keep babies alive but also breathing independently. The only fair way to play God was to enroll patients on a first-come first-serve basis, Chen said. The second baby to qualify had just started treatment. Of the two remaining babies, the final spot would be given to the one whose confirmatory Pompe test result and other paperwork arrived first.

"Dr. Chen, tell me what I can do to help you," John said, eyes wide with excitement.

"Come with me," Chen said.

Aileen and Slonim went to lunch, and John followed Chen up a creaky elevator and down a long whitewashed cinder-block corridor to his small conference room. They settled into two of the six chairs around the table. "What I need most is resources to support the trial," he said. "We need to hire a nurse and a dietitian. I'd like to turn one of our labs into an office for a support team to work. We need computers. These are all things your foundation could buy for us," he said.[8]

"How much do you need?" John asked.

Chen stood up and wrote out line item by line item on the whiteboard. The total: $500,000.

"We can call our new center the 'Megan and Patrick Crowley Center for Pompe Disease,'" Chen said.

"I'll raise the money," John said with no hesitation.

Walking out, he knew it was time to put his fund-raising savvy on the line. He could be remarkably persuasive when he had to be.

Over the next eight months, John and Aileen raised $750,000 through three fund-raising events and an unexpected donation from the neighbor of an old high school friend, Tom Westdyk.

The first fund-raiser was not their idea. Aileen's mother's golfing friends—Mary Stuart, Kathy Scudieri, and Kathy Rosato—offered to plan and host a garden party at their country club. John dismissed the idea at first and then said, "Oh well, whatever little bit comes in will help."

To everyone's surprise—and none greater than John's—the event yielded $80,000. About a hundred relatives and close friends gathered on the second floor of the Beacon Hill Country Club for what was billed a

"garden party." The guests were plied with drinks and hors d'oeuvres before sitting down to dinner and an inspiring speech from John.

"When Megan and Patrick were diagnosed with Pompe last year, we
made a promise to them, and to ourselves, that we would do everything in
our power to change the course of this disease," John said. "The money
that we will raise today is one great step forward to helping us deliver on
that promise to beat nature, now we just have to beat time. As you'll see, we
are blessed to have Megan and Patrick." He introduced the little girl, gor-
geous in a red dress with a matching red bow. "Say hello to everyone,
Megan," he prompted. She waved from her perch in her new red wheelchair, with her name embroidered in black on the back. Her eyes shone
and her face was flushed; she loved the attention. Patrick, who hated the
limelight, had stayed home with Sharon.

For the next fifteen minutes, John talked about the children's diagnoses, his discovery of the experimental treatments being tested, and the
fact that no trials were being conducted in his children's age group.

"There's no doubt in my mind that, with your donations, we can
fund a clinical trial to save Megan and Patrick," John finished, voice quiv-
ering. Aileen's brother Marty, who cohosted the live auction that followed, prodded the tearful guests to bid thousands of dollars for things
they didn't need, from fountains to goldfish ponds and weekend stays at
one another's country homes. The goldfish pond went for a stunning
$8,000.

Perhaps more valuable than the actual money raised was the transfer of
knowledge. John and Aileen immediately recognized a proven formula for
successful fund-raising. That summer, John convinced the Muscular Dystrophy Association (MDA), one of the best-known patient advocacy groups
in neuromuscular diseases, to host a fund-raiser in Boston and donate the
money to Pompe researchers. Leveraging every connection he had, John
got Textron Inc. to donate $10,000 to help underwrite the dinner at a
restaurant near Faneuil Hall called The Rack. (It got its name from its up-
scale pool hall—and, unbeknownst to John until the night of the fund-
raiser, because of the buxom, scantily clad cocktail waitresses.) John was
good friends with Bradley, the son of Textron's CEO, Lewis Campbell.
Bradley had followed John from Marakon Associates to Bristol-Myers.

Aileen, now a believer, made gift baskets for the Boston fund-raiser—

one with pastas and sauces, another with chocolates and champagne. So great was her enthusiasm that she bid on the baskets herself during the silent auction, trying to drive up the prices. John warned her in a loud whisper that time was running out, but, a glass of wine in hand, she batted him away, saying, "You and your Harvard Business School logic—can't you see I'm trying to drive up the price." The next day, grim-faced and hung-over, she and John loaded the baskets back into their car, Aileen still refusing to acknowledge that her bidding tactic had cost the family $1,000. They had bought back the very baskets she had so painstakingly made and driven up to Boston the day before.

The event netted about $50,000, and an Aileen story that John would regale friends with for years. The MDA had agreed to earmark the money for two researchers chosen by John—and he decided right off to divide it between Drs. Chen and Slonim. Intent on covering all the bases, John had pledged $500,000 to Slonim so he could also hire a dietitian and a nurse to support a clinic focused on treating Pompe and related diseases. The money was also to be used to hire an assistant to help Slonim publish an academic paper describing the nonclassical infantile form of Pompe disease—the kind that usually struck older babies and toddlers, like Megan and Patrick. John knew that if Pharming ever began a clinical trial in the United States, Slonim would be the principal investigator.

The final event that fall was one that John and Aileen organized, assisted by a battalion of relatives and friends and the event-planning team at Bristol-Myers. It was held on a high floor of the Millennium Hotel in New York, overlooking Broadway. Aileen, after hours of training in spreadsheets from her Uncle Jim, handled the accounting. Ed Devinney, John's buddy from the Naval Academy, showed up to help him unload a pickup full of donations for the silent auction and carry them through the hotel lobby, up in the elevator to the party room. John's mother designed the invitations and persuaded her hairdresser to get his good friend Ben Vereen, the Broadway musical star, to show up and sing "Impossible Dream."

But nobody could match Bristol-Myers in the sheer breadth of assistance. John had been promoted and reported directly to the chief of the

U.S. pharmaceutical business, who put the full weight of the company behind the fund-raiser. Not only did Bristol-Myers pay $50,000 to under-
write the event, but most of the senior executives sent out personal
invitations to Bristol-Myers's top vendors, who bought tables for $10,000
apiece. Many of these executives, accompanied by their spouses, also attended the event.[9]

The company's event planners donated their time and produced a
video for the evening featuring John, Aileen, Martiniuk, and Slonim talking about the promise of a treatment in the near future. Greg Assink,
whom John had recruited to join his foundation months earlier, flew from
Hudsonville, Michigan, for the event, carrying a picture of Kelsey, his
daughter with Pompe, who was now six years old.

Although they'd been talking on the phone for months, Greg hadn't
met John in person until the evening of the dinner. "I feel like I'm meeting
my twin," Greg gushed when Aileen led him over to John, who was bidding
in the silent auction. The two men shook hands and hugged. They looked
nothing alike—Greg, balding, blue-eyed and blond, stood half a foot
taller—but with their boyish smiles, they exuded the same unabashed enthusiasm. Greg handed John a thick wad of checks. "This is everything
we've collected from our friends and relatives—close to $20,000," he said
with justifiable pride.[10]

John kept Greg by his side for much of the evening, introducing him
to his and Aileen's extended families, the Bristol-Myers executives, and the
Pompe researchers who were among the three hundred and fifty people in
attendance. Martiniuk, whose JV basketball team had a game that night,
didn't come, but Drs. Slonim and Chen were gaily socializing, as was Dr.
William Canfield, the naysaying researcher from Oklahoma whom John
had first met at Randall's conference. Canfield had made a trip to meet
John in New Jersey earlier in the year, looking for funding for a new company he had started, and although John hadn't given him any money, he
had invited him to the fund-raiser.

"Aileen, I think we're finally where we need to be," John whispered to
her, choking up as they stood up from the head table—he in a black tuxedo,
she in a purple taffeta gown—welcoming the guests. "This is amazing. All
of these people and they're here for us, for the kids."

Then he played the video showing him and Aileen at home with

Megan and Patrick, who sat on either side of the couch in the den, their ventilators beside them. Aileen described the children's healthy infancy, their devastating diagnoses, and their rapid weakening to the point that they now needed ventilators to breathe. The camera closed in on John carrying Megan, a floppy white bow in her long brown hair, with Aileen's melodic voice filling the room. "On most nights, Megan always dances with her daddy before she goes to bed," Aileen said. Then the camera focused on Aileen's wide-eyed, cherubic face, seeming to radiate hope, as she blinked, nodded her head, and said, "I just believe, I know in my heart that one day she'll be dancing with him at her wedding. I just know we need to keep pushing the science, and one day they will be cured. They're going to be better, one day, soon."

By the end of the night, the Children's Pompe Foundation had taken in another $150,000.

Greg went home from the event feeling even more taken with the Crowleys than he had been from their conversations over the phone. "They're just like us," he told his wife. "Every aunt and uncle and cousin and grandparent was there supporting them."

The single biggest donation that John and Aileen received that year, however, was not one they had personally solicited. Like most of John's friends, his childhood buddy Tom Westdyk had been helping raise money, and his wife had mentioned the Crowleys' mission to a neighbor who ran a family foundation. The neighbor, moved by the story, invited John and Aileen to her office and told them her foundation would donate $250,000 on the condition the gift remain anonymous. The Crowleys thanked her gratefully.

As 1999 drew near a close, John had money to give out and influence to exert. For the first time, it felt like he had some ability to control the direction his children's lives were taking, and some ability to meld the areas he was good at—business and management—into the world of medicine and disease in which he'd previously been so helpless. He liked being in this position, and he didn't waste any time. He wrote several other checks: one for $100,000 to Chen, another for $60,000 to Martiniuk, and a final one for $100,000 of his $500,000 commitment to Slonim.

All that was needed now, John thought, was for another clinical trial to begin.

12. "Let's Just Do It"

In the fall of 1999, Dr. Chen called John at his office to ask for his help reviewing a manufacturing contract. John had evolved into more than just a benefactor to the Duke doctor. With his legal background and his job at a big drug company, he had become a trusted adviser to both Chen and his Taiwanese corporate partner, Synpac Pharmaceuticals. They had previously told John that their biggest challenge was manufacturing the enzyme. John used his connections at Bristol-Myers to try to help. First, he tried to broker a deal for Bristol-Myers to buy Chen's research program, bringing the Duke scientist and his Synpac partner to a meeting with Bristol's top drug development team. While the company officials wanted to help John, they could not legitimize investing millions in such a risky project in a disease they knew almost nothing about. So John had settled for the next best thing—getting Bristol-Myers to pull a biotechnology drug manufacturing plant off the selling block and sign a contract to produce Chen's enzyme there.[1]

Today, Chen spoke hurriedly, as if he wanted the call with John to be over as quickly as possible. John, as always, pressed for details on the progress of the clinical trial.

"How are the babies doing?" he asked. He knew two additional babies had joined the trial.

"Not doing so good," Chen said.

"What? Why?"

"There could be many reasons," the doctor said tersely.

"What is your hunch?" John pressed.

"Antibodies," came the cryptic reply.

"What are they?"

"John Koncel's body seems to be viewing the enzyme therapy as a foreign substance," Chen said. "His body's immune system is making antibodies to knock off the enzyme. So the enzyme is not having much effect anymore."

"What about the other baby?"

Chen said the second baby in the trial was still doing well, but he hadn't been receiving the therapy as long. He couldn't predict if the other baby would develop the problem as well.

John hung up and sat silently, trying to absorb the blow. He felt like he was floating in a cold sea, and the life preserver he had been reaching for had been violently ripped away. He was supposed to travel to Duke's business school the next week to recruit employees for Bristol-Myers, and he decided that he would drive over to Children's Hospital and find out more.

The day John arrived at Duke, baby John Koncel was receiving one of his weekly infusions. By now, John was not only a major benefactor of Chen's, but he was also such a frequent visitor at the hospital that a nurse led him right to baby John's room. The baby was in the same room as before, this time alone, lying in his crib. John walked over and peered inside at the eight-month-old baby, seeing immediately that the little face that had been so alert the last time he visited looked pale and tired. The baby had a tube in his nose for feeding, which meant he was having difficulty swallowing.[2]

"Oh, you poor little guy," John said, choked up, stroking the baby's head.

"He was doing so well before," the nurse said.

"I saw him myself," John nodded.

"He got even stronger than that. We even let his mom take him home to an apartment nearby. . . ." She gestured unhappily at the baby's limp arms.

"How long has this been going on?" John asked.

"A couple of weeks."

He shook his head regretfully. "And how are his parents doing?"

"They're incredibly strong," the nurse said. "His mother is by his side constantly. She must have stepped away for lunch, but other than mealtimes, she never leaves. His father flies out here from Chicago all the time. I don't know how they do it."

They stood by the crib in silence, listening to the labored sound of the baby's breathing. His nostrils flared with each breath, a sign of the effort it took for each gulp of air.

"I hate to say this," John said, "but he looks and sounds a lot like my own son Patrick did right before we had to put him on a ventilator."

A few days later, John dialed Martiniuk, trying to get an update on his research.

"He's in the lab," his assistant said, promising he would call back.

A week later, John called Martiniuk again. Again, his assistant said he was in his lab, and again she promised that he would return the call.

Frustrated, John realized he had no idea what Martiniuk was doing with the money from the Children's Pompe Foundation. In the weeks after he'd agreed to fund Martiniuk back in April 1999, John had tried to broker a deal between the scientist and a biotech company in California called BioMarin Pharmaceutical, which was interested in developing his research into a treatment. John had concluded, rightly, that scientists weren't experienced in turning research into medicine and could move much faster with the funding and expertise of a drug company behind them. BioMarin was developing a treatment for a related disease, also caused by a defect in an enzyme—but a different one—responsible for processing waste material inside cells. John thought it would be a perfect partnership. He flew Martiniuk and Slonim with him to California to meet with BioMarin. Soon company executives had flown east to follow up. It looked like a match made in drug industry heaven, until BioMarin sat down to make a deal with lawyers for New York University Medical Center and failed to reach an agreement. Martiniuk was disappointed, but John was crushed.[3]

Never one to dwell on failures, John's attention had shifted quickly to Chen, who had called soon after with news of FDA approval to start his trial. Chen had consumed almost all of John's time and attention—and hope—that summer and fall. Now he realized he had no idea where Martiniuk stood with his research. With Chen's trial in trouble, John wanted and needed to know about Martiniuk's progress. Almost a year had gone by since he'd given him the first check, and he didn't even know whether Martiniuk was close to starting the clinical trial for his children.

When no call came in from Martiniuk the next week, John dialed again. This time, the scientist picked up.

"Frank, it's John Crowley. I was just wondering how the research is going."[4]

"Things are going very well, John," Martiniuk said. "It's been very busy. I'm in the middle of a very important experiment now. And I have two grant applications due next week. I'll give you a call after that, I promise."

"I was just wondering if you could send me a progress report or something on your research, Frank," John said.

"Things are going very well, John, very well," Martiniuk repeated.

"Well, how close are you to filing the IND?" John asked, referring to the application to the FDA to begin a clinical trial. "A year's almost up and I was wondering if we were close."

"The research is going great. We're testing the enzyme in older mice to see if we can reverse the defect, and they've been able to recover. We've reversed the defect! They're running on the wheel. I'm doing studies now looking at how low we can dose them. But we need to do more work to file with the FDA. We're going to need more money and more time to get there."[5]

That night, John came home and headed right into his study. Aileen knew something was wrong when he didn't come upstairs first to help her put the kids to bed. After she had put the kids to sleep, she found him on the phone with Dr. Slonim. From the kitchen, as she boiled a pot of pasta for the two of them, she listened to him talking, his frustration making his voice louder and shriller.

"I'm getting worried, Alf," he was saying, now so close to Slonim that he called him by his nickname. "Chen's trial isn't going so well. Baby John has built up antibodies. And I've no idea what's going on with Martiniuk. He says he's getting great results, but he doesn't seem close to filing his stuff with the FDA to begin a trial for the kids. And now he wants more money."

Whatever Slonim was saying seemed to have a calming effect on John. John always trusted Slonim's advice.

"I appreciate that, Alf," John said before hanging up. "I'd just like to find out how far he is from filing the IND."

"Having trouble with Martiniuk?" Aileen asked when John emerged from his study.

"I'm pissed that he doesn't seem anywhere near ready to get papers to the FDA to start a trial," John said. "It's almost impossible to reach him. Alf is going to call and get me an update."

"I didn't know about baby John," Aileen said quietly, as she set the dining table.

"I didn't want to worry you," John said. "It's not all terrible, it's just that the enzyme isn't working on baby John right now because his body's immune system is making things called antibodies to fight the enzyme. Chen is trying different strategies for getting rid of the antibodies. Hopefully, one of them will work."

Aileen was quiet. Ever since she had seen baby John, she had been counting on Chen's enzyme to save her children. The disappointment she felt now was too enormous to absorb. Instead of trying, she changed the subject.

"I've been thinking about what we should do for Megan's birthday," she said. "Let's take her on a special trip out—just the three of us. We'll take her to that cute little toy store at the mall and let her pick out whatever she wants. And then we can go to Friday's with her for dinner."

"What's Megan going to wear?" John asked, giving in to Aileen's need for diversion. This was one way he had adapted since deciding to come back to her that night nearly a year ago. People had their own ways of coping, and he tried not to be so judgmental about hers.

"I found the perfect dress at Baby Gap," Aileen enthused. "It's blue with little flowers."

"It sounds beautiful, honey," he said, kissing the top of her head gently. Aileen gave him a brilliant smile.

That night, after Aileen had gone to bed, John sat at his desk in his study, thinking. He needed another backup. There was only one more horse to bet on—and it was a long shot.

He had held off investing in Dr. Canfield's new company, even after meeting twice with him over the past year to discuss his research. John and Marty, Aileen's dad, had even flown out to Oklahoma City for a day to see Canfield's operation firsthand. But John had continued to hold off, in part because he had been so convinced that Chen's research was the answer, and Canfield was just a skeptic, insisting the Duke scientist's enzyme treatment would never work because it didn't have the right attachments of carbohydrates and phosphates. But also—and perhaps more crucially—Canfield was so far behind Chen and Pharming that John really *hoped* he was wrong. Canfield was still testing his potential drug in test tubes, where Chen and Pharming were in human clinical trials. Megan and Patrick didn't have the time to wait for him to test his treatment in animals and advance into human clinical trials.

But with Chen's success in doubt and Martiniuk's progress uncertain, John decided it was time to reach out to Canfield. He picked up the phone and called Oklahoma City, counting on the time difference to find Canfield still in his office.

"Dr. Canfield, I'm calling with some really good news," John said. "We just got two hundred and fifty grand from a family foundation. We'd like to invest it in your company."[6]

Canfield, who had been struggling to get his company off the ground, didn't say anything. He seemed stunned at his sudden good fortune, and it took him a few moments to respond. Then he bubbled over with enthusiasm. "John, that's the best news I've heard in a long time! Shall I come out there? Do you want to come here? How shall we proceed?"

John told him he would fax over an agreement shortly and, once it was signed, a check would quickly follow.

The agreement arrived at Canfield's office a few days later. At his desk, he reviewed the typewritten pages. In exchange for its investment in his company, the Children's Pompe Foundation wanted a seat on Canfield's company board, 2 percent ownership, and a commitment that the first clinical trial would test the therapy in patients with Megan and Patrick's nonclassical form of Pompe disease. Canfield had known the foundation might seek a board seat and a small amount of equity, but he had never imagined it might try to influence the direction of his research and drug development. He slammed the pages onto the table and picked up the phone.

"I knew it was too good to be true," Canfield fumed to his lawyer, Doug Branch. "I could never agree to tie my hands in that way."[7]

That same day, Canfield called to tell John he couldn't agree with the investment contract. "I want to treat your children," he said quietly, "but I cannot accept these terms. It would be unethical."

John backed down immediately. "Fine. We'll take that provision out, Doctor," he said. "We trust you to design the best trial possible for all children."

"It was worth a try," he told Aileen's dad Marty later. "But we'll have to find another way to work with him."[8]

By January, Canfield had the $250,000 in the bank, and the Children's Pompe Foundation owned a board seat and a small stake in Canfield's nascent company. And Canfield was finding his new investors to be a fountain of assistance in many ways besides financial. He needed to find a chief executive to run the company, and John and Marty agreed to help. When a search firm turned up a potential candidate for CEO, Marty agreed to interview the guy. He called Canfield back, confirming the scientist's impression that the candidate wasn't up to snuff. "He doesn't have the fire in the belly—let's keep looking."

After another couple of weeks went by and no better candidate emerged, Canfield began to call, downcast.

"I don't think I can get the right candidate to Oklahoma to work for a small startup," he said to John in a late-night phone call.[9]

"You may be right, Bill," John said, now on a first-name basis with Canfield. "Hell, maybe I should come there and run the company for you."

No sooner had the words come out than both men paused, each one finding the idea both intriguing and frightening.

"Are you old enough to be a CEO?" Canfield finally ventured.

"I'm thirty-two," John replied.

Hearing no response on the other end of the line, he added, "Michael Dell is thirty-three."

"Well, let me talk to the folks over here about the idea," Canfield said.

"I don't know if I can do it anyway, Bill," John said. "I just threw out the idea, but I just got a promotion at Bristol-Myers. Our families are all here. . . ."

That night, John couldn't sleep. He couldn't stop thinking about his conversation with Canfield. It seemed like such a crazy idea that he knew he should just drop it, but somehow he couldn't get it out of his mind.

The next morning, he called Slonim to see what he thought. Taken aback, the doctor told John that it was one thing to start a foundation donating money to researchers, but an entirely different thing to put himself at the front line.[10]

"Research is so slow and so frustrating. It's one step forward, two steps back. It's emotionally taxing on the most objective researchers. It'll be far too hard on a father whose children's lives depend on the outcome.

"Don't do it, John," Slonim continued. "Your family needs you too much. This will take you away from them."

Next, John called Andy Singer, his classmate from Section J at Harvard Business School, who worked as a biotechnology investment banker at Robertson Stephens. It was Andy who had introduced John a year earlier to officials at BioMarin, helping start the failed conversations about a joint venture with Martiniuk.

Today, Andy, too, urged caution—but for a different reason.[11]

"Nobody will invest in the company if you're CEO," Andy said. "They'll see your conflict of interest. It will be a huge red flag for any potential investor."

John knew Slonim and Andy were right, but he still couldn't let go of the idea.

A few nights later, after the kids were in bed, he broached the topic with Aileen as they sat in the dining room eating dinner together.

"You know the Oklahoma company we just invested the foundation money in," he said. "If I were to become CEO of the new company, what would you think?"

"What—why on earth would you do that?" Aileen asked, shocked. She was accustomed, by now, to being thrown curveballs by her husband, but this latest bombshell didn't even make sense to her. "You *know* you're happy at Bristol-Myers. They've treated us very well. You got *two* promotions; you're going to be the youngest vice president in the whole freakin' company. And they pay for all the kids' health benefits. You can't just walk away from that."

She'd talked him through the crises of leaving the Naval Academy for Georgetown, exiting law practice for Harvard Business School, and resigning from Marakon for Bristol-Myers, but still, she hadn't seen *this* one coming.

"Aileen, I feel like we're running out of time," John said, his face flushed and his pitch rising with passion. "Chen's trial isn't going well. I have no idea where the hell Martiniuk is with his research. Aren't you tired of being told the clinical trials will include other people's babies, not ours? Aren't you tired of being told to stay home and wait for a phone call? I think there's only one person who's going to make this happen for our kids—and that's *me*." His voice grew hoarse with emotion. "Here's a chance for me to get involved instead of waving from the sidelines," he finished, tears flooding his eyes.

"Will we have to move to Oklahoma?" Aileen asked, softening with her husband's fervor, but still wisely honing in on where the job might lead.

"I don't think so, but it will mean I'll be away from home a lot," he said, wiping his eyes. "I won't be able to be around as much for you and the kids."

Aileen set her napkin aside and came around the table to stand by him. "Sharon and I can handle the kids and the house," she said, wrapping her arms around him tightly. "John, I know you're the only one who can get this done. And you know that, too. If you think it's right, then just do it."

The next week, John put together a booklet at Kinkos with his résumé and several years of stellar Bristol-Myers job reviews, and boarded a plane for Oklahoma City, determined to persuade Canfield to hire him.

Canfield had spent the two weeks since John first suggested becoming chief executive fretting over his conflict of interest. He talked for hours to his lawyer, Doug Branch, pondering whether the father of children with the disease the company was striving to treat could possibly be expected to act in the best business interests of the firm.[12]

Doug, a low-key, amiable deal maker, had accompanied Canfield east the previous year when he visited John. He'd been impressed even then with John's exuberance, his Bristol-Myers experience, and his educational background. He pushed Canfield to consider John's enormous personal and professional attributes. "We can manage the conflict," Doug told Canfield, arguing John had the kind of "never say die" attitude that no amount of money could buy.

Unbeknownst to John, by the time he appeared in his pin-striped blue suit in Canfield's corner office on the fourth floor of the Presbyterian Health Foundation Research Park, the scientist had already decided to offer him the job. Now sold on John, Canfield was worried that he might not take the position, so he set about wooing John in the only way he knew how—with a highly technical scientific presentation on his progress so far in developing the enzyme treatment.

For four hours, Canfield stood at the white board in his corner office, drawing diagrams and writing out equations in black marker. He detailed the multiple-step process that he had developed over the past decade for extracting two processing enzymes, and using them to produce a version of the Pompe enzyme with the right sugar attachments to be transported to the lysosomes of muscle cells, where it was needed.[13]

John nodded brightly, if a bit dazedly, hoping Canfield didn't realize he understood very little of the seemingly never-ending lecture. When Canfield finally concluded, John asked only one question.

"How long before it's ready for a clinical trial?"

"One year," came the response.

John had heard that one before, but this time he believed it—because he was no longer relying on someone else. He was going to make it happen.

The job offer came a half hour later when they were lunching at Coach's Restaurant, a sports bar and restaurant within the AAA baseball park in downtown Oklahoma City. And it didn't come from Canfield, but from Doug, who joined them for lunch.

"We really want to offer you the position of CEO," Doug said in his Oklahoma drawl, and proceeded to briefly describe the offer. "We understand this might take some time to arrange, but this would all work best if you were to move to Oklahoma."

John didn't negotiate the salary, which was less than his almost $200,000 take-home pay at Bristol-Myers, or even inquire about the health benefits, so vital to his children's nursing care. He didn't argue about relocating his family to Oklahoma City, fearing that the hint of a reluctance to move might upset the job offer he now desperately wanted. He would figure out those things later.

"I really want to do this," he said, beaming. Pushing all his doubts away, he faced the two men squarely, put on his game face, and echoed his wife's advice from earlier in the week: "Let's just do it."

13. A Rocky Start

SPRING–SUMMER 2000
OKLAHOMA CITY, OKLAHOMA; HORSCHAM, PENNSYLVANIA;
PENNINGTON, NEW JERSEY; NEWTON, MASSACHUSETTS;
NEW YORK, NEW YORK

On the morning of April 3, 2000, John appeared in Canfield's office, looking alert and eager in a sharp gray suit and red tie. In his weathered brown briefcase he carried a legal pad he'd filled at night with questions to ask and plans to put in place. On page 4, under "Mission," he'd written: "Get Canfield's science into human clinical trials within a year." The last part—"within a year"—was circled and underlined twice.

To do that, John knew, he would need to raise millions, maybe even tens of millions of dollars. That's how the chief executive of a fledgling firm spends most of his time, he had been told. In conversations over the phone, Canfield had told him he had almost nailed down the first, or "angel" round of financing—the $1.2 million needed to get the company off the ground. There were many local people ready to invest, including a small local venture capital firm, Chisholm Private Capital, and several wealthy oil executives. John's job would be to finish off the angel round and quickly begin what was called a Series A round—the first major effort drawing in several venture capital firms.

Canfield ushered John into a small office beside his. The office had a single window overlooking the parking lot of the sprawling, modern technology office park that looked strangely out of place against the backdrop of the aging city's skyline.

"You'll have to make do with this small desk and chair for now," he told John apologetically. "I've ordered more furniture, but it's not in yet." Neither were John's computer or phone lines. Canfield also introduced him to Tony McKinney, an intense but affable man with a pronounced Southern accent whom Canfield had recruited from a small Texas biotechnology firm to be the head of drug development. McKinney, a native of Oklahoma, was still amazed he'd been able to find a biotechnology company to come home to.[1]

As Canfield sat with John in his office later in the day, he gave him his first assignment: "Drive down to Chisholm Private Capital, meet the venture investors, and get them to sign on to the deal." Chisholm was one of the only venture capital firms in Oklahoma investing in early-stage research companies, Canfield told John, and the partners were ready to commit to a half-million dollars at least. They were waiting to meet the new chief executive before making a formal commitment to invest.

John was able to get a meeting with the venture capital investors the next day. He showed up at their offices a mile away in a modern high-rise office building downtown. The two partners were waiting for him in a second floor office and greeted him. Their smiles faltered a bit as they absorbed how young John was, but nonetheless the introductions were cordial as they sat down at a small table. John Frick, a fifty-year-old Stanford University Business School graduate, took the lead and began prodding John about his business background. He wasted no time getting to the heart of the matter.[2]

"Ever run a company, son?" Frick asked.

John did his best to talk around the question, describing his experience as a trial lawyer before business school, his foray into the business world as a financial analyst for Marakon, and his quick rise at Bristol-Myers to executive director of the committee that ran the company's pharmaceutical business.

"That's all very good, but really—ever run a company before?" Frick asked again, this time with a touch of impatience and condescension.

"No I haven't, but at Bristol-Myers I was being groomed for a leadership position at the company. I was about to become the youngest vice president there," John said, hoping a big smile and the luster of a successful pharmaceutical company would get him past this shaky ground.

"There's a big difference here," Frick declared, grumpily. "In Bristol-Myers, raising money is mainly a political process. If you're CEO of a small startup, you need to convince investors that you not only have good science, but that you're also an expert at fund-raising continuously. And besides that, your drug development plans I've seen are completely unrealistic. You guys seem to think you're going to go into clinical trial next year. Based on all the data I've seen, it's going to take much longer . . ."

"That data doesn't apply to us," John interjected vehemently. "We're going to do it better and faster and cheaper."

Frick leaned back in his seat, sighing, and rolled his eyes at his partner. "You obviously know that no venture capitalist is going to invest in a company run by an inexperienced chief executive and a scientist who has never worked outside of an academic lab."

"I'm sorry, I, uh, don't understand," John said, horrified at the direction the meeting was taking. "Dr. Canfield has done groundbreaking science that is very impressive, and every CEO starts somewhere. I have all the right academic credentials and excellent legal and business training."

"Young man, no venture capitalist is going to invest in this company, and that's just a fact," Frick said, abruptly standing up. His partner stood up, too, and the two men began walking to the door, leaving John no choice but to rise and follow.

"This will be good learning experience for you," Frick said, patting John's back as he closed the door.

John drove back to the office in shock. Canfield had no explanation for the change that had come over the venture investors whom he had been certain were ready to commit to his new company, but the effect was worryingly predictable. In the world of venture capital, there was almost always a domino effect. Sure enough, that same week, the Oklahoma City oil executives stopped returning Canfield's phone calls. Several of them had been talking to Canfield about making substantial investments of $50,000 to $100,000 or more.

Canfield tried to reassure John. Luckily, he said, he had another source of investment that was almost guaranteed. A small, publicly traded drug company, Neose Technologies, was eager to form a partnership. "Once we get Neose on board," Canfield said confidently, "we'll have the credibility to get Chisholm and other venture investors to sign on."

Canfield scheduled a meeting for the end of the week at Neose's offices in Horscham, Pennsylvania. Before they left, he opened his locked desk drawer and gave his new chief executive the company checkbook. John scanned it quickly and his eyes widened. There was only $37,000 in the bank—barely enough to make payroll for the month. Things with Neose had better work out, or this company was in deep trouble.

Neose was a pioneer company in Dr. Canfield's area of expertise, glycobiology, the study of carbohydrates, which had lagged behind the sexy scientific breakthroughs in decoding genetic material, or proteins. Companies had been making proteins and using them as drugs for the past decade, for the most part ignoring the attached complex carbohydrates or sugars. But glycobiologists like Neose's founder, Dr. Stephen Roth, were now studying carbohydrates, and showing that they played an important role in directing the proteins to which they were attached to the right region of the body. Roth, the former head of the department of biology at the University of Pennsylvania, had founded Neose not to develop its own drugs, but as a service company, to improve other companies' protein medicines by attaching the right carbohydrates.[3]

To keep tabs on the latest innovation in university labs, Neose had started a competitive program to award two $75,000 research grants each year to scientists, no strings attached. The applications from labs around the country gave Neose a window into the work of the top university scientists. In 1998, the company's scientists had chosen Canfield from the 200 applicants, recognizing both the brilliance of his work and its commercial potential.[4]

Neose scientists had known it was theoretically possible to try to treat patients with Pompe and other lysosomal storage diseases by making the protein that is defective in patients—in each case a particular enzyme—with the correct carbohydrate attachments. But the Neose team didn't even consider undertaking such a project with Pompe because they knew how long and complicated the enzymes involved were. It would take years to figure out the structure, let alone make them in a lab, if that was even possible.

When the Neose team reviewed Canfield's application, they realized that someone had actually *already* spent years figuring out the unimaginably complex process. "If he can do what he says he can do, this is a potential gold mine," Roth said to his team. But Roth had been in the business long enough to know the road from the lab to the market is littered with the failures of some of the most exciting and promising science. Now Canfield was pressing for a partnership with Neose, and though Roth and his scientists were impressed, they were still full of questions about whether Canfield's science was ready for prime time.

Accompanied by Canfield and Doug, John flew back east for the meeting at Neose's offices, hoping to seal a deal. Neose's offices were in a converted warehouse in Horscham, an old industrial town about an hour from Philadelphia. Roth and a half-dozen company scientists and regulatory and business officials were waiting in a spare, windowless conference room. As with the interview with Chisholm, they had a list of tough questions to help them decide whether to invest in Canfield's company.

Roth, dapper in a pin-striped suit and a red and blue University of Pennsylvania tie, led the questioning. At age fifty-five, he was about ten years Canfield's senior, far more experienced in the business world, and accustomed to grilling junior scientists.

"How are you getting the PTase?" he began, using the abbreviation for phosphotransferase, the name for the first of the two processing enzymes Canfield planned to use to make his Pompe enzyme.[5]

"We're purifying it out of lactating bovine udders," Canfield responded.

"Cows? Where are you getting the udders from?" Roth asked.

"The stockyards," Canfield said.

"Roger Decker from our company picks them up once a week; they weigh eighty pounds each," John interjected eagerly, trying to be helpful. Canfield scowled at him, making clear he was not to try to add anything to the scientific discussion.

"Never in a million years can you inject cow protein into people," Roth responded, his tone angry. "The FDA would never allow it."

"He's right, you can't do that," said Marjorie Hurley, Neose's head of regulatory affairs. She was a petite woman who was in charge of getting drugs approved by the FDA, and the very notion of trying to get the FDA to sign off on such a scheme had put an expression of pain on her face. "The FDA will never approve a product using a protein derived from cows."

"The bovine version is only for lab work," Canfield said between his teeth. His tone was turning defensive as the questions kept coming. He said he was working on making a different, human version of the PTase enzyme for use in the drug trials.

"What about uncovering enzyme?" asked Roth, naming the second processing enzyme Canfield needed to make his Pompe enzyme.

"Making it in T-293, taken from human kidney cells."

"Oh no—the FDA would never allow that, either," Hurley said. Her big eyes seemed to grow wider with each of Canfield's answers. Kidney cells weren't considered sterile enough to be used as a factory for growing enzymes or any other protein for human therapeutic uses.

"Well, we're planning to change the cell line," Canfield said defensively. He was breathing heavily now as he paced in front of the whiteboard.

"Are you going to make all three enzymes under GMP?" Roth asked. GMP stood for good manufacturing practices, and was shorthand for the stringent and necessary FDA guidelines for producing any medicine that would be injected into a human.

"We haven't entirely thought through that yet," Canfield said, putting the cap on his marker and slamming it on the whiteboard ledge in frustration. Canfield was a high-ranking scientist at the University of Oklahoma, and he was not accustomed to being questioned so aggressively and superciliously.

"And when do you believe you're going to go into clinical trial?" Roth asked.

By now, Canfield was answering in only one or two words. "One year," he said. He stuffed his hands in his pockets and looked down.

"Can you write out the manufacturing process, please?" Hurley asked.

For the next fifteen minutes, with the eyes of the Neose team trained on his back, Canfield stood at the whiteboard writing equation after equation. When he finally turned around, his choppy handwriting in black ink stretched the length of the conference room wall. First, he would make the missing Pompe enzyme in a process similar to Chen's. Then, to attach the right carbohydrates and phosphates to the enzyme, he would use the two processing enzymes—PTase and uncovering enzyme—neither of which anyone was known to have characterized, let alone made in a lab. He described six different purification steps along the way.

"Oh no, you can't do this in one year," Hurley said after a few minutes of intently studying the equations.

"We can," Canfield retorted, only to be interrupted in midsentence by Roth, who had risen to his feet, red-faced.

"This is bullshit. Are you serious?" he shouted, turning and stomping out of the room. A minute later, Hurley and the other Neose officials followed in quick but measured order.

Canfield dropped heavily into his seat between John and Doug, his arms crossed tightly, stroking his beard and looking like the most wronged man in the world.

"This is awful," he mumbled.

John sat silently. It was one of those rare instances in his life when he couldn't think of anything to say or do to make things better.

Luckily, Doug had mastered the art of calming Canfield. He pushed his chair back, crossed his hands behind his head, and said softly, drawing out each word, "Well, Bill, now, this is just business. They'll be back to the table. They're just posturing. Give it a little time. It'll all come together and everything will be okay."

"We've been negotiating with them for months and months. What do they want?" Canfield fumed. "Why are they asking all of these questions? Of course we don't have all the answers—that's why we want to partner with them."

A few doors down, Hurley and the other Neose officers found Roth swearing in his office. "Canfield thinks just because he says it's going to happen, we should believe it will happen—in one year! You have a scientist pooh-poohing the complexity and a CEO who wants more than life itself to get it for his kids. Not a good combination.

"If you're going to make a soufflé for the first time, you can't set out at six to make it for dinner at seven. It's not going to happen, even if you've got the right recipe," he finished.

"I don't know a single company that has taken a drug from a test tube into a human trial in a year," Hurley said, agreeing with Roth. "It will take them a minimum of five years to fine-tube the lab work, set up manufacturing, and test in animals. These guys don't know what they're doing."

"I don't know if we should do anything with a hotheaded guy like Bill Canfield," Roth said.

Roth didn't return to talk with Canfield and his team that day. Instead, Sherrill Neff, the tall, eloquent, white-haired chief operating officer who had sat silently through the presentation, returned to smooth things over. In an apologetic voice, he said he knew the meeting had been tough. Unfortunately, Roth and the others had other meetings to attend that day and couldn't return. But he promised he would be back in touch with Canfield as soon as the team had a chance to reflect on what they'd heard that day. Neff had a kind, thoughtful, almost fatherly way about him that made John like and trust him immediately.

Canfield and Doug flew back to Oklahoma, and John drove the two hours home, feeling like a fool. He'd signed on with Canfield's company without asking enough questions. First, he hadn't known how little money Canfield had in the bank. Next, he hadn't realized the uncertainty of Canfield's commitments from investors. And, finally, as today's meeting had revealed, he had nowhere near understood the complexity of Canfield's development process for the Pompe enzyme. John wasn't a scientist, but he had a sinking feeling the Neose team and the Oklahoma venture investors might be right. Canfield was an excellent academic scientist, but did he have any idea how to turn his breakthrough findings into a medicine? And even if he did have a clue, how plausible was the goal of beginning clinical trials in one year?

When John had made the decision to leave Bristol-Myers, he'd faced this uncertainty on a seemingly smaller scale. His mentor at Bristol-Myers, Brian Markison, had encouraged him to join Canfield. "If it works," Brian had said, "you save your kids, you help a whole lot of people, and you make more money than you ever need. If it doesn't, you come right back here."[6] Should he cut his losses and go back to Bristol-Myers now? He couldn't think of how a first week in a new job could have gone worse.

*   *   *

John pulled up to his house to find Aileen and the kids outside. Megan, now three and a half, and Patrick, now two, sat on his blue Naval Academy blanket in the front yard, their ventilators swishing evenly. Aileen sat between them, while John Jr. rode a tricycle in the street.

"Daddy," Megan shouted, arms outstretched. He ran over to lift her up in the air. Patrick squeaked and waved both arms.

"Why aren't you sitting in your usual spot?" he asked Megan, pointing to the top of the brick steps, where she usually presided over the entranceway.

"I fell down," Megan said, using a combination of speech and sign language.

"Oh yeah—we had a little accident, John. She fell off the stoop," Aileen said, in a singsong voice, deliberately casual because the kids were listening. "Luckily, I caught Megan, but it was a little lesson for us all, wasn't it, honey?" She gave Megan a kiss as she lifted her out of her father's arms so he could greet Patrick.

"Hey there, how's my redheaded stepchild?" he asked, picking up Patrick. John's doting on Megan had become a family joke. Aileen had to remind him repeatedly not to forget his youngest.

"What's wrong with his thumb?" John asked, noticing a big blister on Patrick's finger.

"I'd been wondering that for a few days and I just figured it out," Aileen said. "He's so smart that he's figured out a way of moving his head without using his neck muscles. I guess they'd gotten so weak he couldn't turn his head anymore. So he's been biting down on his thumb and using his arm to pull his head around."

John kissed Patrick's thumb, hiding his face in the boy's hand for a minute as he absorbed the blow Aileen had so casually delivered. The children were growing weaker, just as the doctors had predicted. Megan couldn't sit up on the top step anymore. And Patrick couldn't turn his head without using his arm as a lever.

"Daddy," he heard little John calling from the street. He lifted his face and turned around to see his eldest child pulling open the passenger side door of the family van. A cloud of balloons in every color rose into the air. Aileen shrieked and ran down the street, leaping into the air in her short floral-print dress, grabbing at the balloon strings.

With a start, John realized it was his own birthday. He was thirty-three years old.

Aileen, clutching the strings of the two balloons she had saved, was walking toward him. "Good Lord. I bought thirty-three balloons and now we only have these," she said in a fit of giggles, grabbing John Jr. and swinging his chubby hand.

"Happy birthday, John," she sighed, kissing him. "Let's go inside and have cake."

"Sure," he said.

"You don't look right. How are you?" she asked.

"Oh great—just great," he said wearily, shaking his head and rolling his eyes at Aileen, signaling it wasn't a good day, but he'd tell her about it later. He picked up Megan and her ventilator. Aileen let go of John Jr.'s arm and gathered Patrick and his ventilator, and together they took the children inside.

Within a few minutes Aileen and the children were sitting around the small kitchen table wearing pointy party hats, singing "Happy Birthday." John blew out his thirty-three candles with gusto, grinning as his children cheered.

There was no way he could quit Canfield's company, he thought as he cut the chocolate cake. The children were getting weaker by the day, and he had no other plan for saving them.

That night, as he and Aileen ate dinner, he tossed out an idea he hoped she would go along with for getting Canfield's company some quick cash. "The company needs money right now, Aileen," he said. "I'd like to step up to the plate and help out. The only money we have is in this house, but the good news is that it has already appreciated. I bet I can get a hundred grand out of it if we take out a second mortgage."

"You just started and this company is already out of money," Aileen repeated, blinking her surprise. "What's going on, John?"

"Some of the investors are taking a little longer to line up than we'd expected," John said, keeping his tone casual. "It's just a cash flow problem. Canfield's getting some money and I want to be able to show I can help, too."

"If you're asking if I think it's okay to mortgage the house, you have my permission. Do what you need to do, John," she said, as she had so often before.

In the fifteen months since he had stormed out, Aileen, too, had become more forgiving and supportive. She didn't question John's decisions on business or family finances, even if it wasn't clear to her that he was right.

She didn't ask for details on the company's problems and he didn't offer her any.

John arrived in Oklahoma the next week with a check for $100,000, having taken out the second mortgage on his house.[7] Luckily, Canfield was having a better week. He had been calling down a list of local doctors and dentists, and he had managed to raise another $200,000, mostly in increments of $5,000 and $10,000.

Then John asked Canfield's permission to phone Neose and talk to Sherrill Neff, Neose's chief operating officer. "Let me work something out, business person to business person," John told Canfield, trying to sound more confident than he felt.

Over the next few weeks, John essentially gave Neose a deal so good—and, honestly, so one-sided in Neose's favor—that the company finally couldn't say no. To convince Neose to put in $562,000, John gave the company the option of becoming a partner and owning half of the revenue of the Pompe medicine—with no deadline attached. Partnership requires periodic infusions of cash at key milestones, and by deferring a decision on a long-term association, Neose hadn't committed to any future business dealings. It was a bottom-of-the-line bargain, and a much-needed lifeline for Canfield and John's company.[8]

With the start-up funds in place and their "partner" Neose giving their company some gravitas, John and Canfield set out to raise serious venture capital. John turned immediately to the only old boy's network that he knew. He called Josh Phillips, a buddy from the Friday afternoon pizza parties at Harvard Business School where he used to give out his infamous Kiss-Ass awards.

Only a few weeks earlier, Josh had sent out a blast e-mail saying he'd become a partner in a small Boston area venture firm, Catalyst Health & Technology Partners. Now John e-mailed Josh back, describing his new company and asking if Catalyst might be interested in investing. Josh, who had always admired John's sense of humor and charisma, invited him to make a presentation to his firm.[9]

John used part of the Neose investment funds to hire a consulting firm to help him write a business plan and draft a snazzy, thirty-slide Power-Point presentation. The consultant, Skip Irving from Health Advances in Boston, led a brainstorming session to help John and Canfield christen the company with a new name. Canfield had called it Targeted Therapies Inc., which was serviceable but dull. The new name chosen was Novazyme, a play on the words *new* and *enzyme*.

Several weeks later, in Catalyst's Newton, Massachusetts offices, John debuted the business plan. His new key selling point was that Canfield's scientific approach could be used not only to make the deficient Pompe enzyme, but also enzymes missing or deficient in patients with the other forty-eight lysosomal storage diseases. Even though these diseases were extremely rare, a treatment for just one of them could be priced so high it could yield a fortune. He put up a slide showing Genzyme's projected annual revenue that year from its Gaucher disease treatment—$540 million.

"Imagine the economic potential of a new, improved technology to make a whole line of drugs like Genzyme's," he said. "The market potential isn't just millions or hundreds of millions—it's *billions*." He clicked to a slide that put the market potential at $6 billion.[10]

John acknowledged that a much larger competitor, Genzyme, was developing two enzymes for Pompe disease that were further along in development—Chen's and Pharming's—but he called them "vastly inferior" to Canfield's. Then he presented an outline for developing Canfield's science into a medicine. He had modified Canfield's original time frame, but only slightly. "Novazyme can begin clinical trials for Pompe disease in twelve to eighteen months," he declared confidently.

As he wrapped up his presentation, John searched the faces of the businessmen at the table for clues as to how his pitch had been received. It was hard to read the polite, smiling faces of the group, but John got the signal he wanted from Josh, who turned a little and flashed a thumbs-up that only he could see.

After John left, Josh turned to his senior partner, David Hendren, and said intently, "This company can threaten Genzyme's cash flow." He had recognized something that John, focused on getting clinical trials started for his own kids, had not fully absorbed: Canfield's science represented such a threat to Genzyme's core business that there was a good chance the bigger company would feel compelled to buy the smaller one.

"If it works, there's a big exit potential," Josh said, using venture capital investors' lingo for the opportunity to make a quick sale at a big profit. They agreed that Josh should rush to Oklahoma the next week to check out Novazyme and negotiate a deal before the little company was discovered by other, bigger venture firms.

Negotiations on the terms of a deal flowed easily. Catalyst agreed to put in $1.5 million and commit to raising another $1.5 million in return for owning about 7 percent of the company. The HBS network had lived up to its reputation.[11]

With the commitment for $3 million, John and Canfield were ready to take a break from fund-raising. They thought they had enough money to get them through at least six months, possibly a year. But Roth of Neose had set up a few other meetings with venture capital firms, and though they seemed like long shots, the two men thought it better not to cancel for fear of hurting their already tenuous relationship with the Neose chief executive.

To the astonishment of both John and Canfield, both venture funds not only wanted to invest, but gave them more money than they asked for. Perseus Soros, a new biotech fund sponsored by billionaire George Soros and run by Dennis Purcell, one of the world's most successful biotechnology investment bankers, initially offered $1.5 million. But a week later, when HealthCare Ventures, one of the oldest and most successful biotechnology venture funds, insisted on investing $3 million, Perseus Soros raised its stake to match the $3 million. Catalyst, trying to keep up, increased its investment to $2 million. By the time the A Round was finalized, Novazyme had more than $8 million in the bank.[12]

Standing side by side in their dark business suits at the windows on the thirty-second floor of Perseus Soros's Manhattan office overlooking Central Park, John put an arm around Canfield.

"Doc," he said, grinning, "we've sure come a long way."

14. Failure Is Not an Option

With Novazyme's finances secure, John set about trying to build the kind of company he'd dreamed of discovering when he was just a dad trying to fund research to save his kids. Almost all drug companies proclaimed themselves "patient friendly," but most employees had never met anyone their medicines were designed to treat. Companies were caught up in the pedagogy of science and drug development that held objectivity almost above all else. Patients were statistics in clinical trials, human subjects whose success was viewed in terms of means, medians, and "p values"—the calculation of the statistical significance of the data, often measured in terms of their survival or death. These were calculations intentionally devoid of emotion. Embraced in theory, researchers at most companies tried to keep patients at bay, fearing for the emotional bias they might bring to the rigors of scientific research and drug development.

John was the rare biotechnology executive who had lived in the terrifying world inhabited by the patients his company intended to treat—and still did. And he hated the disconnect he saw between the desperation of patients and the dispassion of clinical medicine.

Now that he was in charge, John wanted to infuse the science and business of drug development with patients' life experience and their families' sense of urgency, the same sense of urgency that drove him. He set about establishing such a corporate culture by inviting patients and their families every week to tell their stories to Novazyme's employees—from the scientists to the secretaries—at what were called Lunch 'N Learns.

That first summer of 2000, Novazyme hosted about a dozen patients, some of whom John knew, others whom he'd never met. Greg Assink, John's big supporter at the Children's Pompe Foundation, showed up carrying pictures of his seven-year-old daughter Kelsey. John intentionally scheduled these Lunch 'N Learns when board members and company consultants were expected, hoping to draw them into his world. Almost everyone came away inspired to work harder. But what John hadn't expected was how the visitors, and one young woman in particular, would affect him.

Her name was Lindsey Easton, and because she lived only an hour away, in Glenpool, a suburb of Tulsa, she was one of the first patients invited to visit. John had been introduced to her family by Dr. Slonim when he started the Children's Pompe Foundation. The doctor had urged John to look up Lindsey's family because she suffered from the same nonclassical infantile form of Pompe as Megan and Patrick. Slonim had seen Lindsey many years earlier, when she was a toddler, but hadn't been in touch with her family for a long time. He didn't even know if she was still alive. John tracked her down to find she had somehow outlived the life expectancy of five years for her disease type. She was, in fact, thirteen, but over the years, she'd lost almost all skeletal muscle strength, and she could—quite literally—move only her eyelids, mouth, and thumbs.[1]

The day Lindsey arrived, John showed up at the reception area, upbeat and smiling. "Hello Lindsey, how are you?" he asked cheerfully, beaming at the girl with big green eyes, long dark hair, and a chubby, expressionless face. She lay strapped in a wheelchair that reclined at about a thirty-degree angle. She responded with a series of grunts.

Lindsey's mother, Laurie Easton, translated quickly: "How do you think I am?" Then Laurie laughed, mock-glaring at Lindsey, and said to her, "Could you please hold your wiseass comments in check for one afternoon?"

John chuckled, realizing that Lindsey, sick as she was, had the same feisty personality as his Megan. He led the young woman, accompanied by her extended family—parents, brothers, and grandparents—from the reception area down a hallway, pointing out Canfield's office, his own, and others. Around the corner, they came to the main laboratory, peeking inside to see a dozen scientists measuring liquids and peering into test tubes. Circling through the empty half of the floor, they returned to the main conference room where the company's thirty employees had gathered for lunch.

Laurie and Lindsey took questions from the audience—the mother sometimes speaking for herself, at other times interpreting for her daughter.

"What do you like to do best?" asked Hung Do, the most curious and extroverted of the scientists on Canfield's team.

"She likes to read—she reads all the time," Laurie answered for Lindsey. "She reads so fast I sometimes can't get anything else done because I have to keep turning the pages. She read the Harry Potter book in three days. If I had invented an automatic page turner, I'd be a rich woman," she finished, drawing chuckles from the crowd.

Hung followed up with question after question, and soon others joined in.

"If the enzyme works and you can move around again, what would you like to do?" Hung asked.

Again Lindsey made some noises and Laurie translated: "I'd like to kick my brother's butt." The room exploded in laughter.

"Are those tubes uncomfortable?" asked Tony McKinney, the head of drug development, on a more serious note.

"Do you receive any physiotherapy?" another employee ventured.

"Are you ever in pain?" Hung wanted to know.

Laurie Easton said her daughter's stomach hurt sometimes when her digestive muscles didn't work well, but that the tubes weren't uncomfortable anymore because Lindsey had gotten so used to them. A physical therapist came over a couple times a week to move and stretch Lindsey's arms and legs so they didn't get stiff.

"It's so wonderful to see all of you working on curing this disease," Laurie said when the questions finally ceased. "For so long, we didn't have hope. And now we learn that not only is there a company working on curing Pompe disease, but this company is right here in Oklahoma. Each and every one of you has brought us hope."

Lindsey's ventilator started beeping, picking up on an obstruction in airflow. Big tears raced down her motionless face.

The room grew silent, choked with emotion. John, at the front of the room, looked red-faced and glassy-eyed. His voice breaking, his lips visibly trembling, John stood up to thank the visitors. "Laurie, Lindsey, thank you for coming here and sharing your stories with us. You, Lindsey, will inspire us to work harder than we ever imagined possible to help you and all other patients with Pompe disease."

At the back of the room, Canfield held his breath, hoping John could maintain his composure. Canfield had been nervous about John's plan to invite patients to speak to the staff each week. He told John that he agreed that it was important for the employees to understand the patient perspective, but he also believed scientists should be removed from the emotion so they were free to experiment without fear of failure. But John, as usual, had forged ahead regardless of his disapproval.[2]

Canfield followed John as he led the Eastons to the elevator, hugged each of them good-bye, and walked briskly to his office. Relieved that John had held himself together, Canfield retreated to his lab.

He didn't see the scene that took place moments later in John's office, down the hall from the lab. John stood with his back against the door, letting tears flow freely. Hearing a doctor talk about the progression of the disease was one thing—coming face to face with it in actuality was quite another. He felt so sorry for Lindsey. He felt so scared for Megan and Patrick. He would work longer, harder, faster. He could not—he simply would not—let Novazyme fail.

15. Cowboys

Years later, John would concede there was one place he never should have ventured: the laboratory. The time, the precision, and the meticulousness required in truly great science didn't play to his strengths. Science could be funded, could be encouraged, and could be inspired, but it could not be rushed. In late 2000, John, who had absolutely no scientific training, crossed the line into making scientific decisions that almost ruined Canfield's reputation, and made Neose believe for a time that his company was a fraud. It compromised his ultimate goal—helping his children—and John never forgot the lesson.

It began with the two scientific problems Canfield had to solve to make his version of the enzyme deficient in Pompe patients, acid alpha-glucosidase. Before adding the two processing enzymes, Canfield needed to make the Pompe enzyme with the right sugar chains attached. To do this, he used an obscure chemical inhibitor called deoxymannojirimycin, or DMJ, which had been discovered years earlier in Japanese fungi. But there wasn't nearly enough DMJ available anywhere in the world to make the kilograms of Pompe enzyme he needed for animal and eventually human testing. He needed to either find a way of procuring more DMJ or find a viable substitute.

Next, and perhaps even more challenging, Canfield had to find a way to make a human version of phosphotransferase, or PTase, the longer and more complicated of the two processing enzymes he used in the next stages of production. PTase was needed to convert the Pompe enzyme into the highly phosphorylated form necessary to be taken into the correct region of the cell. For his lab work, Canfield had extracted the PTase out of cow udders, but as Neose's Roth had so assertively noted, the FDA was unlikely to approve a product made using animal ingredients. So Canfield set about trying to decode and produce one of the most complex proteins known to man. It proved more difficult than Canfield had ever imagined.[1]

Subtly, but steadily, the time pressure John imposed on the company began to affect its science. To be sure, John's sense of urgency did inspire Canfield and his team to work faster than any of them had believed possible. But John didn't quite know when to stop.

To push the science, John relied on the man Canfield had hired to be chief of drug development, the genial Tony McKinney. In his first meeting with McKinney, John outlined his timeline for the development of Canfield's science. Novazyme was to finish animal studies by December 2000 and enter human trials in September 2001.

"Your job is to make this happen. I don't want to hear it isn't possible because it's never been done before. We're doing things differently here," John said, testing out the sentence that would become his refrain. "We're not doing things on the regular drug development timeline. We're doing things on Novazyme time."[2]

"Sure, Chief," said McKinney, even though he had spent more than a decade in the drug industry in sales and new product development, and knew John's timeline would be very difficult to achieve. But McKinney adopted it anyway, moved and inspired by John's sense of urgency and the desperation of the patients he met. McKinney had been at the company only a few weeks when a couple showed up in the lobby, having read about Novazyme and driven from Kansas in the hope of bringing home a treatment to save their baby who was dying of Pompe disease. One of the hardest things he'd ever done was to explain to the parents just how many more tests and experiments were needed to be completed before Novazyme would have a treatment to offer their baby.[3]

McKinney set about immediately developing the design for the animal studies testing Canfield's enzyme in mice, the generally accepted prelude to human clinical trials. The animal tests needed to be persuasive enough for the FDA to approve moving to human testing, the next step in drug development. McKinney sought expert advice from Dr. Nina Raben, the NIH biochemist who had bred a colony of mice with Pompe disease, and Dr. Barry Byrne, the pediatric cardiologist and gene therapy researcher at the University of Florida. Not only did Raben help design the animal studies, but she was so impressed and excited by Canfield's science that she agreed to send a shipment of mice with Pompe disease, which she had recently generated. These mice were in extremely short supply, and were desperately sought by Genzyme and others researching the disease.[4]

By the end of the summer of 2000, McKinney had twenty-four mice with Pompe disease waiting at the animal facility at the University of Oklahoma for Canfield's animal experiments to begin. He also had in place a draft plan to test Canfield's enzyme in mice. Prodded by John, McKinney began to push Canfield to provide some of his experimental enzyme for animal testing.

"I need the stuff—when are you going to give me the stuff?" he said.

"Two weeks," Canfield would reply, in a question-answer pattern that repeated endlessly.[5]

As the weeks flew by and summer turned into fall, it became clear that Canfield was struggling more than he would admit. Not only had he been unable to find enough DMJ for his needs, but he also couldn't even find anyone able to produce it. He had signed a contract with a firm in New Zealand to make the inhibitor, and five chemists were working on the project every day. But each week, the company sent a report of a new snag. Finally, Canfield canceled the contract and assigned two of his own scientists to find an alternative inhibitor, something more widely available.

For many weeks, two Novazyme scientists scoured scientific journals for similar inhibitors. They found several with a comparable chemical structure, ordered them, and began to test them one by one, trying to determine whether any were close enough to DMJ to be substitutable. One inhibitor called kifunensin seemed to produce a similar result—and there was a plentiful supply in the world. Canfield didn't have time for certainty. With McKinney breathing down his neck, Canfield ordered a few laboratory tests validating equivalence, bought eight grams of the chemical, and shifted his attention to the next looming obstacle—making PTase. "I feel like we're building an airplane as we're flying it," he muttered, standing at the whiteboard with his science team, writing out one equation after another. To those outside the science group, he said only, "We're working on it."[6]

Meanwhile, he was beginning to worry that it might not be possible to clone PTase, at least not any time soon. Nobody had ever sequenced the gene that makes the enzyme, much less attempted to produce it, so he had to figure out everything from scratch. Most enzymes were made by one gene, but Canfield thought this one might be produced by two. He knew the identity of one of the genes, but not the other. To find it, he spent days scanning a new computer database of large genes identified in the federally funded Human Genome Project, which attempted to identify all of the genes in the human body. He pulled out a piece of one gene that resembled PTase. Using this segment, he guessed at the structure of the rest of the gene. Then, in a test tube, he put the two genes together with a lipid reagent known to coax genes to make proteins, hoping the product that emerged would be PTase.[7]

The product passed the first test, and an elated Canfield waited in his office for his scientists to perform a confirmatory test. They added the test substance they hoped was PTase to the Pompe enzyme. If it turned into the highly phosphorylated form, they would know the substance they had made was PTase.

But a few hours later, Canfield's scientists reported back that the product they had produced didn't phosphorylate the Pompe enzyme. It was past midnight, but Canfield didn't call it a night. He crossed his arms, a sign that he was upset, and ordered everyone on the science team to report to the conference room.

"Back to the drawing board," he said dejectedly.

The next day, McKinney was in Canfield's office, saying, "We've told our investors that we would have animal results by the end of the year. Bill, when are you going to give us some of the stuff?"[8]

"You can't put science on a timeline," Dr. Canfield said, rubbing his eyes in exhaustion. "These timelines are guides, Tony. We do our best to meet them, but these are not some deadlines to be met at all costs." John, who had been at the company for seven months now, watching Canfield struggle, privately told McKinney to develop a backup plan.

At the next management meeting, McKinney proposed his backup. "Bill, your guys are still picking up cow udders each week at the stockyards, right? And using it to make PTase for laboratory work?"

"Right," confirmed Canfield, his voice barely audible.

"Well, at last count, I calculated we have one hundred kilograms of cow udders in six different freezers here. If the human PTase is going to take longer to produce, why don't we use the bovine enzyme for our first drug candidate? It's similar to the human version. We can produce a second-generation drug using human PTase."

"Extracting enzyme from cow udders is impractical," Canfield said loudly, uncrossing and crossing his arms angrily. "It takes a 20-kilogram cow udder to produce enough PTase to make half a milligram of the treatment. That's only a single dose of medicine. Imagine how many cow udders would be needed to supply patients for a year-long clinical trial, let alone the Pompe patient population for life. Not to mention that—as we've been over many times before—the FDA will never approve a medicine made using bovine enzyme."

John sat back and let McKinney do the arguing.

"But Bill, what about heparin?" McKinney asked, referencing a blood thinner made from pig intestines that the FDA had approved. "It's not impossible for the FDA to agree, however reluctantly, to use an animal enzyme, isn't that right?"

"That's voodoo science!" Canfield burst out, shaking his head.

McKinney looked stunned for a moment and then, sounding a little hurt, said, "You know, Dr. Canfield, with you the glass is not only always half empty, it's a little dirty, too."

John guffawed, breaking the tension, and soon everyone including Canfield was chuckling. McKinney had a folksy way of making observations that others couldn't quite put into words.

Canfield continued to dismiss McKinney's idea, but John, who had helped conceive it, privately assigned McKinney to the task of finding a herd of cows that might be acceptable to the FDA as the source of PTase. To satisfy the FDA, the two men believed, they needed a herd with records of everything the cows had eaten since they were born. Maybe then the regulators would be convinced the animals had no communicable diseases.

"You find the herd," John told McKinney. "I'll deal with Bill."

A month later, with Canfield still working on human PTase and McKinney still searching for a herd, John came up with his own Plan B. He had spent most of the $8.3 million faster than he had believed possible. Not only had he paid $2.5 million to have a small, three-thousand-square-foot manufacturing plant built directly across from the Novazyme research labs, but he and Canfield had also hired fifty new staff members, from scientists to regulatory experts to manufacturing gurus. They would need more money early next year, and he didn't have what he needed to raise the next stage of venture capital funding—scientific data showing the enzyme worked in animals. McKinney had the plan and the mice, but Canfield was still trying to make his medicine.

Novazyme's partnership agreement with Neose said that the company would invest another $562,000 within three months of Novazyme's successful performance of "proof of concept" experiments, or animal studies demonstrating the efficacy of Canfield's enzyme. After that, Neose would also bear half of the costs of drug development—which would slow John's expenditures considerably.

So John set about trying to persuade Canfield that he had a product ready to use in animal testing—the Pompe enzyme made with bovine PTase.

"Bill, I'm not advocating using the bovine PTase in humans. I'm just saying we should use the stuff for our animal testing. We're going to need the money soon. These guys at Neose are just looking for an excuse to invest more. Why not use the stuff you have for the animal experiments so we get proof-of-concept data?"

"It's a waste of time," Canfield replied. "If we can't make human PTase, we're done. Why bother with animal experiments using an enzyme we would never put into humans? I don't see the point. If we can't make human PTase, we have nothing."

"It's not a waste of time, Bill. It's just a way to prove to Neose that the enzyme works. It's a proof of concept," said John. "We get the money we need. When you have the human PTase, we'll do the experiments over."

Reluctantly, Canfield handed over a few vials of his enzyme, but he said he wasn't going to do the animal testing, nor were any of his scientists, who were focused on what he viewed as the make-or-break human PTase challenge.

John's excitement at having won the argument diminished momentarily when he realized he didn't know who would perform the experiments. Seeing John's distress, McKinney, eager to please, volunteered to do the animal experiments. "I used to work as an emergency room tech," he assured his young CEO.

John patted him on the back, thrilled. "If you can inject people, you can surely inject a mouse," he chuckled. The complete absurdity of their attempting to conduct animal experiments would become apparent to them only later, when they learned that these tests must be done in exacting detail to have any credibility whatsoever in the scientific world, let alone with the FDA.

One afternoon in the late fall of 2000, John and McKinney donned white lab coats over their pin-striped suits and stepped into the lab across from Canfield's office. McKinney pulled on a pair of surgical gloves and filled several tiny syringes full of enzyme. John watched from a few feet away as McKinney grabbed three weakly wriggling mice, one by one, and injected their tails.[9]

"Not sure I hit the vein," McKinney said, holding one of the black-tailed mice up to the light. "It's hard to see. This book I read says we're aiming for the tail vein but it's hard to see the vein 'cause the mouse is brown. I'll give this mouse another shot of enzyme just to be sure we got the stuff in the right place."

"Is it going okay?" John asked after the unplanned second dose.

"Oh yes," McKinney said, reassuringly. "I saw some drawback that time. Definitely got the tail vein. This bad boy got himself some enzyme flowing in his blood."

Every week over the next month, McKinney gave the mice another injection or two of enzyme, John looking on nervously. Canfield, shaking his head each time he saw the two men enter the lab, pointedly refused to even watch, let alone participate.

At the end of the month, McKinney killed each of the mice and sliced out their organs. He performed what is known as an enzyme activity test by grinding up the organs and measuring the level of Pompe enzyme. If the mice showed any amount of enzyme in their tissue, he explained to John, it meant the enzyme had been taken in.

To John's delight, McKinney reported back that the experiments showed Canfield's enzyme had been transported into the organs of all three mice. McKinney charted the results on his laptop and showed them to John. He pointed to a dot on a graph that represented tissue taken from an untreated mouse with Pompe disease, which contained less than 1 percent of the enzyme level of a normal animal. Three other dots in different places, but all higher on the graph, represented the enzyme levels measured in the organs of treated mice. The top performing mouse had 25 percent of the enzyme level found in a healthy animal.

"The results are mixed," McKinney told John. "There's some good data, some we've got to work on."

"What do you mean?" John said.

"I mean the results aren't perfect, but they are promising—I see some very promising signals," McKinney said.

John thought it was time to visit Neose. Even if the experiments weren't perfect, from what he could tell, the results showed that the mice with Pompe disease had taken up Canfield's enzyme. Surely they would serve as a "proof of concept." It was worth a try, anyway, to get Neose on the clock to invest more and share in the future costs of drug development.

John and McKinney knocked on Canfield's door and showed him the results. Canfield, stroking his trim beard, shook his head as he looked at McKinney's chart.

"This is not compelling," he said.

"C'mon, Bill," John said. "We're not presenting at a scientific conference. We just want to show the guys at Neose that we're making progress. This doesn't have to be conclusive evidence."

Canfield shrugged and left the room to return to the lab where his scientists awaited his guidance on the vitally important PTase experiments.

John decided Canfield was too much of a skeptic. John's own business school training had taught him not to wait for the perfect result, but to forge ahead with the best information you had. John called Sherrill Neff, the chief operating officer of Neose, and set up a meeting for the next week.

The next day, Canfield made one final argument against presenting to Neose.

"I can't make the trip to Pennsylvania," he said. He was still technically employed by the University of Oklahoma, and as a physician, he was required to be on call for one month each year at the university hospital. His tour of duty was this month, December. "No problem, Doc," John said in his chipper way. "Tony and I will present the data."

As they pulled up to the Neose offices outside Philadelphia on December 14, John stared at the big white letters on the outside of the warehouse spelling the company name and suddenly felt nervous. He remembered the last time he'd visited here, with Canfield, and the rapid-fire science questions that had stumped even the brilliant scientist.

Minutes later, he and McKinney were seated side by side in the conference room across from Roth, the scientist and chief executive who had grilled Canfield the previous time. By Roth's side sat Marjorie Hurley, the tough head of regulatory affairs, and farther down the table, a Neose physician named David Zopf, and Neff, the chief operating officer.

McKinney, overcome with a sudden sense of impending disaster, whispered, "John, maybe you should present the results." John, voice adamant even in a whisper, insisted McKinney do the job.

"You're the one with the science background," John hissed back. McKinney had an undergraduate degree in microbiology from the University of Oklahoma. Clearing his throat, John began to make the introduction.[10]

"Well, we're here because we have some early but, we think, very compelling evidence that our enzyme works in mice," he said, sounding assured as he always did in public. "We believe we have the proof-of-concept animal study here. Tony McKinney, our chief of drug development, will present the results."

McKinney smiled weakly and directed the group to look at the graph on his PowerPoint presentation, on which he'd plotted the enzyme activity levels in the three treated mice.

"Why are your results so variable?" Roth asked. John focused for the first time on the fact that the enzyme activity levels in the three mice differed from one another by five or ten percentage points, realizing he was so far out of his league that he hadn't even known this might be a problem. McKinney had drawn a nice straight line through the middle to show the average.

"Well, it may be due to the fact that it was hard to find the tail veins in the mice," McKinney said. "So some may have gotten more enzyme than others."

Roth's eyes widened.

"Who performed the experiments?" he asked.

"I did," McKinney said.

"*What?*" Hurley's face had taken on the same pained expression John remembered from his first visit to the company in April.

"Are you an expert in preclinical studies?" Roth demanded, incredulous, knowing full well that McKinney was not a trained scientist. In the world of science and medicine, having an undergraduate degree in microbiology was considered barely better than kindergarten. "How do you know the enzyme actually got into the tail vein?"

"We can't be sure, but I surmise from these readings that we got the enzyme into the tail vein," McKinney said faintly. Beads of sweat had formed on his forehead, and his hand pointing at the screen trembled slightly.

The questions kept coming, all or almost all of them leaving McKinney foundering for answers. John felt powerless to help him.

Finally, incredulous, Roth shoved himself violently to his feet and shouted, "This is bullshit. Now I understand why Bill isn't here. He doesn't have the balls to present this crap."

John watched, horrified, as Roth stormed out of the meeting, just as he had after the meeting with Canfield almost eight months earlier.

The next day, Roth phoned Canfield, demanding an explanation. Canfield was a man of few words and he grew even less verbose when under attack. He didn't try to defend himself by explaining that he hadn't wanted John and McKinney to present the results in the first place. Canfield, who hated direct confrontation, had been—and remained—so completely absorbed in the challenge of making human PTase that he hadn't expended the energy questioning John and McKinney before they left to realize the level of sloppiness of their experiment. Distracted and exhausted by his own scientific problems, he had avoided the conflict, retiring to the domain in which he was most comfortable—the lab. But now he was sure the Neose chief was right, and he was furious with himself for not putting his foot down and banning John and McKinney from making the trip. As the chief scientific officer, Canfield knew any science that emanated from the company reflected on him.[11]

Canfield put down the phone and sat silently in his office. Then he picked up the phone and called Doug, his lawyer and confidant.

"I'm worried about John," he said. "We just had a terrible mistake that could ruin us. John insisted on presenting this half-baked data to Neose. He thought that all the guys at Neose wanted was an excuse to invest. Now Neose is furious. You know, I was worried about John's conflict of interest, and now I think it's a problem. He's rushing too fast and cutting too many corners."

"Bill, we can manage him," came Doug's reassuring reply. "This Neose thing sounds terrible, but we can smooth it over. I'll talk to John."

"And why hasn't he moved to Oklahoma?" Canfield continued, anger flooding his voice as he lunged into the topic he complained about frequently to Doug. "You were there, Doug, when we offered him the job and told him he had to move to Oklahoma. If he couldn't do it, he should have said so. Now he's gone and rented office space in New Jersey for himself on days when he isn't here. He hasn't said the words yet, Doug, but I'm sure he's not moving here."[12]

"Bill, it'll be all right, even if the guy doesn't move," Doug said. "I don't see how he can take those sick kids away from all the family support back in New Jersey. John's here almost every week, he's working all night, he works every weekend. What does it matter where his family is?"

"I just don't like it," Canfield said. "If he wasn't going to move, he should have said so before starting. It seems like John Crowley will do almost anything and say almost anything to get a drug to his children. He just ruined my reputation with the Neose guys. They think I sent John and McKinney over there to present those results."

A few days later, on Christmas Eve, Neose's Sherrill Neff called John and invited him to Pennsylvania to talk. Neff was about twenty years John's senior, and after meeting several times, John had begun to think of him as a mentor. It had been Neff who had helped John broker the deal between the two companies following the first disastrous meeting he had attended. John knew that within Neose, Neff was the biggest champion of the partnership between the two companies. Neff saw beyond John and Canfield's inexperience in drug development, recognizing the commercial potential of the science. Neff was a nonvoting member of the Novazyme board, but he often called John after the meetings to offer advice.

This time, Neff seemed much more distant. He was quiet as they drove from the Neose building, only speaking once to ask if it was all right if they ate at a small sandwich shop.

When they finally sat down with sandwiches, Neff got right to the point. "John, I'm concerned. I haven't been around the biotechnology world long, but I've been around long enough," he said, looking directly into the younger man's eyes, his tone firm but devoid of anger. "If you've got a problem, you've got to talk to your investors and your board. You've got to tell them you've got a problem and what your proposed solution is. It's the single best way to keep a coalition together."

John nodded, silent.

"The other day, you and Tony presented your data as great. Not only was it poorly done, but it also wasn't even good data. This business is full of people who are full of themselves and who try to spin data. If you're not careful, you'll quickly develop a bad reputation. You've got to avoid getting a reputation as a shit polisher in this business.

"At our meeting the other day, you tried to polish the shit."

John took a deep breath and tried to smile. Neff had delivered his admonition in such a kind, big brotherly way that John felt it was given for his own benefit.

"I understand," John said, looking up at him. "We're going to hire a director of preclinical studies to do the future studies. We'll do it right. I'm learning."

A week later, at 6 P.M. on Saturday, December 31, the phone rang in John's house. It was Canfield, characteristically short-spoken and terse.

"Turn on your fax machine," he said.

"Why?" John asked.

"Just turn on your fax. I'm sending something over."

John switched on the fax and stepped outside into the den to check on the kids.

A New Year's Eve party Aileen had organized was under way at the Crowley household. Patrick, two, was ignoring everyone from his usual perch on the left side of the couch, watching the Wiggles, a kids' show featuring a group of young Australian men singing and dancing. Sharon was at home in New Hampshire with her family for New Year's, but one of the children's favorite nurses, Helen, sat by Patrick's side, rising often to check on Megan, who was playing with two friends in the adjacent room.

John Jr. appeared at the top of the staircase and shouted, "Where can I hide, Daddy?"

John pointed in the direction of his bedroom, a finger over his lips. "Don't let them hear you or they'll know where to look."

John Jr. had started kindergarten that fall and had finally become easier to manage. His teacher, Laurie, who had become a close friend of Aileen's, had persuaded her to have him tested for attention deficit hyperactivity disorder. When the diagnosis came back positive, a physician had prescribed Ritalin, and it seemed to help John Jr. He was finally able to focus long enough to play a game with his cousins.

As John Jr. disappeared, John peeked into the adjacent room. Megan, now four years old, sat in a small chair, her ventilator at her feet, playing dolls with Angela, eight, who lived next door, and Alexa, nine, who was the kindergarten teacher Laurie's daughter. Their parents were partying with the adults in another room.

"Hey girls, don't let Megan boss you around, you hear?" John teased, kissing Megan's cheek.

She pinned her dad with a withering stare and pointed imperiously at the "No Boys" sign written in crayon and posted on the door.

Laughing, John went downstairs to the basement he and Aileen had just had refinished into a party room with a bar and pool table. In a glittering, low-cut top that tastefully accentuated her ample cleavage, Aileen was serving red and green Jello shots she had spent the past week mixing and freezing. It was still early, but most of the guests had arrived, including

John's naval buddy Ed, Aileen's brother Brian, sister-in-law Kim, her cousin Kevin, and his wife Lisa. In the mix were several new Novazyme employees from their Jersey office—Canfield had indeed been correct that John had decided to stay in the state. Ignoring Canfield's anger at him for not moving to Oklahoma, John had initially rented space at an office center outside of Princeton and hired several people to work there. Not only would it have been very difficult to move his family, but John had also rightly concluded that having a second office in New Jersey made sense. He could attract talented people from the area's enormous pool of pharmaceutical workers who would never dream of relocating to Oklahoma. Just this month, with several new hires bringing their rented space to its capacity, John had moved the office to a white, two-story colonial on Nassau Street in Princeton.

Aileen slid a jello shot into John's mouth. "How are the kids doing upstairs?" she asked.

"They're having a great time," John said. "Megan just banished me. Oh, I almost forgot—Canfield called and said he has something to fax over. Maybe it's a resignation letter he's drafted on my behalf that he wants me to sign," John said, making a joke of Canfield's frustration with him over the Neose debacle. "Let me see if it's arrived yet."

"What's he doing for New Year's?" Aileen called as John ran up the steps.

"He's still at the office," John shouted over his shoulder.

"Geez, doesn't the guy ever take a break?" Aileen asked, popping a jello shot into her own mouth.

In the study, the fax machine was spewing out a series of graphs. John stared at them, straining to understand what Canfield was trying to convey. And then it clicked. John let out a whoop of jubilation and dialed Canfield's office line.

"You did it, Doc," he shouted into the phone. "Congratulations!"

"Call off the cows," said Canfield, ready to make light of the plan to buy a herd now that it was no longer needed. The graphs depicted the results of confirmatory tests that Canfield and his scientists had just successfully completed. At long last, after Herculean effort, they had produced human PTase.

"This will show those guys at Neose," John said. "Now we can begin our animal studies this spring."

"I've already got my team making our stuff with the human PTase," said Canfield.

John hung up, grabbed two bottles of champagne from the refrigerator, and headed toward the basement door. Behind him, he heard Megan's beeper sounding in the toy room and Helen's uncharacteristically angry voice.

"You put that tube back in now, Megan," the nurse was shouting.

John knew exactly what his daughter was trying to pull, and raced into the room to stop her. Megan, who couldn't run to her parents or shout loudly enough to get their attention, had developed her own unique—and very scary—way of summoning them to her side. Perched on her chair, she was holding two ends of the breathing tubes she had disconnected so that her ventilator—recognizing the low pressure—beeped in alarm.

"You know you are not allowed to do that," John said, angrily. "I'm going to tell Mommy."

Megan jammed the two ends together, neatly stopping the anxious beeping, and allowed the tubes to fall to the floor. She let her lower lip jut out and whined, "Daddy, Mommy said I could stay up late."

John decided to give in and save everyone from experiencing one of Megan's meltdowns, legendary in the household for their fury and duration. She would scream for forty-five minutes—the ventilator alarms blaring—if she didn't get her way. "Helen, let's give her another half hour before bedtime," John said.

Then he crouched down in front of Megan, unable to keep the thrilling news to himself any longer. "You know Daddy's been working on making Special Medicine for you, right? Tell Helen what you're going to do when Special Medicine is ready."

Megan straightened her back, pointed at her red wheelchair, then toward the window.

"That's right," John said. "Megan's going to throw her wheelchair out the window when Special Medicine is ready.

"You know Dr. Canfield—you've met him, right. Well, while we're having our party here, he's been working on trying to make Special Medicine. And guess what? He just found the exact right way to make it. Can you believe it?"

"What color is it?" Megan asked, eyes bright with excitement.

"What color do you want it to be?" John asked.

"Blue!" said Megan, pointing at her sapphire blue dress. "Can you call Dr. Canfield and tell him Megan Crowley wants Special Medicine to be blue?"

"You bet," John said. "Blue Special Medicine, coming right up."

16. Losing Support

WINTER 2000–SPRING 2001
CAMBRIDGE, MASSACHUSETTS; OKLAHOMA CITY, OKLAHOMA;
SAN FRANCISCO, CALIFORNIA; PRINCETON, NEW JERSEY

John couldn't afford to let Neose's displeasure demoralize him. He kept telling himself that the company had no real power over him. Neose, after all, didn't hold a voting board seat. All that really mattered, John knew, was the support of his board. If he kept that, the Neose debacle would just be a bump in the road.

But what was brewing on the board would prove more dangerous than anything Neose had handed him.

Unbeknownst to John, one board member, Gus Lawlor, a partner at HealthCare Ventures, had begun his tenure particularly skeptical of the young CEO. HealthCare Ventures, one of the most respected health investment funds in the world of biotechnology, had invested in Novazyme over the initial objections of Gus, who at that time had been the venture firm's newest partner. Gus had opposed the Novazyme investment for one and only one reason—John. Gus saw John's conflict of interest as an insurmountable obstacle.[1]

"I don't believe the guy can be a good businessman and a good father at the same time," he had told his partners. "I don't believe it because I don't think I could do it. What's going to happen if the question is whether he should spend our money wisely or get his kids the drug? He's going to spend away our money."

Gus's partners had argued that that same conflict of interest made John immensely motivated. John's urgency, combined with the fact that Genzyme would likely have to buy Novazyme, made it an excellent investment, they argued. In the end, Gus had reluctantly agreed to the investment—his first as a venture capitalist.

When it came time to decide which partner would sit on the Novazyme board, however, Gus's colleagues decided it should be him. As the most skeptical, he would watch the company the most carefully.

The board membership made Gus nervous. While he was about ten years older than John, it was his first assignment as a partner at HealthCare Ventures, and he was determined not to let it end in failure. He hadn't been born rich. He'd grown up in the old mill city of Lawrence, Massachusetts, the eldest of four sons born to a pharmacist and his homemaker wife. He'd graduated from the University of New Hampshire and the Yale School of Management—like John, a hard worker and a shrewd businessman.

But unlike the younger man, Gus already had more than a decade of experience in management at four biotechnology companies. And he was now responsible for making profitable investments for HealthCare Ventures—and protecting them. He didn't have sick children; nor, from his position, could he afford to let anyone's sick children affect his business judgment. Gus resolved to watch John's every move.

Everything John did in the first few months after the venture investment seemed to confirm Gus's fears—and worse. In addition to the huge conflict of interest, Gus found John inexperienced and arrogant.

The first thing Gus noticed was how quickly John was filling senior management positions with people who had no experience in the area they were supervising. "I'm hiring the best and the brightest," John would report cheerily, when Gus called to check on how things were going at Novazyme.[2]

He also didn't seem to be seeking advice or permission from Gus or anyone else on the board before making big decisions. Gus only heard what was going on at Novazyme when he picked up the phone and called John. To Gus's dismay, he learned only after the fact that John had signed a $2 million contract to build a manufacturing plant in Oklahoma to produce Canfield's enzyme for clinical trials.[3] John hadn't discussed the contract even informally with board members, let alone at a board meeting.

When Gus phoned John to ask why he hadn't consulted the board, John sounded annoyed. Then he didn't believe Gus when he said Novazyme's investment agreements with the venture firms specifically required the approval of 75 percent of the investors before making "major management decisions." John had called back later to apologize and say he hadn't read the investment agreement until now.

"We need to talk," Gus told him. He and another partner flew to Oklahoma City the next week.

In the ground-floor restaurant of Oklahoma City's Renaissance Hotel, Gus and his venture partner delivered a stinging critique of John's record as CEO—less than sixty days after making their investment in Novazyme.[4]

"Your philosophy of trying to hire the best and the brightest is wrong," Gus said bluntly, his blue eyes fixed on John's face in a cold, unfriendly stare. "Nobody at Novazyme has a clue about the clinical side of things."

"That's not true," John replied, stung. "Tony McKinney has ten years' experience in the drug industry."

"He was not in charge of drug development—he was a project manager," Gus retorted. "There's a big difference. Without some experienced leaders, Novazyme is going to make costly mistakes. For one thing, you're trying to do too many things at once. And you have no budget controls. Every time I turn around there are more people hired at the company! You need to slow down and take your time—you've got to give Canfield the time to work out the kinks in his research. It's all right to spend a year or two to get the basic science right."

John nodded sullenly, not attempting to hide his irritation. He stared defiantly at Gus, saying nothing.

"And finally, you need to communicate regularly with your board of directors," Gus continued, undaunted. "You can't just be signing away a quarter of our investment without getting our approval."

"Yes, I understand that. I apologize for the lack of communication," John said stiffly when the list finally wound to a halt. "I certainly appreciate your input."

Gus could tell John had no intention of heeding him.

On the plane back to Boston, Gus turned to his partner and said, "I don't think John Crowley really gives a damn what we investors have to say. We either have to lump it or impose our will."

Nervously, Gus waited for what John would do next. A few days later, John was on the phone saying he and Canfield wanted to add a new, unrelated drug to their portfolio. It had nothing to do with Pompe disease, but Canfield believed that the scientific finding had enormous potential and could be turned into a drug treating many other diseases. "It's a great way for Novazyme to diversify," John exulted.

Gus couldn't believe the idiocy of what he was hearing. "You can't develop what you have in-house already, and you're talking about bringing in something else?" he said. "You absolutely should not do this."

"Thanks for your advice, Gus," John said, cutting the conversation short. "I'll certainly think about what you've said. This new technology fits squarely into Dr. Canfield's expertise in glycobiology. I'll give great thought, though, to your reservations."

Gus hung up, hoping against hope that John had dropped the idea.

But on December 21, as Gus sat in an airport lounge participating in a Novazyme board meeting by phone, John brought up the idea again.

"Steve, what do you think?" John asked, addressing Steve Elms, the partner from Perseus Soros who represented the venture fund on Novazyme's board.

"If you want to do it, we're okay with it," Steve said.[5]

"How about you, Stuart?" John asked, addressing Canfield's mentor Stuart Kornfeld, a professor at Washington University in St. Louis and one of the most respected researchers in glycobiology.

"Sounds like a good prospect," Dr. Kornfeld said.

Dave Albert, the Oklahoma inventor and investor, a friend of Canfield's, also supported the idea. Only after everyone else had endorsed the licensing arrangement did John ask Gus.

"I have ten different reasons why this is a bad idea," Gus burst out. "We don't have the money to finish what we're doing now. We don't have the talent in-house to do what we're doing. I just can't figure out why you want to bring in another product. We can't afford to lose our focus."

"If I can't keep this company focused on lysosomal storage diseases, nobody can," John growled, in a rare and emotional reference during business to his children.

"By the time you realize you've gotten behind in your programs, it's too late," Gus said, unmoved.

"I'm the CEO of the company, and the entire board is behind it, except you," John said, his voice icy. "I don't work for you alone, Gus."

"You don't work for the shareholders?" Gus said, sarcastically.

"I work for all the shareholders," John said through gritted teeth.

John suggested they take a vote. Gus waited, silently, afraid he would lose. But then John pulled back, overriding his anger, suddenly remembering the advice that Josh Phillips's senior partner at Catalyst had given him months ago. "If you ever have to take a vote of your board, John, you've lost the board," David Hendren had said. So John offered a compromise—he and Canfield would do more research on the project and return to the board with more information.

Now Gus was convinced he had to get rid of John. Over the next few days, he phoned the other board members, feeling them out about Novazyme's CEO. He was hoping to find the others similarly frustrated and at least willing to consider firing him.

"CEOs and their boards do run into problems—every five years or so. Here we have a problem every month," Gus told Canfield, who was still the largest shareholder, with 49 percent ownership.

Canfield grunted and said nothing, leaving Gus to construe, correctly, that he stood with John.

"I don't know if John Crowley is the right person to be CEO," Gus said to Dennis Purcell, Steve Elms's managing partner at the Perseus Soros Fund, who had made the decision to invest.

"I don't know either," Dennis admitted. "But if you shoot Crowley now, it will damage, if not kill, the company. Crowley *is* the company."

Gus hung up, concluding that even though some board members thought John could be a headache, there was no enthusiasm for firing him. John was safe for now.

In mid-January, John and Canfield flew to San Francisco for the J. P. Morgan H&Q Healthcare Conference, a who's-who schmoozefest in the biotechnology industry. They arrived with an agenda: to find investors for the next round of financing for Novazyme, which needed to happen much faster than either of them had anticipated.

As John was keenly aware—though he had made no attempts to stop it—Novazyme's bank account was swiftly draining. The company would be out of money by late spring without another infusion of cash, and the list of potential sources of new funding from the existing round of investors was dwindling. John had alienated HealthCare Ventures through his jousting with Gus; he had appalled Neose with his disastrous mouse experiments; and Catalyst didn't have deep enough pockets to give a ballooning Novazyme the kind of cash it needed. There was only one ally with deep pockets remaining from the A Round—the Perseus Soros Fund. John had called ahead of the H&Q meeting and scheduled breakfast with Dennis Purcell, the managing partner at Perseus Soros, and Steve Elms, the partner who represented the fund on Novazyme's board.

On the morning of the third day of the conference, John and Canfield met Dennis and Steve at a hotel restaurant. Dennis, tall and broad shouldered with a jovial demeanor, was in a very good mood as they settled down at their square table. He had built a stunning reputation while working at the bank sponsoring the conference, and John and Canfield had watched in amazement as the other attendees greeted him like a rock star, flocking around him wherever he went. He started H&Q's healthcare investment banking group and raised more money in the stock market for biotechnology firms than almost any other banker. George Soros had recruited Dennis a year earlier to start a biotechnology venture fund, and he had raised about $200 million for it so far. Steve, who had followed Dennis from the same group at H&Q, where he'd been an investment banker for five years, spoke to them in a light, familiar tone.[6]

"You look like a New York City cop," he teased, squinting across the table at John's electric blue shirt. John laughed along, then tried to focus the meeting on financing.

"We're beginning to think about raising our next round," John said. "Would you guys be interested in leading it?"

Dennis beamed, looked at Steve, and nodded, saying, "You guys are making good progress. We could pull together between $10 million and $20 million."

"At what valuation?" John asked, feeling Canfield grow tense beside him. The valuation was the price placed on a company before the next round of investment; the higher the valuation, the bigger the chunk of the company the existing investors owned after the next infusion of cash. Canfield had repeatedly told John that the next round had to be at a high valuation so that he could retain the biggest share of ownership.

"Oh, what could we do, Steve . . . ," Dennis said, looking over at his junior partner. "I'd say between $30 million and $40 million."

John didn't even have to look at Canfield beside him to know that he was upset. In part because of their association with Dennis, John and Canfield had been courted over the past few days by a half-dozen other venture investors and investment banks, all clamoring to be part of the next round of financing. These would-be investors had thrown out valuations twice as high as Dennis was now citing.

"Dennis, why would I do this when the guys at other venture firms are throwing out numbers two and three times as high?" John finally offered.

Dennis, his smile fading, appeared taken aback. "What we're offering is very reasonable for a company that is still a long way from clinical trials," he said.

"I'm just telling you, we're hearing numbers like $70 million and $80 million from the other guys," John said. "We have a fiduciary responsibility to get the best deal for Novazyme."

"We would take care of you and Bill," Dennis said. "We'll give extra options to senior management to make up for any dilution in ownership you experience."

John shook his head, thinking Dennis could never give them enough options to make up for the dilution Canfield would experience at that valuation. His 49 percent made him the largest shareholder, and he was ardently opposed to losing control over Novazyme.

"You know, you guys should go out and test the waters—go right out there and get yourself other investors," Dennis said, his face reddening as he stood up. "Good luck to you both. Let us know how it goes."

The breakfast ended abruptly. John had made another miscalculation, and his inexperience in dealing with the financial world was about to blow up in his face.

At the same conference, meanwhile, Gus had scheduled a meeting with Neose's Sherrill Neff and Stephen Roth to try to win them over to his side in opposing the in-licensing deal John had been pushing at the board meeting. But before Gus had a chance to make his pitch, Roth launched into a description of the disastrous scientific presentation that John and McKinney had made two weeks earlier, which Gus hadn't known about.[7]

"These guys either have no idea what they're doing or they are frauds," Roth declared, steaming at the memory of the meeting.

Gus almost couldn't believe what he was hearing. He had thought he was the only one with a bad feeling about John and Novazyme. What these Neose guys were telling him was far worse than any mere confirmation of similar feelings.

"I've thought they were inept, but I never thought that they were intentionally misleading us," Gus said. "Have you talked to Dennis yet? It sounds like we have a real problem here."

Roth said he and Neff were scheduled to talk to Dennis the next morning, when they planned to fill him in.

The next evening, Friday, the phone rang in Novazyme's satellite office in Princeton. Dennis was on the line, apoplectic with rage.[8]

"What the hell is going on?" he shouted at John. "Neose doesn't believe any of your data. Are you going to begin clinical trials in September or what? Neose is saying there is no way you'll be in the clinic in September."

"I can explain," John said.

"Save your breath," Dennis boomed through the earpiece. He told John to show up with Canfield at his Manhattan office at 9 A.M. that next Tuesday, in just four days, prepared to explain the experiments. Without wasting breath on closing courtesies, Dennis banged the phone down, and John was left holding an empty line.

17. Novazyme Time

WINTER 2000–SPRING 2001

PRINCETON, NEW JERSEY; NEW YORK, NEW YORK; OKLAHOMA CITY, OKLAHOMA

Undaunted by the possible disaster looming above their heads, John and Canfield spent the next four days working late into the night pulling together a report on the company's progress—John out of his satellite office in Princeton, Canfield at headquarters in Oklahoma City. John said he would organize the business side of the report and Canfield was to pull together the science part.

"Let's overwhelm them with the facts," John said to Canfield, cocky even under daunting pressure. "We've achieved more in four months than any other company in biotech history. Sure, we've made mistakes, but every day has been two steps forward and only one step back. We're far ahead of where we were when they made their investment just four months ago. Let's show 'em, Bill."

They had convinced themselves that the venture investors were interfering, even bullying them. On the phone several times a day, they fed each other's anger.

"This is an absolute waste of our time," John complained, and Canfield, naturally skeptical of East Coast finance types, grunted in agreement.

On Monday evening, John came home and went right to his study instead of coming upstairs to say good night to the kids. Aileen knew that meant trouble with the company, and after she had put the kids to bed, she found John still at his desk, surrounded by stacks of papers.

"What's going on?" she asked, leaning against the doorway, framed by the light in the hallway behind her.

"Canfield's flying in tonight. I have to pick him up in Newark and drive him into the city for a meeting with the investors tomorrow."

"Something's wrong," she said, hearing the fatigue in his normally optimistic voice. "You sound terrible. And you look even worse." She moved behind him and began to knead his shoulders gently.

"The sons of bitches think we're frauds," John said bitterly, his muscles tense. "They don't believe the science anymore. Bill and I have to go in there tomorrow and convince them we're for real." He twirled a pen on his desk restlessly. Aileen's hands didn't slow on his shoulders.

Abruptly, he threw his pen across the room and slumped forward, head in hands. "I hate this, Aileen. I just don't want to do this anymore. I hate talking about, thinking about, and agonizing over Pompe disease all day long. And then I have to come home to live it. There's no escape. I just want to quit. I've had it. I'm done."

"Oh, John," Aileen said, pulling him back against her belly and letting her arms loop around his neck and shoulders, rocking him lightly. "You're working way too hard," she whispered. In this moment where all her husband's weariness and pain lay bare, everything else melted away, and all she could think of was easing his strain. "This is too stressful for you. I don't know how long you can keep doing this." Where some saw overreaching or overconfidence, she saw his fierce dedication to his children.

She pushed his papers to one side and slid onto the desk, unbuttoning his shirt and whispering. "It's okay if you're a little late to pick up Bill, isn't it?"

"I'll tell him my wife seduced me as I was heading out the door," John said, looking at her with gratitude, knowing that she understood his tiredness, that she didn't blame him for his weakness. Aileen smiled and hit the switch to turn the lights low.

An hour later, John—more than a little late—found Canfield outside the arrivals terminal at Newark Airport, scanning the crowd wearily. John picked him up, and soon they were in Manhattan checking into their hotel. They left their bags and headed to a Kinkos, where they remained for three hours, struggling to print out the briefing material for the meeting the next morning. It was past midnight when they returned to the hotel with a dozen inch-thick binders.

The day before the meeting, Gus was on edge, fiddling with his blue tie and pacing back and forth on the somber gray carpet of his office. "If they don't know what the hell they're doing, that's one thing—but if they're lying to boot, we're in real trouble," he told Chris Mirabelli, a partner who was a scientist by training. Gus had asked Mirabelli if he would fly down with him to the meeting to help determine whether Canfield's science was a fraud. While Mirabelli might not be able to determine this from just one meeting, his science background at least gave him a better platform to evaluate from than Gus had. HealthCare Ventures had entrusted Gus to make good on the Novazyme investment, and now it looked like the venture firm would not only *not* make a profit, but might also actually lose money. His first assignment could not end in failure.

The next morning, Gus and Mirabelli showed up early for a quick pre-meeting with the Perseus Soros and Neose teams to discuss strategy for questioning Novazyme.

"We need to know if we were hoodwinked," Gus said bluntly, opening the discussion. "Was the scientific presentation to Neose a deliberate attempt to deceive?"

Dennis said he hoped they could come out of the meeting with a plan to get Novazyme back on track. "We need some mouse experiments comparing Canfield's enzyme against Genzyme's. It's worth moving forward only if Canfield's enzyme is better."

When the ten-man group emerged on the twenty-ninth floor of the Perseus Soros building, they found John and Canfield waiting, laptops powered up, in a small conference room with a view of midtown Manhattan. With small, tight smiles of greeting, the group settled around the table and picked up the thick binders in front of them.[1]

Canfield, hoping to dazzle the group with his recent scientific achievements, went first. With slide after slide of a PowerPoint presentation, he detailed the results of four months of nearly round-the-clock experiments that had led to his incredible breakthroughs—producing PTase and finding a replacement for DMJ, the chemical inhibitor that wasn't widely available. But instead of being amazed, the group grew fidgety.

"Stop—just stop," Dr. Roth finally burst out, after thirty-nine slides and one full hour had passed. "We've heard enough. Now get to the point. Please explain the data John and Tony presented."

Canfield paused, frowning and looking over at John, annoyed that the investors seemed so uninterested in his science. "All I will say is that mistakes were made. But that experiment was just a prelude to the animal experiments we have planned." He explained that they had commissioned a series of experiments with an outside investigator, Dr. Barry Byrne, the University of Florida scientist-physician who had worked with McKinney during the summer to design the company's animal studies.

"We will, in a few weeks, have outside validation that our enzyme works in mice with Pompe disease," Canfield concluded weakly. He sat down heavily and wiped a line of sweat from his brow.

Then John, a more succinct and lively presenter, detailed the company's business successes, his eyes scanning the ten men for any sign of encouragement. But their faces were like masks—grim, unmoving, impenetrable. "In the four months since we completed the A Round in September, we have begun a dialogue with the FDA on how to conduct the animal studies," he finished. "We have nearly completed construction of the manufacturing plant, and we've hired sixty employees. And we believe we're still on track to go into clinical trials in September."

As John sat down, Gus looked around at the table at the other investors, feeling annoyed. He hadn't heard anything from John or Canfield to allay his fears that the whole thing was a sham. Instead of explaining why their scientific presentation to Neose had been so flawed, the two men had delivered a sales pitch on Novazyme's scientific and business achievements. They had made an astonishing amount of progress in four months, Gus had to admit, but he didn't trust them not to lie about their results.

"You guys are still going to be in the clinic in September?" Mirabelli, Gus's partner, asked at length, breaking the uneasy silence.

"Absolutely," John said, smiling. Canfield gave a quick little nod of agreement.

"Are you telling me you are still struggling with basic scientific questions and you think you can begin testing in humans nine months from now?" Mirabelli pressed.

"I agree, the timeline is ambitious," John said. "It would not fit the drug development timelines you are used to. But Novazyme doesn't have time to do the science first and then the drug development, given Genzyme's position with two enzymes already in clinical trial. We're going to do everything in parallel. We're working faster than anyone else. We're operating in a different time frame. We're working on Novazyme Time."

Gus, shaking his head, whispered to Mirabelli, "Are we ever going to get a straight answer on the timeline from Crowley?" Again, an uncomfortable silence descended.

Finally, John looked around the table and asked, "Are you less anxious about Novazyme than when you came here this morning?"

Gus, clearing his throat, said, "Well, let me say I'm not more anxious than when I got here."

"Well, we have lots of problems and plans to figure out," John said brightly. "But I'm very optimistic."

Dennis, who had been sitting silently during the whole presentation, his hands locked together on the table in front of him, looked up at this cheery reassurance. "You better figure them out," he snapped, "or you'll have a big fucking problem."

John looked down, his smile gone.

Gus knew then that Dennis had finally come over to his side. If John didn't get things back on track, he would be fired.

The meeting had ended without Gus and the group being able to determine for certain whether or not Novazyme's science was fraudulent, and Gus wasn't ready to let the question go. To know for sure, Gus thought, they really needed to hear from an insider at the company. He and Mirabelli flew back to Cambridge that afternoon, having arranged for the physician-scientist, Dr. Pedro Huertas, whom John had hired a month earlier to be Novazyme's chief medical officer, to fly up the next morning for a secret meeting. Gus had prevailed upon John to hire Huertas as part of his campaign to raise the level of experience of senior management. Huertas came from Genzyme, where he had been involved in developing a drug for a disease similar to Pompe. His academic credentials were stunning, with a doctorate in biochemistry from Harvard University, a medical degree from Harvard Medical School, and an MBA from the MIT Sloan School of Management.

Gus had asked Huertas to come prepared to provide an off-the-record assessment of Novazyme's science, hoping the scientist would be candid since he'd gotten the job through Gus and because his mentors at Harvard Medical School were scientific advisers to HealthCare Ventures.

The next morning, Huertas sat with Gus at one end of a long conference table in his firm's bright second-floor conference room. Sunlight streamed through the windows, which overlooked the courtyard of One Kendall Square and, beyond that, the long brick buildings of Genzyme.

"I don't know how much I can help you, Gus. You must remember I have only been at Novazyme for about one month," Huertas began.[2]

"Well, just tell me your feelings so far," Gus said, smiling. He was wearing a rumpled tweed jacket and glasses, and looked more like a professor than the hard-nosed venture capitalist that he was.

"My feeling so far is that Canfield is a really smart guy, but he's as dogmatic as they come," Huertas said, his Chilean background still evident in his accent. "He's suspicious of outsiders, keeps the details of his work to himself and a small group of scientists. I think his approach is right, but my feeling so far is that neither Canfield nor anyone else has a clue of how to develop a drug."

"Do you think there's fraud going on?" Gus pressed.

Huertas drew up short for a moment. Gus had asked him to prepare to be candid, but he'd had no idea that Novazyme's backers were worried that there might be deception. "My feeling is these guys are just inexperienced, but I don't think there's fraud," he said carefully.

Gus leaned back in his chair, breathed deeply, and said, "I have to say, Pedro, any amount of incompetence seems like a blessing compared to the alternative. I appreciate your feedback very much. I know this isn't easy for you, but you have to appreciate our position here." Relieved, he smiled at Huertas as he walked with him to the elevators, saying, "And of course, as I said before, nobody knows we had this discussion."

Less than a week later, Gus was shocked to learn through the investment grapevine that John and Canfield were traveling around the country trying to raise money from other venture funds. Instead of improving re-lations with his existing investors, John appeared to be trying to blunt their influence by finding new money.

"I have to admire the guy's gumption," Gus said to Mirabelli, with a kind of amused exasperation. Then he added seriously, "But it's another sign of Crowley's inexperience that he thinks he can get new investors without the support of the existing ones. Doesn't he know the new guys will wonder why the existing investors aren't in the next round?"[3]

The venture capital world was an old boy network. Soon, partners at the funds John approached were on the phone to Gus asking why Health-Care Ventures wasn't leading, or at least participating.

"John Crowley is a problem," Gus declared to each caller. "The com-pany has an inexperienced chief executive and an inexperienced chief sci-entific officer, and they don't give a damn what their investors think." The company was struggling with scientific questions, was behind in animal ex-periments, and had deep feuds between management and the board, Gus told the callers. Before signing off, he made sure to tell them that he was as close to giving up on a business relationship as he'd ever been.

It worked. In less than two weeks, John was getting nowhere. John saw fifteen different firms in two weeks, and despite his considerable powers of persuasion, failed to convince a single one to give him even a tentative commitment.

When the last one turned him down in a call to his cell phone on Fri-day afternoon, John looked at his watch. It was nearly 5 P.M. He had liter-ally minutes to reach someone before offices on the East Coast closed for the weekend. Novazyme was almost out of money, and he didn't want to lose the weekend. He picked up the phone and dialed the Perseus Soros of-fice, reaching Steve Elms. "We'll do the financing with you guys on the terms you think are fair," John said, getting right to the point.

Steve had already heard through the grapevine that John was making no progress with his venture capital road show. "All right, John, but you know you're going to get your ass kicked," he said.

"I'm prepared," John replied grimly.

On Monday, John showed up at the same Perseus Soros conference room where his venture investors had berated him two weeks earlier, pre-pared to grovel.

"I told you this was going to happen," Dennis began, shaking his head. John capitulated immediately, saying, "There are some things I'm good at, and some things I'm not."[4] He had learned to be humble when he had to be.

Dennis proceeded to lay down the terms of the deal. "The premoney valuation will be $35 million," he said. That was within the $30 million to $40 million range John and Canfield had rejected earlier, but John didn't dare argue. He was just relieved that he hadn't gone any lower.

"Whatever you believe would be fair is fine with me," John said.

"It's not quite so easy," Dennis stopped him. For this deal to even happen, Dennis said, he needed Gus's firm to participate.

Soon Dennis was on the phone telling Gus about John's change of heart. "I'm inclined to give them more money," Dennis said. Novazyme's management's blunders didn't take away from the reality that its science represented an enormous threat to Genzyme. If Novazyme could just complete one or two experiments validating Canfield's science, the venture investors might be able to sell to Genzyme and bail out with a big profit.

"I don't want to throw good money after bad," Gus replied warily. "But before saying a final 'no,' I'll talk to my partners. I'll be back to you in a few days."

Meanwhile, Gus and the rest of the directors arrived in Oklahoma, where Novazyme was holding its board meeting for the first time. Gus noted with relief that the idea of in-licensing a new drug, which he had so vehemently opposed, was not on the agenda. Maybe, he thought, Crowley was finally coming to heel.

The early morning was all routine board business. In the late morning, John had scheduled the ribbon cutting on the new $2 million manufacturing facility. Gus and the other board members followed John on a tour of room after room of sparkling stainless steel equipment across from the company's research labs in the same office complex. Then they joined Novazyme's sixty employees crowded into the corridor outside, talking excitedly.

"We at Novazyme are passionately driven by our mission to discover and develop drugs that profoundly enhance human life," John began forcefully, vibrant in a navy suit and red tie.

"This manufacturing plant is being dedicated for a brave young lady," he said, looking down at a girl in a long-sleeved blue dress, reclining a few feet away in her wheelchair. The new facility, he said with gusto, would be called the Lindsey Paige Easton Biologics Manufacturing Facility. John had decided to name the new plant after the young lady who had moved and inspired him on her last visit.

"Every day that we didn't have our own manufacturing plant, every day that we don't have enzyme, somebody in the world suffers greatly from one of these diseases," John said. "We've dedicated this plant to you, Lindsey, so everybody knows, every time they enter this doorway, why it is we are doing what we do." He pressed his lips together to compose himself, as Laurie Easton, standing beside her daughter, wiped away tears.

John cut the ribbon to applause that continued for several minutes. From his position in the back of the crowd, Gus noticed the young employee to his right interrupt her clapping twice to wipe away tears. In the front of the room, near John and the sliced ribbon, Lindsey Easton, sat motionless except for her big eyes scanning the crowd from behind a pair of eyeglasses. Her face hadn't changed and she didn't seem to have shifted position since she appeared in front of the audience ten minutes earlier. Gus, uncomfortably aware of his ignorance, wondered if she could move at all.[5]

Lunch followed, and Gus knew very well that it wasn't coincidental that John had scheduled one of the Lunch 'N Learns he talked about so enthusiastically. Along with the other board members, Gus sat at the back of the second-floor conference room, uncertain what to expect. Other than the quick look at Lindsey that morning, he had never met a Pompe patient; in all the months he'd worked with John, it had never occurred to him to ask to meet one. That was the domain of doctors; his expertise was finance.

The room was crammed with the company's employees, most of them young and scrubbed looking. They fell silent as a gray-haired woman who looked to be in her mid-fifties walked in, leaning on a cane and clutching her husband's arm. John introduced her as an Oklahoma resident, a mother and grandmother, who suffered from the adult-onset form of Pompe. The woman, speaking softly and matter-of-factly, said she was diagnosed with Pompe when she was forty years old. But for years before, she had felt something was wrong, though no doctor had been able to find the problem. As a child, she was always the slowest runner, the last one picked on the kickball team. After she married and had children, she noticed her legs feeling extra heavy one day and that she was getting winded just walking up a flight of stairs. She saw one specialist after another over five years until an endocrinologist finally diagnosed the disease.

"I've gotten slowly weaker over the past fifteen years since I was diagnosed," she said. "Now I can't walk up stairs at all. But I still take time to enjoy life. I try to stay fit by walking every day. I've taken up painting. If no medicine comes along, I know I'll keep getting weaker and in a few years I'll need a wheelchair.

"I can't even begin to tell you what it means to have the hope of a treatment that might stop me from getting weaker. It makes me think about living instead of dying. I think again about growing old with my husband," she said, looking lovingly at the man standing patiently beside her. "I think about seeing my grandchildren grow up. Before Novazyme, I didn't let myself hope for a future—but now I find I can't let go of it."

Looking at John smiling and thanking the woman for visiting, Gus thought—*really* thought—for the first time about what his life must be like. He wondered whether John's children were mobile like this older woman or had to be pushed around in a wheelchair like Lindsey. If either of his own two children had the disease, what would he have done? He knew the answer before he finished the thought. There was absolutely no question in his mind. He would have set out, just like John, to drive science toward a cure.

Gus returned from his visit to Oklahoma with a new respect and sympathy for John. He was driving his board crazy, but he had put together a real company filled with zealous young employees. Gus had even told John as much as the luncheon concluded. As he'd joined the end of the line for take-out Chinese food now spread over the conference table, John had come up behind him. "Gus," he joked good-naturedly, "I'll bet you've been wanting to try some Oklahoma Chinese cuisine your entire life."

Gus laughed, but was unable to shake the mental picture of this aggravating, exasperating man at home, pushing one of his children lying limply in a wheelchair. "John, what you've done here is pretty impressive," he admitted. "You've established a remarkable corporate culture. It's unlike any other biotech I've seen before."

Still, Gus was determined not to let these feelings cloud his decision on whether to invest more of HealthCare Ventures's money in Novazyme. He kept reminding himself that the inspiring corporate culture aside, Canfield was not one inch closer to getting the scientific data they needed to move ahead.

And then, as if reading his mind, John was on the phone to Gus, reporting exciting data from Dr. Barry Byrne, the University of Florida scientist who had been testing Canfield's enzyme in sixteen mice with Pompe. "I'll fax it over and you and your partners can take a look for yourselves," John said.

A few minutes later, Gus was standing by the fax machine reading that Byrne had treated eight mice with Canfield's enzyme over several weeks, and compared the strength of their leg muscles with eight others that had received no medicine. Byrne reported the muscle strength of the eight treated mice had been restored to almost normal. He had measured the strength by running an electric current through samples of muscle from each of the mice. The stronger the muscle, the more it flexed when stimulated with the current.[6]

It was far from the proof Gus and the other venture investors were seeking that Canfield's enzyme worked better than Genzyme's two experimental treatments—and Byrne hadn't yet performed any confirmatory experiments, so it wasn't necessarily even proof that Canfield's enzyme worked at all. But Byrne's results were the first indication from someone independent of Novazyme that Canfield's approach held promise.

"I still don't know about Crowley, but maybe we should think more strongly about putting in more money to give Canfield time to generate some credible data," Gus said, striding into his partner Mirabelli's office to show him the data. Mirabelli shuffled through the papers, considering.

"I think we've got Crowley more under control. He has heard us and brought on more guys with more experience," Gus said, referring to Dr. Pedro Huertas and several other new hires. "Maybe Dennis is right. We give Novazyme a little more cash, and we sell it for a profit and get out."

"No point in throwing in the towel now," Mirabelli agreed, handing back the papers.

Back in his office, Gus got John on the phone. "Are you still on track to go into clinical trials in September?" he asked. In the venture world, certain milestones, like beginning a clinical trial, enhanced the value of the company—making it a good time for the original investors to sell.

"Absolutely, we're on the money," came John's unhesitating answer.

Gus sighed. He didn't really believe him, and despite the go-ahead from Mirabelli and his own urgings in that meeting, still struggled with whether it really was worth the risk to invest more money—and then an idea sprang to mind for protecting part of his next investment, if he was going to make it. He cleared his throat and phrased his words carefully.

"John, I liked the data you sent over," Gus began. "We'd like to be part of the B Round." Then the part he knew John wouldn't be so happy with: "You know, I'm going to talk to Dennis about investing in two stages. What I'm going to propose is that we give you $8 million now—and $8 million when you file your application to the FDA to begin clinical trials in September."

"That sounds fair," John said. But even from the other end of the line, Gus thought he could hear the enthusiasm draining.

John hung up, closed the door, and sat silently in his satellite office in Princeton, watching a spring rain douse the cars in the parking lot.

Gus had called his bluff. How could John argue against hitching half the investment to the start of clinical trials without admitting he would never be in trials by that fall?

The people Gus had made him hire—from Huertas, the chief medical officer, to Bill Fallon, the new head of manufacturing—had convinced him that it was truly impossible to begin human trials in September. John still hoped he would be close, but he wasn't yet ready to admit any expected delay. If he changed the timeline, he believed his investors would flee.

What was he going to do? He now had seventy people employed, and he was spending more than a million dollars a month. Eight million would only get him to September. And if Novazyme wasn't in clinical trials by that time, John was sure Gus and the others would fire his sorry ass on the spot.

Where would Megan and Patrick be then?

He stared at the rain silently funneling down the windows of the parked cars, turning the pavement a dark gray and slicking the lawn with flecks of silver.

There was, he finally decided, only one way of doing what he needed to do—getting the company more money, saving himself from his investors' wrath, and giving his kids a prayer of getting treated soon. It was a solution that had offered itself several times over the past few months, but one he hadn't wanted to give in to. Now, he realized, it was the only way.

He would take the money his venture capital investors were ready to offer and race the science as fast as he could over the next six months.

And then he would sell Novazyme.

18. Making Memories

As Aileen watched the ordeal of the past few months, she had come to be-lieve it was far from certain John would get their children treated in time. "I don't know if I can make this work," he had said to her repeatedly as he grappled with the funding, the science, and the venture investors. Seeing her husband's struggle, Aileen rushed to play the role of comforter she had assumed in the marriage. Not a day had gone by in the past two years when John had not been completely focused on trying to cure the children. She decided to plan a vacation.

John dismissed the idea at first, unable to conceive of how he could get away while trying to close the next round of financing with his wary in-vestors. Only when Aileen pushed, saying, "The biggest tragedy would be if you spent all this time trying to save the kids that you didn't get to enjoy them while they were here," did he finally relent. Aileen promised that she would take care of the arrangements.

Aileen remembered the "wish" Megan had been given by her mother's friend Kathy Rosato and Kathy's daughters at the first fund-raiser two years ago. The "wish" was from the nonprofit Make a Wish Foundation—dedicated to making the dreams of children with life-threatening illnesses come true. Aileen had accepted it graciously, but she had never intended to use it. She didn't return calls from the Make a Wish volunteer, and she told John they should give the "wish" to another child who needed it more.

"Our children aren't dying," she'd said firmly. "They'll be getting an enzyme, and then they'll be fine."

Now, two years later, Aileen's resistance to using the "wish" had disappeared. Each time Chen's clinical trials had gotten postponed, each time she overheard John talking about a new obstacle at Novazyme, she had let go a little bit more of the promise of a cure. With Sharon to help, she had resolved to embrace a new mission, which she would articulate when people asked when the enzyme therapy would be ready. Shrugging, she would answer, quite sweetly and truthfully, "I don't know—I'm just trying to keep the kids as healthy and happy as I can."

One morning in early March, Aileen dug Megan's "wish" from under a pile of take-out menus at the bottom of the kitchen drawer. The "wish" was a folded blue piece of paper emblazoned with a silver star attached to a Make a Wish volunteer's card. Aileen called the volunteer and said her daughter was finally ready to use her wish, and she wanted to go to Disney World. When the volunteer called back, she had made all of the travel arrangements except for the flights. She wasn't able to find a single commercial airline that would fly the children with a supply of oxygen in the cabin, which they needed in case of a respiratory emergency. It was against federal air regulations to carry oxygen in the cabin because it was flammable.

Aileen, trying not to lean on her exhausted husband, realized she had no choice but to ask him for help. The only way to get the children to Disney World was to find a private plane to fly them there, she said. "Could you please ask Brad if his dad can help?" Lewis Campbell, the father of John's friend Bradley was the chief executive of Textron who had helped underwrite the Boston fund-raiser. As she had expected, her lovably predictable John frothed and raged that he already had too much to do, then picked up the phone and dialed Brad. By the end of the day, Lewis Campbell had agreed to let the Crowley family use his firm's corporate jet.[1]

On the third Saturday in March, the Crowleys' blue minivan rolled up beside Textron's private jet at Trenton Mercer Airport, just a short ride from their house. Aileen could tell her husband was more excited about riding in a private plane than about the Disney visit. He jumped out of the car and ran up the steps to check out the cabin before returning to help load the kids, the luggage, and the medical equipment onto the small plane.

Once everyone was on board, including Sharon and their regular night nurse, Yvonne, John, in his trademark navy shirt and khaki shorts, leaned back in his tan leather seat extra slowly. He puffed out his chest and marveled aloud, with boyish enthusiasm, that his seat could swivel, even though it would only move a few inches with three backup ventilators jamming the short aisle. The big bulky batteries of the ventilators were piled on top of the toilet in the rear, making it unusable.

Soon John was striding into the cockpit to discuss the model and make of the plane with the pilots (it was a Cessna Citation 7) and the weather ahead (clear skies, good visibility with scattered low-level cloud cover). Out the window, he spotted some former Bristol-Myers colleagues getting on the next plane over and ran outside to talk to them—eager to be seen also traveling on a corporate jet. As she stood in the doorway watching him, Aileen overheard him say, deliberately casual, "I'm just taking the kids down for a quick trip to Disney World. We'll chase you down there."

When John was back on board, the pilot said the flight would be delayed because he needed extra fuel to handle the weight of so much medical equipment. They were an hour behind schedule when the little plane finally charged into the air. So much for the big shot corporate executive.

For the two-and-a-half-hour flight, Megan, who hadn't been on a plane since she was old enough to remember, stared outside through her red Minnie Mouse sunglasses, fascinated by the clouds swirling by. Patrick cried and Aileen held him on her lap. John Jr. played his Game Boy quietly in the rear seat.

"This is a nice way to travel," John kept repeating, opening the cabinets and refrigerator several times to pull out snacks and drinks.

When the plane landed, Aileen saw two Make a Wish volunteers and a dog parked nearby in a red pickup. They said they were there to drive John to the other end of the airport to rent a van. "Jump in back," the driver said to John, leaving him no choice but to climb into the bed of the pickup, which was filled with hay. As he settled awkwardly onto a bale, Aileen pulled out her camera and clicked a picture, teasing, "Oooh, Mr. Big Man on his private plane—now look at you."

"Wave to Daddy, everyone," Aileen shouted as the truck revved its engine and roared away.

"No, look at Daddy's hair!" Megan cried gleefully. "I've never seen Daddy's hair look like that before!" The pickup was accelerating onto the highway, and John was hunched over, grasping the sides, his carefully combed and gelled coiffure standing straight up into the streaming air.

The Make a Wish Foundation arranged for families visiting Disney World to stay nearby in a fifty-acre village run by a nonprofit called Give Kids the World. The group was started by a successful hotelier who wanted to make sure children with life-threatening illnesses could visit Disney World. While Aileen checked in at the front desk, John led the kids and the nurses around the village. The "villas," where the families stayed, were built around a village center that had a pool, rides, a fishpond, a movie complex, and an ice cream parlor. Clowns and jugglers performed everywhere.

As they entered their two-bedroom villa, Aileen heard John joke, "Megs, why go to Disney World when we have all of this here?"

"What? You have *got* to be kidding," Megan retorted with a withering look. "That's fine. *You* stay here. *I'm* going."

By now, Megan and John had become almost like a comedy duo. Of their three children, Aileen knew Megan was most like her husband: funny, confident, and happiest in the limelight.

Aileen had promised her two youngest they could go to Disney World that day *if* they took naps, and she quickly settled Megan and Patrick, with their ventilators and IV poles, into one bedroom. John, Aileen, and John Jr. would share the other, while Sharon and Yvonne had reservations at a hotel nearby.

The excitement of the journey had exhausted Megan and Patrick, who needed more rest than healthy children, and within minutes they were asleep. As John Jr. watched TV, John, Aileen and the nurses unpacked the luggage and medical supplies, including a dozen boxes of surgical tubes, medicines, and diapers shipped ahead. Because of muscle weakness, Megan, four, and Patrick, three, couldn't control their bowel movements and still needed diapers.

At 4 P.M., the gang was back in the handicapped van, John at the wheel, heading to the Magic Kingdom. Traffic jammed the roads, making it a slow trip. It took an hour to make the ten-mile journey. John, swearing, pulled into the Disney World parking lot. He followed the blue painted lines leading to the handicapped section until an attendant leaped in front of the van, waving a flag.

"I'm sorry, sir, but the handicapped parking lot is full right now," he said.

"This cannot be happening," Aileen said, pinning John with a stare that said *Do something*.

"I feel like Clark Griswald hearing that Wally World was closed," John quipped, alluding to the Chevy Chase comedy, *National Lampoon's Vacation*, in which a family travels across the country to a theme park and arrives to find it closed.

Rolling down his window, John said politely but firmly, "I'm sorry, sir, but we're here for my daughter's Make a Wish trip. We've come a long way for this." He was certain that invoking the magic words "Make a Wish trip" would cause the man to apologize and usher them in.

But the attendant shook his head and repeated, "I'm sorry, but the handicapped parking lot is full."

"Sir, I have two *seriously* disabled children here, and they're going into the Magic Kingdom. *Right now*," John said, his voice dangerously level. Then he pointed ahead to a flower bed shaped like Mickey Mouse and said, through clenched teeth, "See those beautiful flowers there? Well, I'm going to park this van right on Mickey Mouse's head if you don't get out of my way."

As Aileen breathlessly awaited the outcome, the handicapped van lurched forward and the attendant leaped aside. "Mister John, no!" Sharon yelled from a rear seat. The kids gleefully clapped their hands and cheered. The van circled the lot twice, then pulled into a spot marked "No Parking" in bright yellow.

"I *dare* them to tow a handicapped van," John said, still fuming as he jumped out.

Aileen leaned into the back of the van, whispering to Sharon, "It's going to be harder than I thought to get him to relax."

"You're telling me," Megan chimed in, rolling her eyes.

* * *

Megan led the way into the Magic Kingdom, one hand in her father's, the nurse Yvonne pushing her red wheelchair. Patrick followed in his wheelchair, holding Aileen's hand. Her parents, Marty and Kathy, had flown to Orlando and joined them at the villa that afternoon, and they brought up the rear, John Jr. between them.

The river of people on Main Street USA flowed jerkily by, coming to a halt every so often as tanned, chubby children stopped and gawked at the tubes coming from Megan's and Patrick's necks. After a few minutes, Megan pulled her hand out of her father's and put it under her chin, her posture when she felt self-conscious. With a pang, Aileen realized that her daughter who had been so confident despite her handicap was now old enough to notice when people stared at her. Behind her, Patrick, always uncomfortable in crowds, twisted and made whimpering sounds of discomfort. Aileen looked up to see that they were still a couple hundred yards from Cinderella's Castle, and she began to think maybe the whole trip had been a crazy idea.

Suddenly, the crowd broke into a cheer. The children who'd been staring at Patrick's ventilator swung away, bouncing with excitement, and with a wave of relief, Aileen saw Mickey Mouse up ahead beside Casey's hot dog stand, heading in their direction. He seemed to see the wheelchairs from afar because he reached his arms out and bounded in their direction. John Jr., scared of the life-sized characters, dived behind Patrick's wheelchair.

Seconds later, Mickey Mouse knelt in front of Megan's wheelchair.

"Mickey Mouse, this is Megan," John said proudly, making the introduction. Mickey Mouse threw his arms around Megan and touched his face to her cheek, making a loud kissing sound.

"I love you, Mickey," Megan gushed. She took her chin off her hand and looked up from one parent to the other, bursting with excitement. "Can we live here, Daddy?" she asked.

Hearing Patrick squealing behind her, Aileen grabbed Mickey Mouse—who was, by now, fawning over other children—and drew him toward her youngest son. "I have someone else here who's dying to meet you," she said. As Mickey bent down to nuzzle his neck, Patrick flapped his arms excitedly.

* * *

Next, the Crowley entourage—parents, grandparents, kids, and nurses—
moved in the direction of the Toon Town Hall of Fame tent, a big store
that shot off into smaller rooms where the characters met visitors. When
they got to the store, a long line awaited them. The attendant took one
look at the wheelchairs and the big circular Give Kids the World pins on
Megan's and Patrick's chests and ushered them in the back door.

"What character do you want to see first?" he asked.

"Cinderella," shouted Megan. John and Aileen followed as Megan was
led into a back room where the princess met visitors.

"Oh, hello, Megan," cooed Cinderella in her familiar powder-blue
ballgown, her voice low and velvety. "Can I kiss you?" she asked.

Megan nodded vigorously and Cinderella bent down, leaving the imprint of her bright pink lips on Megan's face.

Back in the waiting area, Aileen watched as John pulled out a tissue to
wipe Megan's cheek, and his daughter covered the imprint with her hands
and loudly admonished, using her new favorite line, "You have *got* to be
kidding."

John burst out in laughter—and for the first time since the vacation
had started, Aileen realized that even he was caught up in the magic.

For her part, Megan would refuse to wash her face for the rest of the
week-long trip.

The next morning, the phone began to ring again for John, who was managing every detail of the latest round of venture capital financing from
Disney World. The only phone in the villa had a yellow receiver and a
standing Mickey Mouse on the base. Aileen picked up her camera to document John in serious discussion with Mickey Mouse under his chin. She
listened as he made concession after concession.

"Wow—you really gave it to them," she teased when he had finally
hung up. John put on a pair of Mickey Mouse glasses and picked up the
receiver to pose for another picture, re-creating the conversation the way
he wished it had gone. "You asshole, you listen to me," he shouted into the
phone, waving his arms furiously. "We're going to do this *my* way, you
understand?"

It was so nice to see John able to joke about his work, Aileen thought on the ride back to Disney World that afternoon. Of late, she knew he'd been bowing under a "the weight of the world is on my shoulders" attitude.

"What are you going to see today, Megan?" John asked.

"I'm going to go on *every* ride *two* times," Megan replied.

"How about you, Patrick?" Aileen said, making sure he didn't feel left out. He pointed at the rear window—wanting to go back home.

"You know, Aileen, he'd be happier lying in bed at the hotel watching Disney cartoons," John said.

"I know, but he needs to get out," Aileen said, turning back to look at Patrick. "You wait, honey, I just know you're going to have a good time."

And for the next hour at Disney World, Patrick forgot he had wanted to go home. He waved to Megan as they rode together with their parents, nurses, and grandparents on It's a Small World, a little boat ride that went through a tunnel with children from different countries waving and singing and dancing. But once he got off the ride, he began to cry again, pointing in the direction of the exit. John and Sharon took Patrick back to the hotel, while the rest of the crew continued to shepherd Megan and John Jr. through the Kingdom.

Two hours later, John came dragging into view at Cinderella's Castle, where the group was waiting for Story Hour with Belle to begin.

"You'll never believe my afternoon," he said, and Aileen knew he was about to launch into one of those horror stories that was only funny in retrospect.

"Go on, tell me about it," she said, shaking her head and sighing. "What happened this time?"

John said Patrick had screamed all the way to the Monorail, hating the heat and the crowds. When they finally got on the train, John's cell phone rang, bearing bad news from his secretary—he had bounced the paychecks of seven nurses that week.

"Jesus Christ," he had shouted, proceeding to loudly direct the transfer of money from one account to another. All the while, Patrick continued to cry hysterically. Sharon, trying to divert him, tried music—belting out the theme song for the Mickey Mouse Club: "M-I-C-K-E-Y M-O-U-S-E, Mickey Mouse."

John said he hadn't been able to hear over her screechy voice, and he'd roared at her to be quiet—and then noticed Patrick's favorite little plastic

Peter Pan had fallen on the floor. Still on the phone, he handed it back to Patrick, who flung it back down.

"If I wanted it, asshole, I would have asked for it," Sharon mimed in a high-pitched voice for Patrick, evidently smarting from John's shushing. Sharon's foul mouth had always amused John, and he was guffawing loudly when a primly horrified woman's voice from the seat across said, "Children, quick, cover your ears!"

"You wouldn't believe it, Aileen," John continued. "Perfect Family was watching us curse up a storm in, of all places, Disney World. There was the thin, blond mother; the tall, handsome dad; and two daughters—dressed in identical Laura Ashley dresses. It was *classic*."

Aileen howled with laughter. She—and only she—knew exactly what he was talking about. The previous Christmas, they had settled upon a defense mechanism for the flood of cards bearing the faces of families with healthy, beautiful children. It was hard to look at the cards without feeling overwhelmed with some degree of envy. Those families were flaunting what John and Aileen wanted more than anything else and might never have: healthy children, a normal family, a carefree life. The technique was very simple, and she wished they'd thought of it sooner. Perfect Family was perfectly easy to mock.

"Another Christmas card from Perfect Family," Aileen had taken to saying in a singsong voice, handing John the next picture.

Aileen was still giggling about her husband and Sharon making such a scene in front of the latest Perfect Family when Belle appeared, announcing that the show was about to start. Then the princess began to invite members of the audience to act in her play, and Megan's wheelchair caught her attention. She picked John to join her onstage and play the beast. A born ham, he smiled and bounded onstage.

When Belle said, "The beast is angry," John roared. When the evil Gaston stabbed the beast, John fell heavily to the ground. John knew the story well because Megan watched the Belle video at least once a day, so he didn't need to be told to lie on the ground motionless until Belle had tended to his make-believe wounds and helped him to his feet.

When Belle said "Thank you for coming" and brought the play to an end, Aileen could tell John was perplexed. He had been waiting expectantly—and taking a step in Belle's direction—just before the play ended. Then Aileen remembered that the movie version ended with Belle kissing the Beast. "You know, kids," Aileen giggled. "Daddy was waiting for Belle to kiss him."

"It's not going to happen," Megan said in her perfect preadolescent imitation, shaking her head and smirking with her voice. "*Never* going to happen."

Then Belle jumped off the stage and greeted Megan. She presented Belle with a picture she had drawn for her.

Aileen watched as John tried to coax Megan to go back to the hotel.

"You have *got* to be kidding," Megan shouted. As usual, she got her way with her father, and the next time Aileen caught sight of them, John was holding Megan up on a horse on the Cinderella Carousel, her ventilator slung over his shoulder.

They were still in the park when night fell because Megan insisted on staying to see the fireworks. As Tinkerbell danced across the sky and the children screamed with excitement, John kissed Aileen and whispered, "Honey, you were right. How could we *not* bring the kids to Disney World?"

Aileen relaxed into the hammock of his arms and drifted on the comfort of the warm tropical evening, watching the riotous explosions of color against the dark sky. Whatever the future held—whether John's Special Medicine got delayed, defeated, or never even made, whether Patrick would someday walk or Megan never breathed without a ventilator again—at least now they had something lasting to hold on to. They had these memories of having fun together as a family.

19. The Bluff

SPRING 2001

OKLAHOMA CITY, OKLAHOMA; CAMBRIDGE, MASSACHUSETTS

The Monday after his return from Disney World, John flew out to Oklahoma City, filling a legal pad on the plane with the plans racing through his head. He was still convinced he had to sell Novazyme, not only because he knew there was no way to get the drug ready in time, but also because he'd come to understand it would take tens of millions of dollars more to produce enough enzyme for the trials. He was an optimist, but even he couldn't see how he could raise that much money based only on animal data in a quickly cooling financial market.

Still, he kept these realizations to himself. If he admitted that the September trials were not feasible, he worried that every worker at Novazyme might let up and fall even further behind. And he didn't believe for a minute he could afford to level with his investors—at least not while keeping them.

The idea of selling Novazyme was not entirely new. Genzyme had been courting John about a potential acquisition since he'd introduced himself several months earlier to chief executive Henri Termeer at a biotechnology conference in Laguna Niguel, California. From what John could tell, Genzyme had made deals to develop Pharming's and Chen's enzymes, run into problems with both, and needed to find some way to salvage its drug development program for Pompe disease. So John thought that his plan of selling to Genzyme was entirely within the realm of possibilities—except for one thing.[1]

On his notepad he wrote "Obstacles," and beside it, in capital letters, "PRICE." After the latest round of financing, his venture investors were even more firmly in control of Novazyme, and their demands for a significant return on their investment were increasing. Would he ever get Henri to offer enough for Novazyme for his investors to go along with a sale?

It would be extremely difficult because John's three venture investors—HealthCare Ventures, Perseus Soros, and Catalyst—had together already put in more than $24 million, including the $8 million pledged contingent on the September commencement of trials. Like most venture funds, they hoped to at least double or triple their money. Together, they owned a little over half of the company, which was valued at $51 million after the most recent B Round. That meant that for the investors to make their desired return of twice or thrice their investment, John would have to sell Novazyme for between $100 million and $150 million.[2] It was hard to imagine how Genzyme might pay anywhere near that amount considering that he had heard through the biotechnology rumor mill that the company paid only a fraction of that amount in its two previous deals for Pompe enzymes—$17 million for Pharming's rabbit enzyme and $20 million for Chen's program.[3]

"Genyme prepared to pay $20 million, tops," he wrote.

Next, under "Obstacles," he wrote "BioMarin." When he had mentioned Genzyme's overtures in the past, his investors had made clear that unless that company made an extraordinary offer for Novazyme, they preferred to wait an extra year or two until Canfield could move his science into human clinical trials, and then take the company public. These investors were salivating over the story of BioMarin Pharmaceutical, the tiny biotech firm that had been interested two years ago in Martiniuk's enzyme. That company had gone public in 1999 with no products to sell—just a single experimental medicine in human trials for a related disease even rarer than Pompe. BioMarin's market cap had soared above $1 billion, and some of John's investors were convinced that Novazyme could turn into another BioMarin in a couple of years.[4]

Waiting two years might mean a windfall to investors, but it was out of the question for John. His children weren't going to live that long, and neither were many other Pompe patients worldwide.

But while he wasn't willing to wait until the company could go public, John knew this was a business, not a charity. The thought of asking his investors to accept a sale at a lesser profit for the sake of his kids didn't even enter his mind. He knew the hard truth: in the world of venture capital, his children's lives meant absolutely nothing.

There was only one way to get Genzyme to pay a high enough price. It would not be for the purchase of a third enzyme for Pompe disease, especially one not even tested yet in human beings. But Henri might pay a whole *bundle* more if he believed Novazyme was developing a better treatment for his company's core business, threatening its flagship, $540-million-a-year-in-revenue Gaucher disease drug, Cerezyme.[5]

And it wouldn't be a lie, exactly. Canfield had always said his technology of adding the right sugar combinations could make enzyme treatments for most of the forty-nine diseases caused by different lysosomal enzyme deficiencies. John had said as much in his own business plan, which promised a new enzyme therapy every eighteen months. But Gaucher wasn't even on the list of the top six candidates for Novazyme enzyme development; it made more business sense to develop medicines for the many untreated diseases first than to compete head to head with one of the biggest biotechnology companies in the world.

Unless, of course, you wanted Genzyme to buy your company.

In the business world, what John and Canfield did next was known as the "strategic positioning" of a company for sale. Everywhere else, it was known as bluffing.

The next day, as John sat with Canfield in his corner office, he put on the table what senior management at the company already sensed, though never voiced aloud: the September goal for beginning clinical trials was out of reach. He told Canfield his belief that the investors wouldn't put in the next $8 million come September, and the company would then be out of money again. The economy was slowing down, which would make it difficult to find another source for the tens of millions in additional funds needed to enter clinical trials.

"A deal with Genzyme may end up being our best bet, Bill," John said.

Canfield knew about the talks with Genzyme; he'd even participated in some, though at the time neither man had thought they would sell to the larger company.

"I think it's time to move Genzyme to the front burner," John said. "The big question is whether we can get Henri to pay enough."[6]

Canfield nodded, stroking his beard and thinking. The two men had very different personalities. Where John had a hard time saying "no," Canfield had the opposite tendency—wresting a "yes" from him was harder than finding good Chinese food in Oklahoma City. Still, John had learned during their year-long relationship that if he presented an argument in purely rational terms, Canfield might fret, but if it made sense he would eventually go along with it.

"I don't like the idea, but I think you may be right," he said at length.

"I think it's the right thing to do," John nodded.

Then, one eyebrow cocked, he changed his tone and asked archly, "Bill, have you begun testing your technology in Gaucher disease yet?"

"No . . . but I *could*," Canfield replied, quickly picking up John's drift.

"Let's see how quickly Elvira can do some experiments on a Gaucher enzyme," John said.

Canfield called in the recently hired director of preclinical studies and told her she was in charge of a new project to make a better version of Genzyme's Gaucher treatment. "Make this your top priority," Canfield said quietly. "Keep a record of all experiments. We may need to present results very soon."

When she had left, John, his tone still light, suggested they brainstorm for names for the Gaucher treatment they were now developing. Genzyme had named its first-generation Gaucher drug Ceredase, and its improved version Cerezyme.

"How about Ceravance?" John said, again slyly crooking his brow.

"I like it," Canfield said with a smile.

"Then I'll work on filing the trademarks today," John said. "And what about a code name for these merger talks?" To keep discussions secret, senior executives often gave them code names, seeking to avoid having their own employees illegally trade on the information.

"Project Echo?" Canfield suggested.

"Naaah," John said, grinning. "I've got a better one. We need sixty to ninety days to get this to the point where Genzyme knows it *has* to do a deal. We're going to wrap this package up and put a great big bow on it. Let's call it Project Bow."

Canfield, who often found John's brashness discomfiting, laughed, shaking his head at the audacity of it all—and the name stuck.

That day, John phoned Henri Termeer's right-hand man, Jan van Heek, the executive vice president of worldwide therapeutics at Genzyme.[7]

"We have some good preclinical results and some other things we want to share with you," John said, referring to Dr. Barry Byrne's tests that appeared to show Canfield's treatment strengthened the leg muscles of Pompe mice.

Van Heek—like Henri a native of the Netherlands—sounded thrilled and said he would call back with a meeting date. He called Henri to tell him there was finally some movement on Project Rodeo. The talks with Novazyme had had a series of code names, all of them far less imaginative than Project Bow. At first, Genzyme called the discussions Project Cornhusker, but then someone pointed out that Cornhusker was the University of Nebraska's mascot. Wrong state! Then the talks were known as Project Sooner, after the University of Oklahoma's football team, but that was soon dismissed as too obvious. The latest name, one that hadn't been challenged to date, was Project Rodeo—suggesting something western, but covering a broad enough area that it wasn't obvious the company in question was in Oklahoma, where only a handful of biotechnology firms existed.

On April 4, John and Canfield arrived at Genzyme's headquarters, a series of interconnected old brick buildings in Kendall Square in Cambridge, Massachusetts. Van Heek, a tall, lean man with a chiseled face topped by a helmet of thick brown hair, led them down a hallway so long and narrow—a legacy of the buildings' original use as a fire hose manufacturing plant—that John felt claustrophobic. He was already nervous at finally being within the walls of one of the biggest, most successful biotechnology companies around, and the walls seemed to be creeping in on him. Inside a pencil-shaped conference room, a dozen senior drug development officials waited around a rectangular table.

Taking a deep breath, John began his pitch with a corporate update, intending to demonstrate that his company had both the momentum and resources to move forward alone, without Genzyme. Unlike some of their earlier, long-winded presentations, attempting to overwhelm their viewers with facts, this time John and Canfield aimed to be brief, with only eighteen PowerPoint slides between them. John said Novazyme now had over seventy employees. It had built a new manufacturing plant that was fully operational. And most important, it had completed a new round of financing.

Then, gaining confidence, John reached once more, as he was prone to do.

"Novazyme has $15 million in the bank," he said boldly. ("I'm rounding the numbers a little," he had chuckled to Canfield earlier in the day.) John also said they would begin clinical trials in September even though he knew that would be impossible.[8]

When his turn came, Canfield didn't present Dr. Byrne's data, which he knew Genzyme had seen in the press release from March. Instead, he showed off a fresh round of mouse experiments that his new preclinical director had just finished—with outstanding results. "As you'll notice, the glycogen appears to be completely cleared in the cells of the mice who received the enzyme," he said, with a note of triumph.

What Canfield didn't say—and to be fair, no company would get into such detail in a presentation to a competitor—was that he couldn't be certain the test to measure glycogen clearance was accurate. McKinney had been trying to buy a glycogen test, but couldn't find any company willing to sell one, so Canfield's team had used a makeshift one they had designed. It was promising, but Canfield hadn't yet performed the extensive secondary tests required to validate its accuracy. Canfield also didn't say that the enzyme used in this new round of experiments, as with Byrne's, was the old version made with bovine PTase, which he didn't intend to take into human clinical trial. Although Canfield had made human PTase, he had not succeeded—despite several months of effort—in using it to make a batch of the Pompe enzyme that produced good results in mice. He was still tinkering with the process, trying to determine how much of each ingredient to use, and under what conditions, to make the enzyme correctly.[9]

Canfield concluded by noting that the experiment showed that his Pompe enzyme cleared much more glycogen from the cells of mice than did Pharming's and Chen's conventionally made enzymes, both of which Genzyme now owned.

And then, as if it were an afterthought, Canfield said, "One more thing. We have a new initiative we want to tell you about."

On the screen at the front of the room, he put up a slide entitled "Project Advance." The slide read, "Genzyme Corp. generates about $600,000,000 a year with 80% margins" from its Gaucher medicine, Cerezyme, as if those in the room didn't know.[10]

Then he clicked to the next slide, which was titled "Next Generation Cerezyme Opportunities." He noted that Genzyme's seven-year-monopoly under federal law for bringing to market a new treatment for a rare disease was due to expire the next month. Cerezyme was an effective treatment for Gaucher disease, in which patients became steadily more disabled with swollen organs and deteriorated bones, "but the medicine isn't perfect. It doesn't effectively reach patients' lungs and bones.

"Ceravance is an improved third generation product," he continued, using the name John had coined in his office only a week earlier. On the slide, a little R with a circle around it floated over the word Ceravance, indicating that the name was trademarked.

At this, van Heek, who had gotten up and was pacing at the back of the room as Canfield presented the scientific results, stopped and shook his head, half in disbelief, half in dismay. Now John was sure the $2,500 spent on a patent attorney to apply for that trademark was well worth it.[11]

Only a few days later, van Heek was on the phone inviting John and Canfield back to Cambridge to discuss an acquisition. With a boyish grin, John knocked on Canfield's door and gave the doctor an exuberant thumbs-up. "Project Bow is moving forward!"

As they rode in the backseat of a Boston Coach limousine to Genzyme's offices, John asked Canfield to make a bet on the offer Genzyme would make.

"Not a cent over $50 million," Canfield said.

True to form, John highballed it. "I'm saying $100 million," he said grandly.

At Genzyme, John and Canfield were ushered into a smoky glass-walled conference room adjacent to Henri's plush offices on the fifth floor of the main building. John sat himself at the head of the long wooden conference table, and Canfield settled into a seat on his right. They waited about fifteen minutes until Henri and van Heek appeared with a man they introduced as the company's head lawyer and senior business development executive, Peter Wirth.

Henri was in his fifties, tall and elegant, with wavy brown hair that parted on the side. He greeted each of them with a big smile and a long handshake, and asked John how his children were doing.

"I hope we can work together to do something for your children and all other children with Pompe," he said in a soothing voice, his Dutch accent pronounced.

"Peter is going to go over numbers with us," he continued, "but the numbers aren't important. What's important is that we can move this drug development program faster together than apart."

It was a line John had repeated often in his discussions with van Heek, telling him that he wouldn't do a deal unless he was convinced it would get a treatment to patients more quickly. He never actually brought up Megan and Patrick, but everyone knew he had his children in mind.

John and Canfield sat tensely, staring at Wirth, who spent the next half hour outlining the prices of other comparable deals. He noted that Genzyme had paid $17 million for Pharming and $20 million for Chen's program. He knew Novazyme's own investors had valued the company at $35 million before the latest round of financing.[12]

"The fair price for Novazyme is $48 million," Wirth said in conclusion.

John could see Canfield out of the corner of his eye leaning back in his chair, arms crossed and looking at the table, gloomily. "Well, if that's your price, we've just wasted a lot of time," John said. "My venture investors are never going to go for that, Henri, and you know that."

Wirth jumped in to back up his numbers. John interrupted, saying he wasn't quarreling with the calculations. "I'm sure the numbers are sound," he said. "But the question is, 'At what price can we get a deal done?' And $48 million? My investors would never go for that."

"What's your price?" Henri asked.

Caught off guard, John didn't reply at first, then stammered, "I'll, uh, we'll have to ask our board." In truth, he didn't really know. It wasn't his company to sell. It belonged mostly to his venture capital investors and Canfield. John owned less than 5 percent of the firm.

"I'm sure there's a way we can figure this out," Henri said, smiling. "Why don't you go discuss it with your investors. Find out at what price they would do it."

John had regained his bravado. "I could never recommend anything under $100 million—and I don't even know if that would be within range," he said.

Henri's eyes widened, and he said, "We may be a long way away."

"What you didn't factor in is that we're making tremendous progress right now—and we don't have to do this deal," John said defiantly. "Look at the trajectory we're on. At the point where you have to have us, we'll be too expensive for you."

Henri raised his eyebrows. There was an edge in his voice for the first time as he said, "We'll always be able to afford you."

Back at the stately Charles Hotel in Cambridge that night, John and Canfield wrestled with what to do. John had learned from the lashing he took from his venture capitalists in January that he needed to get their input and keep them well informed. He'd been making a special effort with Gus, and was surprised at the difference it was already making in their relationship. He had finally learned how the game was played—you needed to treat your investors as partners. A year ago he'd thought it was enough to take their money and merely check in once a quarter. How wrong he had been. They needed to feel valued and involved. And to John's surprise, the investors actually had real value to add beyond their financial investment because of their experience and long-standing contacts in the biotechnology industry.

After he and Canfield finished dinner, John dialed Gus and found him still in his office working.

"We're pretty far apart," John said dejectedly.

"I'll swing by and grab a drink," said Gus, whose office was just a few miles down Memorial Drive.

In a matter of minutes, he sat down on the other side of the table from John and Canfield, stirring his gin and tonic with a lime. As a jazz band played, John went over the meeting with Genzyme, blow by blow, ending with the $48 million offer.[13]

Gus asked a lot of questions. John felt, for the first time, Gus was genuinely trying to help him figure out what made sense for Novazyme as a company, not just for himself as an investor. He was almost fatherly in the way he listened and probed.

"The questions you have to ask yourselves," Gus said, "are 'Would I rather deal with my son-of-a-bitch venture investors, or would I rather deal with Henri and Jan?' And 'How certain am I the science will work?'"

John looked down at the ice cubes he was stirring in his glass. He'd drained the cocktail without even noticing. "My gut tells me to call Henri and Jan and tell them we're too far apart," he admitted.

Gus said he was inclined to agree. The first offer was simply too low to begin negotiating.

Sleep was hard to come by that night. What if Genzyme didn't come back to the table? John thought over and over. He had to be prepared for that possibility. He hadn't admitted to Gus or anyone other than Canfield that he didn't think they could make human trials by September. He and Canfield were the only ones who possessed all the information to truly weigh the options, and Canfield seemed to be deferring to him on this question.

At 6 A.M., exhausted and restless, he headed to the glass-enclosed hotel pool and swam fifty laps. With each powerful stroke through the water, he weighed the pros and cons of walking away from the Genzyme talks. Once he'd finished his laps, he hoisted himself out of the pool and sat on a bench, still deep in thought. Should he ask van Heek for time to present the Genzyme offer to the full board? Could he push van Heek for a better offer?

Suddenly, he noticed a swimmer had stopped in the middle of the pool and was staring at him, mouth agape. Two other men toweling off near the deep end were also looking at him sideways. John looked down and realized he was sitting there stark naked. He had been so preoccupied that his thoughts had skipped ahead to the locker room, and he had taken off his swimsuit!

John jumped up and tried to hoist up his swimsuit, but it was stuck around his ankles. Now two other older men had stopped swimming and pulled down their goggles in disbelief. Everyone seemed to be staring at him, like in some nightmarish high school dream where you showed up in class naked—except, in this case, it was true. Cursing, John began hopping as fast as he could toward the men's room, his wet swim trunks flopping around his ankles and calves, but it didn't feel like he could get there quickly enough. Everything seemed to have slowed down.

"I've officially lost it now," he told Canfield later that morning, regaling him with the story as they rode together to Logan Airport. John never failed to find humor in stressful situations, and today was no exception. Canfield shook his head, smiling, and moved on. "Have you called Jan yet?"

John's ruminations overnight and in the pool had led him back to where he had ended the discussion the night before with Gus. If he began negotiations with Henri at $48 million, there was no way he would end up in the range that his venture investors would accept.

"You still feeling the same way as last night?" John asked Canfield.

"No doubt in my mind," came the response.

John dialed van Heek and got him on his cell phone immediately. "Pricewise we're so vastly apart, it would be counterproductive to spend the political capital and emotion to close the gap," John said.

"Well, if you're sure," van Heek said, disappointed. "If you change your mind, we'd be very happy to continue discussions."

At home that weekend, John threw himself into family life, trying not to dwell on whether he'd blown his chances of ever selling Novazyme. He found himself entrusted to take care of Patrick and John Jr. while Aileen escaped to the stores on Saturday afternoon, Megan at her side. Aileen had already imparted her passion for shopping to her young daughter.

Inside a nearby Kohl's, with Megan in the child's seat of the shopping cart, ventilator in the basket, Aileen headed gaily toward her favorite housewares section. Mother and daughter scanned the shelves with the same keen-eyed intensity. Aileen picked up several dark wooden picture frames and put them in the basket. She was looking at thank-you cards when Megan grabbed a pack. The shiny golden angel on the front had caught her attention, and she held them up for Aileen to see. "Wow, those are beautiful," Aileen gushed. "The cards say, 'Thank you for your baby gift,'" she read to her daughter. "How nice is that?"

An hour later, as they stood in line at the checkout counter, Aileen noticed that Megan was still holding the angel cards. While she unloaded the cart, she casually took the cards out of Megan's hands, setting them aside.

"My cards. Don't forget my cards," Megan said, pointing to them.

"Megs, we're not getting those cards today," Aileen said, patting her head. "They say, 'Thank you for the baby gift.' Do we have any babies in the house anymore?"

"I want those cards," Megan said.

"We're not getting them, honey."

"Oh, yes we *are*," Megan insisted, tears beginning to well up in her eyes and her face turning a deep shade of red. A moment later the piercing alarms on her ventilator went off.

"Look, Megan—*enough*, do you hear me?" Aileen shouted, pointing her finger in her daughter's face. "Megan, look at me. I don't care if you need a goddamned machine to help you breathe; you're not getting the freakin' cards."

Megan wailed louder, throwing her arms back and twisting in her seat, the alarms continuing to shriek.

Aileen looked up and saw the checkout lady staring at her, mouth open. She glanced to either side and saw everyone at the other registers staring, too. Flustered, she hurriedly paid for the picture frames and fled—as much as someone pushing a cart with a child and a fifty-pound ventilator could flee, anyway.

When they got home twenty minutes later, Aileen carried Megan inside and handed her to John. "Here you go," she fumed. "I'm done."

"Daddy, Mommy wouldn't buy me anything at the store," Megan said sullenly.

"You wait, young lady, until I tell Daddy about the scene we just caused," Aileen said. She turned to John, shaking her head. "I totally lost it. I don't know if I can ever be seen in that place again. They'll probably call the police."

"The unflappable, perfect mother lost it?" John teased. "I can't wait to hear this story."

Aileen stomped upstairs, took a shower, and burrowed into a new book she had just bought on child discipline. When she came back downstairs an hour later, Megan was sitting on her father's lap.

"Mommy, Daddy's going to get me the cards tomorrow," she said. Her tone was sugar-sweet, and her eyes had regained their customary sparkle.

"No, he is not," Aileen said. "John, I am not going to let you spoil that child. The nurses are all complaining that she has to have her way. She has to learn that you don't go to the store and get everything you want just because you have a meltdown."

John wiped the smile from his face and somberly agreed. "Mommy's right, Megan." Two sets of eyes stared at Aileen contritely.

"I promise I won't do that again, Mommy," Megan said.

As Aileen turned away, out of the corner of her eye she saw her husband lean toward Megan and give her an exaggerated wink. "That was supposed to be a secret, silly," he whispered. Her daughter squeezed both eyes shut in a brave, sweet attempt to answer his wink, and Aileen bit down on her lips to suppress a smile of her own.

20. The Deal

Henri Termeer spent the next two weeks pondering what to do about Novazyme. The question was whether he should pay a significant premium for the company in order to move his own drug development program for Pompe disease forward. Henri was a seasoned chief executive, having spent seventeen years at the helm of Genzyme, and before that a decade at a big European drug company, Baxter International. The choice he faced, Henri believed, was either to buy Novazyme or to put his Pompe drug development programs on hold and wait to see what happened with Novazyme's product. He had already invested more than $50 million in his two drug development programs, including acquisition costs for Chen's and Pharming's enzymes, and he couldn't justify investing more money in them believing, as he did, that Novazyme was likely developing a better one. On the other hand, he hated to lose momentum, having learned that once lost, it was virtually impossible to regain.[1]

Still, Novazyme was not a sure bet. The technology was early in its development, and even the animal data had not been replicated. His own scientists doubted the results and had repeatedly advised him not to buy the company. Wait and see how the science develops, they said. Buy it in a year or two after there's more data.[2]

Henri might have waited, had not Novazyme's recent presentation and van Heek's urging forced him to think about the acquisition more broadly. Van Heek repeatedly reminded him that Novazyme might be able to use its enzyme targeting approach to improve upon Genzyme's big-selling Cerezyme, and that the same approach might improve upon another drug candidate that Genzyme now had before the FDA, awaiting approval. Henri concluded that tiny Novazyme would not only force him to delay his Pompe drug development program, but could also grow into a real threat to his company's bread-and-butter market product.[3]

"If they're right, what we're doing in all our programs is irrelevant," Henri finally concluded to van Heek two weeks later. "Let's go for it."

The next week, at van Heek's invitation, John was back in Cambridge, Massachusetts, sitting with him at the Charles Hotel, where they'd met several times over the past six months. The two men had an easy rapport, and they were beginning to like and trust one another. At six foot four, van Heek towered over John. He had a warm, earnest, and affable manner that John trusted. Like Henri, he had been raised in Holland and spoke fluent English with a strong Dutch accent.[4]

For his part, van Heek found himself charmed by John's sense of humor and moved by his passion and drive. "You mentioned a number in your meeting with Henri," he said now. "One hundred million. I think I can get Henri close to your price."

John, looking nervous, said he had no idea if his board would do the deal for $100 million. Having decided not to go to the board with the $48 million offer, he had been waiting to see if Genzyme would come back with something higher before approaching his investors, sensing that they would have wildly divergent opinions, some of them completely unrealistic. "I threw it out as a number. I think it's an absolute minimum."

"Oh, c'mon, John," van Heek said, aghast.

"Jan, if it was up to me, at $100 million I'd sign right now," John said, embarrassed that he couldn't be more enthusiastic about what was already a very generous offer. "But I need to talk to my board first. Let's take the next week and see if we can get a deal done."

John scheduled an emergency meeting of his board for the following Monday. Then he called the directors separately on the phone to see where each was leaning. As he had expected, the board members' opinions varied considerably, with some wanting to consider the offer and others dismissing it outright. "I can tell you now, we'd never do $100 million," said Steve Elms of the Perseus Soros group, recalling the BioMarin deal.

At the meeting, John discussed the valuations of comparable deals that Genzyme's lawyer had first presented. He told the board about Genzyme's first offer of $48 million and the current one of $100 million. "I need some direction from you on what price would be acceptable," he said.

The venture investors, who only a few months ago had thought Novayzme might be a fraud, were convinced they owned something very valuable. If Genzyme wanted Novazyme, it must be onto something.[5]

"A hundred million dollars—that's only a twofold return for us," said Elms. "That's not going to be acceptable. Any buyer would have to pay at least $500 million," reminding the group that BioMarin's stock market value had reached $1 billion with one drug in clinical testing. If they waited a few more months until Canfield's enzyme was in human testing, the company's value would skyrocket.

"Steve, we're a preclinical company," John said. "If we crossed the $100 million range, we'd be the most expensive preclinical sale ever."

"Look, if $100 million is the offer, we just built an enormous amount of value in the company," Gus said, jumping in to side with John. "And the markets could get colder." He reminded the others that they would need to put significantly more money into Novazyme to get it far enough to go public. "And don't forget, drug development is fraught with risk," he finished grimly.

John looked from Gus to Steve and said, "Can I get you guys to cut the difference?"

"If you can get $225 million, we should close this deal tomorrow," Gus declared.

"You're right, Gus. If we get $225 million, we should sell," John said—and with that, an unspoken consensus emerged that $225 million was the target number.

John called van Heek after the meeting to report the board's $225 million selling price.

"John!" van Heek said, taken aback.

"Let's see how close we can get," John soothed. He knew he would never get Genzyme up to $225 million, but he hoped that if he could get the company higher—maybe up to $150 million, he might get his board to go for the deal.

In a flurry of phone calls, van Heek increased his bid to $125 million; John stuck to $225 million. Van Heek proposed $137.5 million. They were stuck at that number. Van Heek said Henri would never go higher, and John said it wasn't nearly enough to get his board's support.[6]

At home over the weekend, John thought of a compromise. He phoned van Heek and said, "Bill and I want to do it, but you've got to help us." He laid out a plan for a purchase price of $137.5 million up front with the balance of the $225 million—$87.5 million—coming years later, and even then only if Canfield's approach produced two new drugs for Genzyme.

"That way I can tell my board I got them $225 million—even though part of it would only come later. And you can tell Henri you're at $137.5 million, and you would only pay more for success."

"Henri thinks he's already paying for success," van Heek said morosely.

"C'mon, Jan. You only pay more than $137.5 million if one or two of the drugs is approved. If even *one* is approved, you get back the full value of the deal in one year's revenue."

"All right, John, I'll talk to Henri one last time," van Heek agreed.

A few hours later, he called back excitedly. "Henri says we have a deal."

John phoned Canfield with the news, but neither of them celebrated yet. It was one thing to get Genzyme to the convoluted calculation of $225 million; it would be quite another to convince his board to go for it.

But suddenly the little company was hot. No sooner had Henri agreed to the deal than Genentech Corporation, one of the two biggest biotech companies in the world, and admired for its pioneering cancer drugs, jumped in with an offer. John had been coaxing Genentech along in parallel discussions for months, not just as a backup, but also because like most people in the biotech industry, he was dazzled by the company's science. He was also friends with Myrtle Potter, the company's chief operating officer. The two had worked together at Bristol-Myers, and John liked and respected her. Potter proposed a collaboration in which Genentech would invest $22.5 million for 10 percent ownership of Novazyme and pay the majority of the future cost of developing the drug. This was a way for John and Canfield to get the money to develop the Pompe enzyme without having to give over near-complete control to another company. It also offered investors an infusion of cash while holding out for the potential bonanza of going public in a couple of years.[7]

From a financial point of view, it seemed at first like an impossible choice. John talked to his board members and found that they differed widely on which way to proceed. He asked his investment bankers at Morgan Stanley to quickly produce a financial analysis of the two deals, and scheduled another board meeting for the following Monday.

On Sunday night, at home in his study, John groaned as he read the report from Morgan Stanley, sent only an hour earlier by e-mail. Even for an objective third party, it was a decision without a clear answer. Closing the door to his study, he read the report slowly a second time. Canfield wouldn't be there for the board meeting the next day because he was hiking with his son in the mountains of New Mexico, but John had bought him a satellite phone to take along and turn on every night at 10 P.M. so they could talk for ten minutes. He still had a few hours before that call in which to make up his mind about the deal he would recommend.

John knew he would need to be clear and persuasive to get Canfield on his side. But which side was he on? Putting down Morgan Stanley's presentation, John began making his own list of pros and cons on a legal notepad. Under the pros for the Genentech deal, he wrote "great science." Next, John wrote "mutual respect among scientists." Genentech's scientists had met with Canfield, and were excited about his scientific approach. Genzyme's scientists, by contrast, didn't bother to hide their disdain for Canfield's science. John also knew he could work well with the business side at Genentech. Having known Potter for several years, he trusted her implicitly.

Under the Genentech proposal, Novazyme would remain a separate entity. That meant that if Novazyme were successful, it could go public at some point at an enormous profit, just like BioMarin. He wrote "significant upside—like BioMarin" as another pro.

Below that, he wrote "control." He and Canfield would undoubtedly have more control over the future of the company under the Genentech scenario, since Novazyme would remain independent, with John as the CEO. However, he wouldn't lose *all* control if he went with Genzyme; early on, John had told Henri he would sell to Genzyme only if he came with his company—as a senior vice president in charge of all drug development programs for Pompe disease. Henri had readily agreed, deciding that John's energy and motivation outweighed the downside of his enormous conflict of interest as the father of two patients. Still, he would have nowhere near the power of being CEO of Novazyme.

Under the "pros" for Genzyme, John also wrote "money in the bank." The Genzyme acquisition would give investors $137.5 million right away. With Genentech, the investors would have to wait for a couple of years until the company was ready to go public.

Rubbing his hands over his weary eyes, John sighed and set the notepad down on the table. He didn't know that only a couple of years later, Harvard Business School students would use this very dilemma as a case study and vote on whether John had made the right choice that night.[8] Many CEOs have to make such difficult strategic choices, but perhaps never in history had the survival of his or her own children also rested on the decision. Setting aside the merits of the business deal, John arrowed straight to the question closest to his heart: Which deal was better for his Megan and Patrick?

In the months since Disney World, they had grown noticeably weaker even to John, deeply immersed and distracted as he was by Novazyme's problems. He had also noticed that Aileen didn't point out the children's lost milestones to him anymore. Like John, she had begun to try to keep the worries about "her" area of their lives—the home and the children's day-to-day well-being—to herself, unless there was something she thought John could do to help in the short term. But it was hard for him not to notice that Patrick could not sit up at all now without support, and that Megan, while she could still sit up, fell over more and more frequently. How much longer could they go on?

Which company was most likely to get a treatment to his kids quickly?

Genzyme, he reiterated mentally once again, was the only company in the world that sold a treatment for a lysosomal storage disease—Gaucher. Genzyme had also developed a potential treatment for another lysosomal storage disease and taken it through clinical trials, where it was currently awaiting FDA approval. There was no question that Genzyme was expert at manufacturing these types of drugs; Genentech, on the other hand, had thus far been focused on treatments for cancer and other diseases.

From his year at Novazyme, John knew that any drug development program would run into obstacles. When that happened, he asked himself, which company, Genzyme or Genentech, would fight harder to keep the program alive?

At Genentech, Canfield's enzyme would be one of dozens of drugs in development. At Genzyme, Henri had promised him that the Pompe development program would become the largest in the company's history. It would be vital to Genzyme's future, and Henri and he would fight for its survival.

"This program will keep Henri up at night," he said out loud.

And what if Canfield's enzyme didn't work? It was easy to believe your own corporate spin, but despite his eternal optimism, John was at heart a realist. Canfield still hadn't fine-tuned his process for using human PTase and the DMJ replacement, kifunensin, to produce the Pompe enzyme. The results he was touting to Genzyme and the investors were from experiments using Pompe enzyme made the previous year with bovine PTase, and the FDA might never accept that.

If John were at Genzyme, he'd have backups: the Pharming and Duke enzymes. Even if they were far from perfect, they had saved the lives of some patients. If Canfield stumbled, these enzymes might be a bridge for his kids, keeping them alive until something better came along. They could be his insurance against the failure of his own company's product.

With that thought, John knew where he stood. He put his feet up on his desk, looked at the clock, and waited for 10 P.M. to call Canfield.

The next day, June 18, John awoke feeling clearheaded. Canfield had agreed with the decision to push the Genzyme deal, and John had slept well, confident that it was the best. Now he had to focus his energy on convincing his venture investors to go with Genzyme. He knew that the investors at Perseus Soros and Catalyst were leaning toward the Genentech proposal, but that Gus at HealthCare Ventures was an advocate for the Genzyme deal.

John was in the shower, going over his arguments in favor of Genzyme, when Aileen burst through the door, her face panic-stricken.

"Where's John Jr.?" yelled Aileen, who rarely lost her cool. "I can't find him!" John raced outside, pulling a towel around him. He ran through the children's bedrooms upstairs, leaving splotches of soapy water on the walls and floor. Megan and Patrick were in their bedrooms, waking up, but John Jr. wasn't in his. He dashed through the first floor of the house screaming his son's name, then opened the front door and sprinted around the outside, still clad only in his towel, calling, "John!"

Running back inside, he shouted, "Aileen, call the police." As she picked up the phone, the day nurse, who'd also been looking for the little boy, called out from upstairs, "Guys, guys, calm down, guys—he's in his bed." Aileen and John looked at each other in astonishment. Upstairs, they found their son curled in a fetal position under a mound of bedding at the foot of his bed. Neither John nor Aileen had seen him asleep under all the covers.

Collapsing onto the bed, John pulled his son into his arms, tears of relief spilling onto his cheeks. Aileen knelt beside the bed and wrapped both arms around the two of them. "Hi, Mom and Dad," the little boy said, opening his eyes sleepily, looking from his parents to the nurse. "Why is everybody in my room?"

Three hours later—soap suds washed off and hair neatly gelled—John sat at the head of the table in Morgan Stanley's top floor conference room, overlooking lower Manhattan. Light streamed in through the big windows that looked over the city, the soaring Twin Towers of the World Trade Center marking southern Manhattan a few blocks away. Dennis and Steve from Perseus Soros sat to his right, Gus to his left, and beside him, Josh Phillips and his senior partner, David Hendren, of Catalyst. The two other board members—Stuart Kornfeld, the brilliant scientist, and David Albert, the Oklahoma inventor—dialed in. Canfield, still hiking, didn't participate. In front of every board member lay a navy blue, hard-covered spiral-bound book containing Morgan Stanley's financial analysis.

John began with an abbreviated PowerPoint presentation to summarize the arguments in favor of each of the deals. Then he moved into his personal recommendation to go with the Genzyme offer.[9]

"The Genentech deal offers the potential for more upside, but the investors keep all of the risks of drug development," he said. "On the other hand, the Genzyme deal gives us a big, immediate return to investors, and the potential of still more money. If our technology works, this is a good deal, not a great deal. But if our technology doesn't work, the Genzyme deal is the deal of the century."

"I don't know," Josh said, shaking his head. "I just feel like we're stepping away from a great deal of value."

"Well, I'm sorry you're disappointed," John said a little sarcastically, the tension of the past few weeks spilling over. John knew it was a good deal for the venture investors as long as they didn't get too greedy. "I hope all of your deals are as disappointing as this one."

Josh backed off immediately, saying, "I *am* disagreeing, but we understand that when management unanimously thinks it's time to sell, we can't stand in the way."[10]

Dennis jumped in. "Do you think there's any more value on the table? Can we get Genzyme any higher?"

"This is as far as we're going to push Henri," John said, firmly.

"Could we use the Genentech term sheet as leverage?" Dennis pressed.

"It would imperil the deal and cause bad will. I could never go work at Genzyme after pushing Henri any further," John said, even more adamantly. He was certain he'd pushed Henri as high as he would go, and he didn't want to imperil his relationship with Myrtle Potter by using Genentech as a stalking horse.

"It's a good deal and we should take it," Gus said. Dennis, finally convinced, nodded in agreement. There was no need even to take a vote.

"I want you to know you did a really, really good job," Dennis enthused after the meeting ended, patting John on the back. When the room cleared, Gus came up to John, smiling, and said, "I think you will be happy. I think this will be good for you *and* your family, John."

John stepped outside to the sunny spring day and grabbed a cab to Penn Station. It was early afternoon—the meeting that decided the fate of his company, and caused him so much sleeplessness, had only lasted a single hour. As he rode the New Jersey Transit train home, he sat back and thought about how, two years earlier, he could barely get managers at Genzyme or Pharming to return his calls. In a few weeks, he would be in charge not only of Canfield's experimental medicine—but also of all other drugs in clinical development for Pompe disease in the entire world. How far he'd come from the days when he had struggled even to gain entrance to Randall's Pompe research conference!

Now, one way or another, with Canfield's drug or with some other enzyme, he felt certain his children would be treated. All he had to do was keep the pressure on Genzyme to move quickly into clinical trials. He had already done the hardest part—he was part of the Pompe world, in a position of influence; he had given the science the necessary funding boost and steered Canfield's enzyme toward trials and FDA approval. The rest, he was sure, couldn't be any harder than that. He picked up the phone to tell Aileen about the meeting.

"Hey honey," he said. "Do you still like clam chowder?"

"So you got the board to go with the Genzyme deal," Aileen said, picking up on the reference to Boston. "Honey, you are amazing."

"How're the kids?" he asked.

"Oh, just great," she said, with the merest hint of sarcasm. "Patrick just finished speech therapy. Megan's in physical therapy. Their vents are acting up today. Sharon and I have been running between them trying to figure out what all the beeping is about. It's just another great day in the Crowley household. What time are you going to be home?"

21. Genzyme

At 8:30 A.M. on September 26, John strode across the brick courtyard at One Kendall Square in Cambridge to begin his first day of work at Genzyme. He wore a navy suit and carried his old leather briefcase over his right shoulder. It was a beautiful fall day, and students from the nearby MIT wandered by in shorts and T-shirts. Other than his suit, John thought he could easily pass for one of them. He was only thirty-four, but he still looked years younger with his short, trim physique, full head of hair, and unlined, olive complexion. Almost every time he introduced himself, the other person registered shock that someone so young was Novazyme's CEO. John's standard response was to laugh and say, "Well, if it's any consolation to you, I feel a hell of a lot older."

In truth, John thought, he couldn't be further removed mentally and emotionally from the young man he'd been when he graduated four and a half years ago from Harvard Business School, across the Charles River and only a couple of miles away from Genzyme's headquarters. His life had been so different then, so carefree, it seemed someone else had lived it.

John remembered the day he'd graduated from Harvard—and remembered thinking that nothing could get between him and his plans for a great life for himself and his family. How could it? Not with a Harvard MBA, a Notre Dame law degree, Annapolis training, and the strength of his and Aileen's tight-knit extended families. Perhaps his class's choice of graduation speaker—Ray Gilmartin, chief executive of the drug company

Merck & Co.—was a signal of the direction his life would take. Perhaps it was more than coincidence that in his own Class Day speech, he had asked his fellow students to use their Harvard MBAs "to combat disease, to fight racism, to promote the entrepreneurial spirit in your own countries."

John stopped at Bean Town breakfast shop for tea and a bagel with peanut butter before heading into the long brick 1400 Building, Genzyme's headquarters at the time. In his briefcase, he carried a legal notepad covered in his distinctive longhand scrawl—his plan for taking over the company's Pompe program. During the three agonizing months since his board had agreed on that June day to sell to Genzyme, John had steamrolled his way through negotiations on all the finer points of the deal, including the positions he and Canfield would assume at Genzyme after the acquisition. As of today, they were both senior vice presidents at Genzyme. Canfield would manage research operations in Oklahoma; John would direct the companies' combined programs to develop a treatment for Pompe disease, which would soon become not only the most expensive drug development program in Genzyme's history, but among the costliest in the history of the biotechnology industry.

On his way to Henri Termeer's fifth-floor office, John passed the same conference room where they had haggled over a price a few months earlier. Even after agreeing on the deal, the negotiations had been fraught with turmoil, and John knew that Henri had repeatedly overruled his senior scientists in deciding to sign the final papers. John, worrying about how these scientists and others at Genzyme would receive him, had been strategizing for weeks about how to get along.

It was September, the month when he had once hoped to get the trial started—the one that would treat and save Megan and Patrick. Instead, he was beginning a new job. Doctors had repeatedly told him that children with the nonclassical infantile form of Pompe, like Megan and Patrick, could survive until age five—maximum. Megan would turn five in December, which was only three months away. If his children were to survive, he needed to quickly build a cohesive team and drive a treatment into a clinical trial. He was running out of time.

Henri, gracious as ever in a dark suit, button-down shirt, and bright red tie, greeted John warmly. "It is so wonderful to see you. I am so thrilled to have you here," he said, reaching for John's hand. But if John was expecting any direction on how to do his job, he didn't get it that day. Instead, as they sat briefly together, Henri asked for John's thoughts on transitioning into a leadership role at Genzyme. Drawing from the notes he'd jotted down, John told Henri he wanted to meet one on one with all of Genzyme's senior staff working on Pompe disease over the next few weeks. During that time, he hoped to keep a low profile and hold off bringing in his own management team. Only after he'd met the key players and developed an action plan would he bring on his team.[1]

Henri nodded approvingly. "Yes, John, that makes sense. I like that." He said he had only one piece of advice, for now: "Keep your people at Novazyme motivated." He wanted to avoid a frequent casualty of acquiring a company, which is to lose some very talented employees who fear their roles will be substantially diminished. Then Henri's secretary appeared, telling him he had another meeting waiting. He stood up, patted John on the back, and said, "Go get 'em. Let me know if you need any help."

A minute later, Genzyme's newest senior vice president and director of the Pompe disease program stood outside the CEO's office with absolutely no idea of where to go next. He hoped someone had remembered to find him an office.

Trying to look as if he knew where he was going, he strode confidently down the hallway, turned right into van Heek's office, and asked his secretary if she happened to know where he was supposed to sit. After a flurry of phone calls, she led him through a maze of hallways, into another building, and to a tiny corner office she'd secured. John thanked her and stepped inside, trying to keep his expression composed—he'd seen attic bedrooms that were bigger. The ceiling was so low on one side that he could barely stand up.

So much for his hope of wielding power and influence from an office near Henri's and van Heek's; he wasn't even in the same building. John shrugged it off—for the moment, anyway—and sat down to get right to work.

Van Heek had given him a list of phone numbers of the company's employees involved in Pompe disease. The first person he should meet,

John had been told, was the newly hired medical director of the Pompe program, Dr. Hal Landy. John dialed his number and set up a lunch for that very day. John told Landy he would come by his office to pick him up. "I'm looking forward to it," Landy replied politely.[2]

Somehow, despite knowing that Landy's office was on the floor below Henri's, John still got lost trying to find it. He wandered through four different floors in three different, interconnected buildings before finally finding himself outside Landy's door.

He was waiting, his door ajar. About ten years John's senior, Landy was of medium height and was square-faced with a big forehead, tightly cropped dark hair, and an intense expression. He wore his shirtsleeves rolled up and his collar open, and his tie hung loosely like a pendant. "It's so nice to meet you, John. I've been hearing you were coming," he said, shaking hands.[3]

As they walked outside, Landy filled John in on his background: He was a pediatric endocrinologist who had spent years coordinating clinical trials for a Swiss biotech firm, Serono. Under his direction, Serono had won government approval to sell a synthetic version of human growth hormone for children with a deficiency. He said he had joined Genzyme only two weeks earlier.

The two men agreed to try a nearby Mexican restaurant. They settled into chairs on the outdoor patio on Kendall Square, with Genzyme's headquarters on the left and the brick building housing Gus's venture firm on the right. After the waiter took their order, they exchanged a few pleasantries, and then John began peppering Landy with questions about his experience thus far at Genzyme.

"So who's in charge of the Pompe program?" John asked.

"There *is* someone—a very nice man, in fact," Landy said. "He's not very senior at the company, though."

"Does there seem to be any kind of comprehensive plan for developing a Pompe treatment?"

"Not that I can tell," Landy replied. Aside from the Novazyme enzyme, he said, Genzyme was working with three other potential treatments for the disease. There were the programs to develop the Pharming and the Chen enzymes, as well as a recent effort John hadn't known about to produce an enzyme similar to Chen's but easier to manufacture.

"There is a 'core team' for each enzyme. I'm going to be assembling my own team to bring all of them together. You can be on my core team if you'd like," he declared, taking a swig of iced tea.

John didn't reply at first, shocked that Landy seemed to think he was the one who was taking over leadership of all the Pompe programs. As the waiter plopped their meals in front of them, John wondered—should he set Landy straight right now or wait until he had more information? John grabbed his burrito with both hands and bit into it. He decided it would not be prudent to pick a fight now and tried to make a joke of Landy's comment.

"Maybe I'll form my own 'core team,' too. Then we'll have six core teams," he quipped, flashing his boyish grin. "And we all won't talk to each other. That couldn't be any worse than what it is today!"

But Landy wasn't laughing, sensing the murky territory between himself and this young hotshot CEO. He moved swiftly to claim it.

"John, you do drug development for the Novazyme program—I don't need to know anything about that," he said, frowning, deliberately imparting to John his subordinate position—as a leader of only one of the four potential Pompe treatments under development.

"You *do* need to know about that," John retorted, sarcasm flooding his voice, shoving the crumbling bits of his burrito around his plate with his fork. "I would think as *medical director* of the Pompe program, you would need to know about *all* the programs, Hal."

There was nothing but tension at the table as the two men finished their entrées. All John could think of was that he needed to get out of there, to find out what was going on, before he alienated Landy any further. Pointing at two wasps that were now circling, he joked stiffly, "Let's get back to the office before I get killed by these things." The discussion—and the lunch—ended before the waiter could even ask if they wanted coffee or dessert.

Back in the safety of his office, John closed the door, sat at his desk, and put his head in his hands. One day into the job and he was already being challenged for his job title. His status at the company—to judge from his office—appeared to be nonexistent.

Should he call van Heek or Henri and demand that they set Landy straight? He thought back to a class he'd taken at Harvard Business School called "Coordination, Control, and Management of Organizations." An inexperienced executive would go running to the boss for help, he decided. A seasoned player would lay low, gather more information, and go to the boss with a clear plan of action. He would stick to his original plan.

Reluctantly, John picked up the phone and scanned down the list of employees he'd been told played significant roles in the company's Pompe programs. The next name was Bob Mattaliano, a senior scientist, and John sighed, hoping that he would be more accommodating than Landy. Moments later, he was back on the line, making another lunch date. And so began John's marathon of interviews over the next three weeks, during which time he talked at length to almost fifty people.

Several people John interviewed were on the "core team" that was developing Dr. Chen's drug. This was the same enzyme John and Aileen had been so hopeful about after it showed promise with baby John Koncel, who had subsequently regressed when he built up antibodies. A second group of employees that John spoke with were part of a core team in Europe, handling the development of the Pharming enzyme. Scientist Bob Mattaliano led the third core team, trying to develop a Pompe enzyme grown in a more productive line of Chinese hamster ovary cells (CHO cells) from the one Chen had chosen. Mattaliano and his team had begun this project only a few months ago, but they had some early, encouraging data in mice.

From all these interviews, John concluded there was no overarching drug development plan. Including Novazyme, the four groups developing potential Pompe drugs operated almost independently of each other. "It would be comical if my children's lives didn't rest on the outcome," John muttered to van Heek in disbelief.

Genzyme itself was large and unwieldy. Founded in 1981 by a Tufts University Medical Center researcher, the company had experienced exponential growth based mostly on revenue from its first drug, the treatment for Gaucher disease. Even though Genzyme now had about five thousand employees spread over the world, Henri had preserved the same freewheeling culture the company had had at its inception, believing it essential to retaining the entrepreneurship that had made his firm successful in the first place. John, who lined up his shoes in his closet and color-coordinated his sock drawer, found the structure difficult to understand, let alone navigate.

For one thing, according to Henri, John was supposed to be in charge of the Pompe disease program—but nobody reported to him. Landy reported to someone in the medical and regulatory affairs division. The woman who ran the core team in charge of manufacturing Chen's enzyme reported to the head of the U.S. manufacturing division. And the scientists on each core team reported to the head of the science division. These divisions—medical affairs, manufacturing, marketing, and science—looked to John like silos without bridges, standing tall but having little to do with each other.[4]

With no choice but to forge ahead, John told van Heek that it was time to announce he was taking over leadership of all the Pompe disease programs. He drafted a memo that van Heek sent around describing the formation of the new Pompe leadership team, which would oversee the company's drug development programs for Pompe. The memo said that John would be the team's chairman and that it would be comprised of eleven other members. There were eight people from Genzyme, including Landy and Mattaliano, the scientist trying to develop an enzyme that was easier to manufacture. Four came from Novazyme, including John; Tony McKinney; Bill Fallon, the manufacturing guru; and Julie Smith, a smart woman John had recruited from Bristol-Myers, who he'd put in charge of closing the Genzyme deal.

Conspicuously absent was the name of William Canfield.

It was hard to say who was more upset—Canfield or Landy. Canfield believed that John had done nothing less than betray him, and stopped returning his calls. John had promised that they would continue to work as a team after the acquisition, and nothing could have been a more blatant breach of that pledge than denying him a spot on the leadership team.[5]

John hated to leave Canfield off the team, but concluded—after days of wrenching soul-searching—that he would be too divisive a presence. Every time Canfield was in the same room as the Genzyme scientists, the meeting would degenerate into a series of attacks and insults. It wasn't always Canfield's fault; sometimes the Genzyme scientists initiated the digs. But Canfield, dogmatic about his approach and often abrasive with those who disagreed with him, didn't seem able to bite his tongue and make nice.[6] John needed to build a coalition fast, and the only way he could expediently eliminate the tension was by removing one side from the argument.

As for Landy, until he saw the memo, he had been certain he was the one running the show—and to his credit, the misunderstanding wasn't his fault. Having led the clinical side of a major drug development effort at Serono, Landy had taken the job at Genzyme only because he had been promised a hugely expanded role. The senior managers who hired him had been unaware that Henri and van Heek had agreed to give John leadership of all the Pompe programs. Now, even as they apologized profusely, they told Landy they were powerless to change the situation. Henri and van Heek were in charge, and they were sticking with their commitment to John.[7]

Determined not to let hurt feelings get in his way, John tried to move on. He scheduled a kickoff meeting of the Pompe leadership team for the week before Thanksgiving. To establish its significance, he didn't hold the meeting in Genzyme's offices but reserved a conference room at the trendy and expensive University Park Hotel on nearby Sidney Street.

About twenty people were invited to attend the meeting, including the new twelve-member Pompe leadership team and a few others. As they settled around the U-shaped conference table at the hotel, John rose to give a welcoming speech.[8]

"I am so happy you have all agreed to join my team," he said. "I know we all realize the significance of what we're doing, but before we get going here, I'd like to relate a very personal story. Last year, only a few months after I joined Novazyme, a family from Kansas appeared at our doorstep in Oklahoma. They came trying to save their tiny 'floppy baby' who was dying of Pompe disease. And they were begging for some of the treatment they had heard we were working on. We hadn't even entered animal studies as yet." Everyone in the room knew what that meant—the family had been turned away empty-handed. "The point," John went on, "is that it was completely unrealistic for this family to expect any treatment, but also that this reflects the hopelessness that patients and families with Pompe struggle with every day. I think it's important for the twenty of us here in this room to realize, truly, that we represent the best and only hope for these patients and their families.

"The first order of business of the Pompe leadership team is to present Henri with a drug development strategy for Pompe disease within the next sixty days," he said. Toward that effort, John wanted everyone to begin by participating in a simple but vital exercise. "I'd like us to talk about our vision for what the world will look like for Pompe patients five years from now. Let's begin by each of us describing our vision."

John paused, waiting for someone to volunteer, but nobody raised a hand. The Genzyme employees leaned back in their seats and looked at the table. Determined not to be fazed, John forced a laugh, and said, "Well, I guess we're all feeling a little shy today. Let me tell you my vision. I have a vision that five years from now we have a good treatment for the disease. We will completely understand the biology and the science around Pompe. And by then we'll be researching wholly new ways to treat the disease that will make these enzymes obsolete."

Two Novazyme alumni, Tony McKinney and Julie Smith, raised their hands and added to that vision. "I would like to see us not only with a treatment for Pompe, but I would hope that there are also others on the market for some of the related diseases where patients have no hope today," McKinney said.

"My vision is that there would be newborn screening so Pompe babies would be identified as soon as they are born and treated immediately," Julie added gamely.

John looked around again for others who might speak, and found none.

Hal Landy stared at his feet, fuming. "This kind of exercise was interesting when you were twenty-five—not when you've been in the workplace for twenty years," he mumbled to the person beside him.

"He's like a car salesman," scientist Mike O'Callaghan whispered to Mattaliano. O'Callaghan, a gaunt, white-haired New Zealander, was another of Genzyme's top scientists.

Shrugging, John barreled ahead into the PowerPoint presentation he had prepared, outlining the history of the development of treatments for Pompe disease. He began with the Dutch physician and researcher, J.C.

Pompe, who made the link between the enlarged heart he saw in one baby he autopsied and the glycogen filling the muscle cells. John described early attempts at enzyme replacement therapy that failed. Enterprising doctors and researchers had purified the Pompe enzyme out of human placenta and infused it into a patient. Unfortunately, the patient showed little sign of improvement, which suggested to researchers that replacing the missing enzyme wasn't an effective treatment for Pompe.

Then, in the 1970s, researchers began to learn how enzymes got to the crucial sections of cells. They revealed that the sugars attached to the enzymes played a vital role in directing them to the lysosomes of cells. This body of research explained why the experiment with the placental Pompe enzyme had failed. That enzyme had already been excreted from the lysosomes, where the sugars needed to get inside had been trimmed down. So these placental enzymes, when infused, didn't have the sugar chains needed to enter the lysosomes.

O'Callaghan, shaking his head, pointed out to Mattaliano that the slides John was showing still bore the Novazyme logo.

"How long does it take to change that to the Genzyme symbol?" he whispered. "It's like the junior varsity has taken over."

John summarized the four drug development programs for Pompe that Genzyme now owned and then paused, trying to decide how to end the meeting. He had been wrestling with whether to show the team a segment about him that had appeared a few weeks earlier on the *Today* show. Was it tactically smart to remind people about his children when he needed to be seen as an objective leader interested in saving all patients?

But things were going so badly, John decided to take the risk. "And now, here's a recent episode of the *Today* show that will give you a flavor of what my personal family's hopes and challenges are," John said. He hit the "play" button.

"There's been a lot of talk of heroes in the last several weeks," host Katie Couric said, referring back to the terrorist attack that had shaken the nation two months earlier. Introducing the Crowleys, she said, "This is one father who is going the extra mile."[9]

The tape showed Megan, in a red polka dot dress, and Patrick, sucking his pinky finger, beautiful young children who looked almost like any other kids—except for the tubes coming out of their throats, indicating that they needed ventilators to breathe. The reporter, Anne Thompson, told the story of Megan and Patrick's diagnoses and of John forming the Children's Pompe Foundation, becoming CEO of Novazyme, and driving toward a treatment to save his kids.

Then the reporter, camera honing in on John's face, asked, "If Megan and Patrick die, will you have failed them?"

Slowly, voice heavy with emotion, John responded, "I'd go back to the promise we made to them three and a half years ago that we would do everything we could—and I think we have."

"We wish the Crowleys our best," Katie said, smiling into the camera—and the tape ended.

"Well, that's my family," John said, a little awkwardly.

When the lights came back on, several people were in tears. Landy swallowed several times, trying to clear the lump in his own throat. The tape had touched the father, pediatrician, and idealist in him. He had three sons himself, the youngest born with such a severe defect in his joints that he'd been in a body cast for the first few months of his life. The tape reminded Landy of when his wife, also a physician, was pregnant with that baby. A test had revealed that the baby might have severe birth defects. Doctors had raised the possibility of abortion. Landy and his wife had decided to continue with the pregnancy, believing that they, as doctors, were qualified to care for such a disabled child, if anyone was.

The child, it turned out, wasn't as disabled as the doctors had feared. But he had still needed a lot of extra care as a baby and young child. Seeing Megan and Patrick on the screen, beautiful and precious and horribly weak, Landy remembered the overwhelming love and helplessness he'd felt in the face of his own child's situation.

Now, looking at John standing quietly beside the television monitor, instead of seeing a power-grabbing, Ivy League know-it-all in a pin-striped suit, he saw a desperate father who loved his children and had committed all his enormous talent to one goal—finding a cure for their devastating disease. Landy had gone into clinical research for the very same reason—to help sick people. To think, he realized, that this guy standing before them, awkward and ill at ease, had been able to pull together a $137 million company in one year! If anybody was qualified to run the Pompe program at Genzyme, Landy thought, John certainly was. A turf war over leadership of the program suddenly seemed juvenile, and in that moment, Landy conceded it.[10]

He was the first person in the room to rise. Picking up his papers, he walked over to John.

"Wow," he said quietly to the younger man, his face flushed. "That was—that's very powerful. Thanks for sharing it with us."

22. Tough Choices

WINTER 2001–SPRING 2002
PRINCETON, NEW JERSEY; CAMBRIDGE, MASSACHUSETTS

When John arrived home at 9 P.M. on Friday, the kids were already in bed. He tiptoed into their bedrooms and kissed them. John Jr. slept soundly, but the younger two stirred. Megan raised one arm and waved it with her pinky, pointer, and thumb extended, signing "I love you."

John had been away from home all week, staying at what was fast becoming his second home, the Charles Hotel in Cambridge. If he decided to remain at Genzyme after the one-year requirement of the acquisition agreement, the family would move to Boston. Otherwise, they would stay in New Jersey, where they were close to John and Aileen's extended families and the network of nurses, speech therapists, physical therapists, and occupational therapists they had painstakingly recruited over the past four years.

Downstairs, John heard Aileen in the kitchen. He found her pouring cream into a pot of meat sauce and knew she was making his Aunt Michele's sinfully rich recipe. She poured the sauce over plates of bow-tie pasta and set them on the table.

"How are you?" he asked, as they sat down.

"Oh, I'm fine," she said listlessly.

"Honey, you don't seem very fine at all," he said. "Tell me about your day. How'd the little troopers do today?"

"They're fine—they're fine *now*. They weren't so fine a few hours ago."

"C'mon, Aileen—what happened? If you're not going to tell me, who are you going to talk to?"

"Nobody," she said, her carefully controlled voice breaking a little. "That's just it. I have nobody to talk to, John."

"Oh, Aileen," he said, getting up and giving her a hug. She turned her face into his shirt and breathed deeply, leaning into his support and regaining her composure.

When he sat back down, she told him she had taken Patrick upstairs to bed and had been undressing him when his ventilator started beeping. She checked the settings, and the vent seemed to be working fine, but the beeping continued. Patrick, distressed, pointed at his tracheotomy and cried, so she pulled the tube out of his throat to see if was clogged with a mucus plug, which happened at least once a week. It was plugged, so she'd suctioned it and tried to stick it back inside, but the hole in his throat seemed to have closed. It was one of those emergency situations that occurred with terrifying regularity every few months, literally bringing the children within minutes of death. It required skill, calm, and luck to overcome.

As Patrick turned grayer, Aileen screamed for Sharon, who was downstairs with Megan. Sharon ran upstairs and after several attempts finally pushed the tube back in. By then Patrick had passed out, his lips blue. It took a minute or two for him to regain consciousness, with Aileen pumping the bag attached to his tracheotomy tubes to force air into his lungs.

Megan, aware something was wrong with Patrick, was crying downstairs when Aileen found her. Aileen carried her up to bed and was reading her favorite "Beauty and the Beast" bedtime storybook when she pointed at her throat and signed she was having trouble breathing. Aileen checked the ventilator settings, which were fine, and then, thinking back to her son's mishap minutes before, pulled her daughter's tube, too. The airway was clear so she quickly stuck it back. In a few minutes, Megan felt better and fell asleep.

"It's nothing that hasn't happened a hundred times before," Aileen said, looking down at her plate. "It just got to me today. I don't know why."

"Aileen, you know you do a great job with the kids. The best. You couldn't do it any better," John said, stroking her hand. "You know, I've always said you're our best nurse. And certainly the best looking."

"I don't want to be the kids' nurse, John. I want to be their mother," Aileen said, tears starting to fall again.

"I know. I know this is really hard for you. I've been away too much. It's hard for you to have the children's lives in your hands alone, day after day. I know you've got Sharon, but you need me, too. I promise, we're almost there," he said, leaning in to look into her face. Aileen nodded, wiping her eyes.

"I've almost accomplished everything I need to do at Genzyme. Then I'll be here for you and the kids all we need," he continued soothingly. "I think people at Genzyme finally get what we need to do. The Pompe leadership team is all set. They watched the *Today* show tape of us. I think they understand now what it's like for a family to live with Pompe disease."

Aileen blew her nose on the table napkin and changed the topic. "Megan's fifth birthday is coming up, John. I've been talking to her about what she wants to do. What do you think we should do?"

"Aileen, we need to do something big, really big," John said, excitedly. "Think of it—nobody expected Megan to live until she was five. And the tough little girl has made it. We've got to do something big, real big. And we finally have the money."

It was one of the best immediate effects of the sale of Novazyme to Genzyme: The major players, including John, had made millions. Canfield, with the largest share of the company, earned about $30 million. The two big venture firms each exited with $28 million. And John, who owned less than 5 percent, mainly from stock options given to management, netted $6 million.[1]

Suddenly, after struggling for ten years with credit card debt and the $140,000 in John's student loans, John and Aileen were rich. They paid off the debts—a drop in the bucket of the $6 million. Then they splurged. John bought himself a Rolex Submariner watch, the same kind his dad had been issued as a Special Forces Marine. John had inherited the beaten-up watch when his father died and had tried many times to get it repaired, but it never worked. He bought a three-year-old Jaguar XK-8 on eBay, in British racing green. And he and Aileen made a down payment on an enormous new $2.7 million house in Princeton. It was unfinished and needed months of work before they could move in, but it gave everyone in the family something wildly exciting to think about. Megan talked constantly about how her new house was so big that she was going to be able to ride her electric wheelchair inside. A year ago, she had gotten the wheelchair, which she could operate herself using a little steering device, but she had only been able to use it outside. John Jr., focusing on the details, told everyone there were seven bedrooms, six bathrooms, and two kitchens. Aileen had been meeting with an interior decorator and had already picked out some big, comfy chairs and couches and floral draperies.

But perhaps the best gift that their new wealth had brought John and Aileen was the end of their constant worries about money. Where John had complained since the day they were married about all the bills and financial obligations—the mortgages, the student loans, the support for his grand-parents, and, of course, the medical bills of late—now Aileen watched in disbelief as he wrote out check after check without saying a word. "It sure helps to have a gazillion dollars," she giggled.

As Aileen finished dinner, John began to throw out one extravagant idea after another for Megan's birthday—clowns, ponies, cakes the size of houses. "Okay, okay, I have it now," he said, finally. "I'm going to talk to Megan tomorrow and see what she thinks."

At Genzyme, John was painstakingly establishing his leadership of the Pompe program, but there was one reality no amount of doggedness was going to change: money. By selling to Genzyme, John had clearly guaran-teed millions of dollars more for Pompe drug development than he ever could have wrung out of his jittery venture capitalists at Novazyme. But even Genzyme wasn't in the business of overspending on drugs that might never work.

To prepare for next year's budget, John calculated the cost of continu-ing the development of all four of the company's potential treatments for Pompe: $80 million in the coming year. Henri was prepared to spend more money on Pompe than any other drug development program at his com-pany, but $80 million was out of the question. He gave John a budget of $50 million, still by far the largest development budget at the company, and said, "It's time to rationalize your costs."[2]

It was a euphemism for one of the toughest decisions in the drug in-

John and Aileen Crowley were married in Indianapolis on August 18, 1990.

John, twenty, with his best friend, Ed Devinney, during a day they snuck off from the U.S. Naval Academy in 1987.

Aileen and John help their two-year-old son, John Jr., hold his newborn baby sister Megan for the first time.

Moments after Megan nearly fell out of his arms, John walks back to his seat at the Harvard Business School graduation, holding on to her, his son John Jr., their bears, and his diploma.

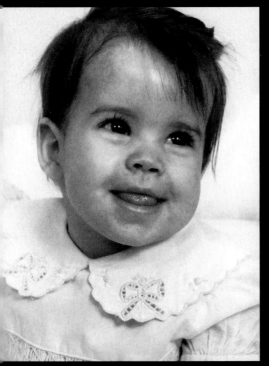

Megan, while she could still smile, at nine months old in a portrait that adorns a hallway in the Crowley house.

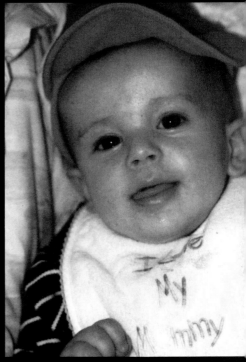

One of Aileen's favorite pictures of Patrick, who was such a chubby, content baby that it was difficult to believe he was sick.

Months before Megan was diagnosed, John, Aileen, Megan, and John Jr. enjoy a fall day in San Francisco, looking like the perfect family they would later envy.

The Crowley kids baking cookies at home in Pennington, New Jersey. Megan's fifty-pound

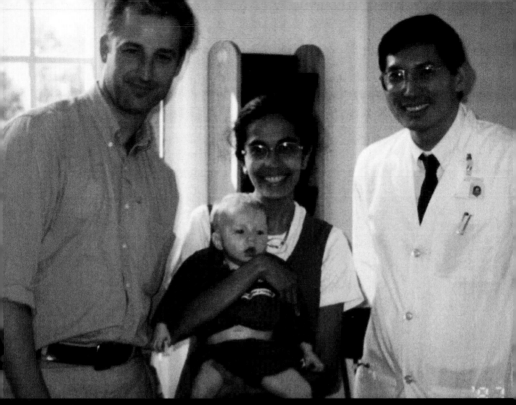

Dr. Y. T. Chen (right) and his protégé, Dr. Priya Kishnani (center), show off baby John Koncel, the first patient to receive the doctors' enzyme replacement therapy, summer 1999. Barry Koncel, the baby's father, looks on.

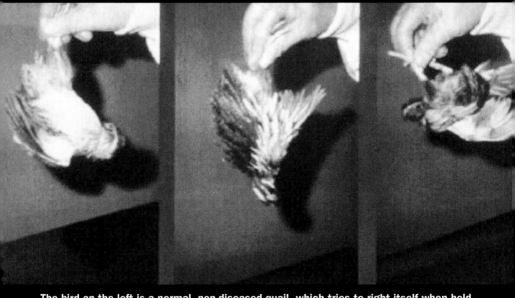

The bird on the left is a normal, non-diseased quail, which tries to right itself when held upside down. The center quail has Pompe and hangs limply. The third quail, on the right, has been treated with Dr. Chen's enzyme replacement therapy. After treatment, the

Human muscle cells taken from a baby with Pompe disease before treatment and after twelve weeks of therapy. In the second picture, the glycogen pools have receded and the muscle cells have smoothed and grown.

Megan accompanies her dad to a Children's Pompe Foundation fund-raiser at the Tavern on the Green in winter 2001.

The visitor to Novazyme who most inspired John, Lindsey Paige Easton, returns for the dedication of the company's manufacturing plant in her name.

Even though we were on vacation Daddy was busy at work on the Mickey mouse phone! He is our star

A page from Aileen's 2001 Disney World trip scrapbook. John, after finishing a tough conversation with his venture investors on the only phone in their vacation apartment, hams it up for Aileen.

Arms raised, Megan, with her brother Patrick, celebrates having finally arrived at Disney World on her family's Make-A-Wish trip in spring 2001.

Winnie the Pooh and Tigger pose with John, Aileen, Nana (Kathryn Holleran, standing at right), Megan, John Jr., and a nurse, Helen (sitting at left). Patrick stayed home with Sharon that day.

Tony McKinney and John on a cruise for Novazyme employees in February 2001. The cruise was one of John's team-building events.

Dr. William Canfield, left, with John Crowley.

Genzyme's headquarters in Kendall Square when John worked for the company. Genzyme has since built a new headquarters nearby.

Henri Termeer has served as Genzyme's chief executive for more than twenty years.

John's favorite portrait of Aileen and Megan. He keeps it on his desk at work.

Aileen and Patrick ride on the Ferris wheel during their trip to Ocean City in summer 2002. Megan and John are in the cart below.

Megan's first time ever on a beach was during the family's trip to Ocean City in summer 2002.

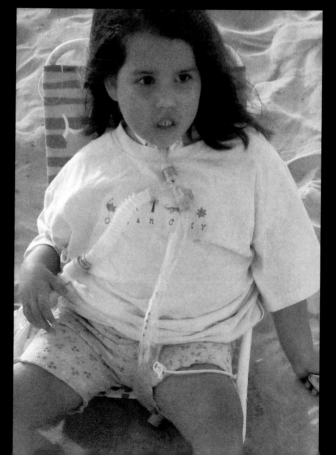

Sharon Dozier and Megan wait for the school bus to take them to her first day of kindergarten in fall 2002.

Dear Mr. and Mrs. Crowley,
Megan and Patrick,

*May the Blessings
of Christmas
bring you Peace
and Joy throughout
the New Year*

Most sincerely
Debra-Lynn Day-Salvatore
and
The Institute for Genetic Medicine

The Christmas card from Dr. Debra-Lynn Day-Salvatore, which arrived at the Crowley house on December 24, 2002, with an accompanying note saying the children's clinical trial had been approved to begin in the next two weeks.

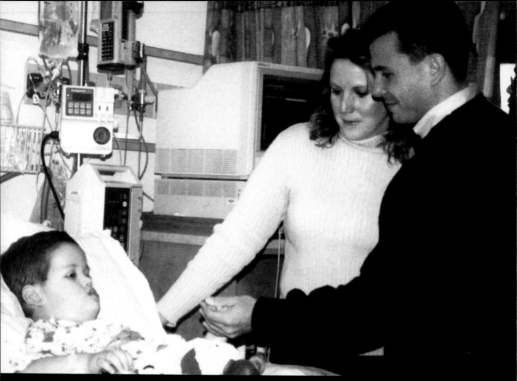

John and Aileen check on Patrick after pressing the button to begin his infusion of Special Medicine on January 9, 2003.

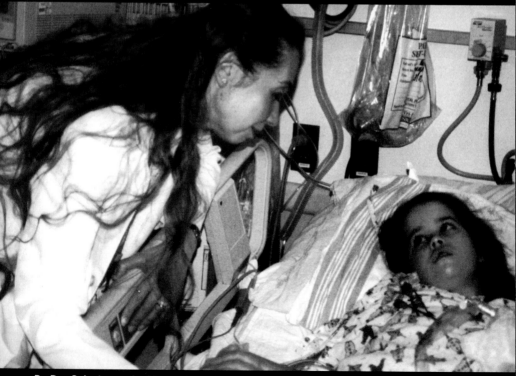

Dr. Day-Salvatore asks Megan how she feels soon after beginning her first treatment with Special Medicine.

John and Aileen embrace at Patrick's bedside.

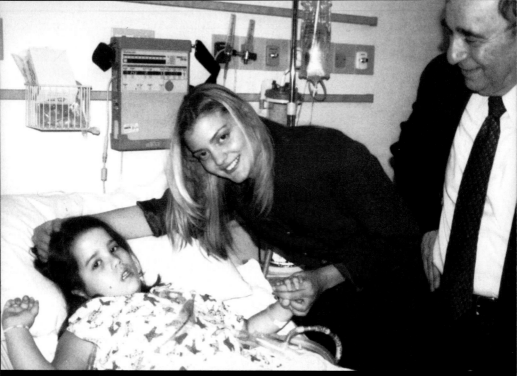

Dr. Alfred Slonin with nurse Linda visit Megan in the hospital the day after she received her first treatment.

Megan, stronger after six months of treatment, heads off for a ride in her dad's convertible. It's the first time in years that he's taken her out alone.

The Crowley family on vacation in Ocean City.

After several years of therapy, Megan Assink, who has Pompe disease, can smile, talk, and walk with braces. In this picture taken on Christmas Eve 2005, she dances for her parents, Greg and Deborah, who laugh in the background.

This picture, taken when John was still in the early phases of fund-raising for the Children's Pompe Foundation, ran in *Family Circle* magazine with the line, "Too weak to walk, but not to hug." Megan and Patrick continue to inspire their father on the journey to find a cure for Pompe.

dustry, aside from the fact that his children's lives could depend on the right answer. In the next two months, John needed to pick the one enzyme with the greatest potential, throw all of Genzyme's money and staff at it, and shut the other enzymes down.

Having been indoctrinated in more than a year of daily conversations with Canfield about the importance of having the right sugar chains attached to the enzyme, John was certain that his approach was best. John also had every reason personally to want Canfield's enzyme to succeed. If it were chosen as Genzyme's single, $50 million enzyme, John would almost certainly control the clinical trials since he was the president and general manager of Novazyme—now a Genzyme subsidiary, under the terms of the merger. If he were in charge, he would somehow make sure Megan and Patrick were in the first clinical trials. That was, in large part, why he had pressed to be made director of all the Pompe programs.

John would have made a strong pitch to go with Novazyme's enzyme except for one caveat—Canfield was still struggling in the lab. He had made many different versions of the Pompe enzyme using the new ingredients of human PTase and kifunensin, and none seemed to work nearly as well as the earlier bovine-based versions in mouse experiments. In their due diligence before the acquisition, Genzyme scientists using Canfield's enzyme made with the new ingredients had also been unable to replicate the stunning early results he and John had presented months earlier.

Henri had gone forward with the deal anyway, believing in Canfield's approach, and concluding from his scientists' complaints that it needed some tweaking to work right. Failure at one point in time didn't mean failure forever, as far as Henri was concerned. He'd gone forward with a Gaucher disease drug that had failed in the first trial, overruling almost everyone around him who urged restraint. It turned out that most patients in this trial were given too low a dose, and that the drug produced dramatic results at higher doses. That drug, Cerezyme, had become one of the most successful in biotechnology history.[3]

Canfield was working obsessively through nights and weekends to find and fix the problem with his enzyme, but John knew it was anybody's guess how long it might take. The Novazyme enzyme was not the right choice for his children and other Pompe patients who might die if they didn't get a treatment within the next six months. For them, it would be better to choose one of the other enzymes, even though they apparently lacked the right sugar chains to get to the lysosomes of muscle cells in large numbers. Genzyme could return to Canfield's enzyme as a second-generation treatment once he'd worked out the kinks.

But which one of the others would be the best pick?

At night in the Charles Hotel, John read over volumes of scientific documents describing what was known so far about the three other potential enzyme therapies. Now that he was inside Genzyme, John had access to far more data about animal studies and clinical trials than had ever been published.

His thoughts first turned to Chen's enzyme—perhaps that would be the best choice. John would never forget the sight of baby John Koncel sitting up in his mother's lap, lifting his arms and smiling, after only a few weeks of infusions. But John would also never forget the sight that followed two or three months later. The child was no longer sitting up, he was breathing with difficulty—slowly, he was regressing.

John read that baby John's parents had taken him home to Illinois, where he was still alive but very weak, needing a ventilator to breathe and battling almost constant infections. A second child on the same enzyme, after initially improving, had also lost almost all the gains the drug had won for him. But there was still some hope. A third infant had done so well on the Chen enzyme—without any regression—that he was walking and about as strong as the average two-year-old.[4]

The child with the stunning improvements was the only one of the three whose body naturally made a minute amount of the enzyme correctly. It appeared that as a result, his body did not treat the infused enzyme as foreign, and thus didn't create antibodies to fight it. Like this child, Megan and Patrick also made a tiny amount of enzyme—less than 1 percent—which was why they hadn't died as babies. If Chen's drug were chosen, John felt certain his children would respond well to the medicine. Chen's protégée, a passionate young doctor named Priya Kishnani, was now running a small second trial with eight babies for Genzyme, designed to include only infants six months old or younger who could breathe on their own and made small amounts of enzyme themselves.[5]

Yet first Chen and now Genzyme had struggled to manufacture enough of the enzyme even to run these tiny trials. The second trial now under way had been delayed repeatedly because the contract manufacturer couldn't make enough of the medicine and one batch after another failed to pass inspection. John didn't know how long it would take to find a better way to make the drug, if it was even possible.

The third potential drug candidate was the Pharming enzyme, the rights to which Genzyme now owned. Over room service pasta dinners, John pored over all the records of the tiny clinical trial that Pharming had conducted in 1999. Four infants had been infused with Pharming's rabbit enzyme in its first trial, and one had responded so well that he was now as strong as an average two-year-old. The other three infants had seen their hearts grow dramatically stronger, but they had had variable gains in strength in the rest of their bodies. Two of these three babies had regressed after a time; the third continued to gain strength, but very slowly.[6]

As John read on, he saw the Dutch researchers had drawn very different conclusions from Drs. Chen and Kishnani about the patients' varied responses. The baby who responded the best did, indeed, make a tiny amount of enzyme himself, but the one who improved next best produced absolutely no enzyme. Both of these two top responders were the babies who had received the therapy when they were very young—three months old and two and a half months old, respectively—and not yet severely affected by the disease. The Dutch researchers believed that patients treated when they were very young, before they had lost a significant amount of muscle strength, had the best prognosis.

In addition to four babies who were treated, John discovered five other Pompe patients who had also received the Pharming therapy. Three of them were juveniles or adults when they received the treatment, and included Tiffany, Randall House's daughter. They gained some strength, not in any way comparable to the babies, but still meaningful.[7]

Tiffany, for one, felt energetic enough for the first time in several years to go to school after starting treatment and having an operation to correct severe scoliosis of the spine. She hadn't been able to attend high school because of fatigue and respiratory infections, relying instead on a tutor at home. But a year ago, she had enrolled as a freshman at the University of Texas in San Antonio. She was still in a wheelchair and needed support from a breathing machine at night, but even the modest gains in strength and endurance had measurably changed her life.[8]

But as John read on, he saw that Pharming's manufacturing problems also made it an imperfect candidate. The enzyme was still being purified out of the milk of transgenic rabbits. Not only were the rabbits difficult to milk, requiring sedation to calm them down, but over time they made less and less enzyme. Pharming had also raised a herd of cows with their genes altered to produce the human Pompe enzyme in their milk. But to the great disappointment of scientists at both Pharming and Genzyme, the cows' milk contained so little enzyme that it was almost impossible to purify it out.[9]

If Genzyme were to put its efforts behind the Pharming drug, John learned, it would mean maintaining a supply of tens of thousands of the rabbits, which John viewed as almost comically impossible. It would not only be a logistical nightmare, but growing medicines in live animals posed a substantial threat of contamination.[10]

And what if it ended up being John's decision to shut down the Pharming treatment? The Dutch researchers who had developed it and the patients still on the medicine were passionate proponents of its benefits, and had already expressed fear that it would be discontinued. If the drug was not chosen and the rabbit enzyme was discontinued, these patients, including Tiffany, would have to be switched to the chosen drug candidate. What if they didn't do as well on the new medicine? Who would they blame?[11]

The final option was the one Genzyme scientists had developed internally to try to get around the manufacturing problems with the Chen and Pharming products. Genzyme already had extensive experience growing enzymes in Chinese hamster ovary (CHO) cells, the method Chen had used; the company's Gaucher treatment, Cerezyme, was made this way, in enormous, temperature-controlled bioreactors in a big manufacturing plant in Allston, a section of Boston across the river from Genzyme.

Where the type of CHO cell that Chen had chosen produced a very low yield of Pompe enzyme, scientist Bob Mattaliano's team began with a cell line known for its high productivity. They injected the gene that made the human Pompe enzyme into the cells and added different chemicals to coax them into producing it. After substantial trial and error, they thought they had a good sample and tested it by injecting it into mice. It seemed to work—not nearly as well as Canfield's had appeared to in Novazyme's early results, but it still held promise. And this enzyme was so easy to make that Genzyme could produce oceans of it.

Should Genzyme throw $50 million a year at this approach that showed some modest improvement in mice but hadn't been tested in humans? What if it didn't even work as well in human beings as the Chen or Pharming enzymes?

The more John thought about the choices, the more he realized that there was no way to know, for sure, which way to go. This level of playing God appalled him. It seemed almost inconceivable to think that his children's futures and the hopes of all Pompe patients in the world rested on a choice he would make based on incomplete information. And yet in the business world—as he had learned at Harvard and preached at Novazyme—choices were always made based on incomplete information. For all the talk of patients, management's allegiance to shareholders was paramount. Resources, businessmen would say, must be conserved to make sure the company continues to make money, which in turn allows it to continue to make medicine.

On that scale, painful as it was, stopping production of three of the four Pompe enzymes was the lesser of the evils that John faced.

A solution emerged from the science side. Soon everyone, including John, decided that the only way to know how to proceed was to conduct a massive comparative study of the four enzymes against each other. But it couldn't be done in humans, which was the optimal way to test a potential new medicine. Novazyme's and Genzyme's internally developed enzymes needed much more animal testing before the FDA would allow them anywhere near a human being. So the comparative study would have to be done in the next best medium—mice. It was a risky proposition given that everyone knew that drugs worked differently in mice than in humans, but at least there would be some uniform basis for comparing the four competing enzymes.

John agreed on the need for the study. But privately he worried that the level of acrimony of the internal debate over the merits of the different enzymes might spill over into the experiments. Genzyme's scientists thought so little of Novazyme's science that they had resisted even doing the Novazyme deal. Would they set up the experiments so that the Novazyme enzyme was likely to fail? If they did, John was certain he would never know. He was out of his league at this level of science, and he knew it.

There was only one person John knew and trusted at the company who had the scientific credentials to go toe to toe with Genzyme's scientists: Bill Canfield.

"I need you, Bill," John said, cradling his office phone between his ear and shoulder. "Will you join the Pompe leadership team?"

"So now you need me," Canfield said bitterly. He had not even begun to forgive John for leaving him off the leadership team. It had taken John multiple attempts, and days of leaving voice mails and messages with Canfield's secretary, to get him on the line at all.

Eager to get Canfield immersed in the scientific aspects of the debate, John quickly dove into an explanation about the test tube and mouse experiments planned to compare the four enzymes.

"It's a waste of time," Canfield scoffed. He believed that the Pompe enzyme was best taken up by the lysosomes of muscle cells if the right sugar chains were attached with phosphate molecules at the ends. He'd processed his enzyme so each of the seven sugar chains finished with two phosphate molecules. The other three enzymes weren't processed after they were made in the CHO cells or rabbit milk. They had some differing amounts of naturally occurring sugar chains, but not nearly enough of the right kind, according to Canfield. The only one that had a prayer of reaching the lysosome at some level was Chen's, which had two phosphate molecules at the tip of one sugar chain. On Genzyme's internally developed enzyme, only one of the sugar chains had a phosphate molecule at the tip. The Pharming enzyme had sugar chains with varying amounts of phosphate molecules, but they were blocked by other molecules.[12]

"Bill, the experiment is going to happen with or without you," John said, stuttering a little as he tried to appeal to Canfield's rationality over his injured dignity. "You're the only one I trust to make sure it's done properly, that our enzyme has a fair shot."[13]

John knew from others at Novazyme that Canfield was still nursing hurt feelings about being sidelined. John didn't doubt his decision, but he felt ashamed of how he had handled it. He ought to have flown to Oklahoma and explained it face to face, he thought to himself, rather than in a brief, awkward telephone conversation. Expediency had overridden sensitivity in the sprint to save his children's lives, and he had deeply hurt his former partner. John took a couple of shallow breaths, waiting for Canfield to answer.

As stubborn and moody as Canfield could be, he was—as John had always known—also supremely rational. And he wasn't about to miss an opportunity to be involved in a decision that could define the future of his life's work.

"When do you need me in Cambridge?" he asked gruffly.

23. The Mother of All Experiments

WINTER 2001–SPRING 2002
PRINCETON, NEW JERSEY; NEW YORK, NEW YORK; CAMBRIDGE,
MASSACHUSETTS; FRAMINGHAM, MASSACHUSETTS

Megan's fifth birthday was, as John had planned, a page out of a princess story. Both he and Aileen conceded that it was way over the top for a five-year-old, but they wanted it that way. Now that they had, as Aileen joked, "a gazillion dollars," they wanted to use it to celebrate their joy that Megan was still alive on the birthday that one doctor after another had said she would never live to see. Each knew the other was also wondering how many more birthdays Megan would have.

At around 11 A.M. on Sunday, December 16, a white stretch Lincoln Navigator SUV limo pulled up to the Crowley house. Megan, prim and pretty in a black velvet dress, surrounded by six girlfriends, had been waiting in her wheelchair at the upstairs window as her mother took hot rollers out of her hair. "Mommy, the limo's here. Let's go," Megan shouted, wrenching two hot rollers out of her hair.

"Geez, Megan, you're going to burn yourself," Aileen admonished. "This is just going to take five seconds."

And true to her word, Aileen had Megan ready seconds later. Her shoulder-length brown hair hung in graceful curls around her. Megan looked in the mirror, eyes smiling for the cheeks that couldn't move.

"You look beautiful, honey," Aileen said. She put a pink birthday hat on her daughter's head and carried her down the stairs, Sharon following with her ventilator. A throng of relatives waiting in the den and kitchen shouted "Happy Birthday" as Megan appeared, luminous. John plucked Megan out of Aileen's arms and carried her outside to the limo, sparkling bright white in the sunlight of the 50-degree winter day.

"Where do you want to sit, Princess Megan?" he asked.

"I want to be right in the middle!" she said excitedly.

John strapped her into a car seat in the center of the backseat and plopped down beside her.

"You can't come, Daddy," Megan chided, looking annoyed. "It's girls only."

John chuckled, kissed her, and said, "I know. I'll be waiting at home with your brothers. Don't rush too fast to get home to the boys."

Megan's six girlfriends—Sharon's three granddaughters, Haley, Cara, and Taylor; two neighbors, Angela and Whitney; as well as Aileen's friend's daughter Alexa—scrambled in next. Nana (Aileen's mother), Laurie, (Alexa's mother), and Sharon's daughter Misty followed. In the back, Aileen and Sharon took apart Megan's red wheelchair and loaded it in the trunk, along with a backup battery and ventilator.

It took a half hour to get everyone and all Megan's medical equipment inside the limo. But finally, with Megan and her giggling entourage of eleven, the vehicle sped up the New Jersey Turnpike into Manhattan. The group was late for their lunch reservation.

An hour later, the limo stopped on Central Park West in front of the entrance to Tavern on the Green, the famous garden restaurant in Central Park. John's mother Barbara was waiting for them at the corner table for thirteen they had reserved in the greenhouse section. As they ordered their meals, Aileen's brother Marty, who lived in the city, showed up with seven bouquets of roses, presenting one each to Megan and her friends. Megan accepted her bouquet excitedly and then looked at Aileen. "Boys aren't al-lowed, you know," she said. Uncle Marty laughed and said, "Not even boys with flowers?"

"Nope, it's an all-girls party," Megan said, shaking her head.

Uncle Marty stayed long enough to see Megan cut her white chocolate birthday cake and return to the limo. It drove next to the Lunt-Fontanne

Theater, where the group watched the Broadway production of Megan's favorite story, *Beauty and the Beast.*

"Can we come again tomorrow?" Megan said to her mom as they rode back at five o'clock that evening.

"You make sure to ask Daddy," Aileen said, smiling and diverting the question, "because he planned all of this for you."

They got home to find the kitchen and den decorated with pink and white balloons. John had taken Patrick and little John to the mall to buy decorations and a big cookie cake with a pink icing rose that read, "Happy Birthday Princess Megan." Everyone stayed and sang "Happy Birthday" again; John grew tearful as his little princess blew out the five candles, thrilled with the attention, and entirely oblivious to the larger significance of the day.

That night, with the relatives and guests all gone, the deflated balloons and crumpled crepe streamers wadded in the trash cans, and the remains of the huge cake in the freezer, John read his precious daughter to sleep with the story "Beauty and the Beast." Megan looked up at him, her eyes still sparkling, and said, "That was such a fun day, Daddy. Can we do it again tomorrow?"

It took most of December to design and begin what became known at Genzyme as the Mother of All Experiments. McKinney came up with that name at a Pompe leadership team meeting, reading down the long list of experiments planned and exclaiming, "Jesus, this is the mother of all experiments!" And the moniker stuck, despite the attempts of several serious-minded officials at Genzyme to give the experiments a more "appropriate" name.

Each drug development group—the one in Europe developing Pharming's enzyme, scientists in Oklahoma working for Canfield, Chen's team at Duke, and Mattaliano's group at Genzyme—prayed their drug would "win." Losing, everyone knew, meant marginalization of their research and, in some cases, wholesale layoffs.

To placate the various factions, the scientists decided to use several different methods to test the efficacy of the enzymes. These included a biochemical analysis, in which they ground up mouse tissue and added a chemical to measure how much enzyme had been taken in. In another biochemical analysis, they compared how much glycogen had been removed. They also performed a histological analysis, slicing up tissue, putting it on a slide, and staining it to see how much glycogen remained. They compared the enzyme activity and glycogen clearance in several different types of mouse tissue, including samples from the triceps, quadriceps, and hearts. They tested the enzymes at three different dosages. And they also performed experiments to compare the levels of antibodies produced in the mice to get a clue about which enzyme might be least foreign to the body. In all, they would analyze nearly five hundred tissue samples. They would be tested in Canfield's lab in Oklahoma as well as Genzyme's in Framingham.[1]

To make it a blind test, the formulations group color-coded the different enzymes whose identities were kept confidential. In the test, they would be known only as green, blue, yellow, and magenta samples.

It took almost two months to complete the almost five hundred experiments and one exhausting week to compile the results. And there was, indeed, a winner.

On January 31, John pulled up at Genzyme's science center, a four-story brick and glass building that was part of a campus of a dozen buildings the company occupied in Framingham, an old industrial town about twenty minutes west of Boston. The science team, which included Canfield, Mattaliano, O'Callaghan, and several others—had met several hours earlier to discuss the results of the Mother of all Experiments and learn the identity of the winning enzyme. They were waiting only for him to arrive.

John found the scientists assembled in a small, cold, second floor conference room, occupying nine of the ten seats around the rectangular table. John took his seat, greeting everyone briefly. Mattaliano said the science team had spent several hours reviewing and analyzing the massive amount of data generated by the Mother of All Experiments, and that he would now present the most important of the conclusions. He launched into a PowerPoint presentation of the results. The first slides showed the results of a series of biochemical analyses, in which the muscle samples were ground up and a chemical added to test for the presence of the Pompe enzyme. In this test, the magenta enzyme was taken up best, outshining the others by far. But in the next series of slides, when numerous different tissue samples were studied to see which enzyme had cleared glycogen best, the yellow and green performed better than the magenta. And this type of analysis was considered the more relevant test in Pompe science because it indicated that the enzyme treatment had entered the lysosomes and done its job, metabolizing glycogen.[2]

"Of the top two, the yellow enzyme appears slightly superior in some muscles, but not by enough to be statistically significant," Mattaliano said, as he clicked to change slides.

John, hoping Novazyme's was the yellow or the green, snuck a look at Canfield, who hadn't said a word yet. His arms were folded tightly across his chest, and he was brooding down at the grains of wood in the conference table. Novazyme's must be the yellow, John thought, and Canfield looked upset because it didn't perform significantly better than the second-place finisher.

"Now let me show you what these enzymes are," Mattaliano said. "We were just unblinded ourselves to the color coding a couple of hours ago."

For first place, there was a statistical tie between the top-performing yellow enzyme, Chen's, and the green, the internally developed Genzyme enzyme, the one Mattaliano had helped develop for easy manufacturing. Novazyme's, the magenta, came in third in the overall assessment, and Pharming's a distant fourth.[3]

John was shocked and, to some degree, embarrassed. Even though he'd known Canfield was struggling to get his enzyme to work right, John had been sure it would outshine the others—or at least work as well.

"How is it that the Novazyme enzyme was so much better on the enzyme activity test and did so poorly in the glycogen clearance?" John asked, hoping there was some mistake with the final analysis.

Mattaliano smiled. "We were wondering the same thing," he admitted. "We discussed it at length a few hours ago." He said that the scientists' best guess was that the Novazyme enzyme, with all the extra phosphates at the end of the sugar chains, was taken up by some other part of the tissue before it could get to the lysosomes of the muscle cells. Endothelial cells, in the linings of blood vessels, also had receptors with an affinity for the sugar

chains. Perhaps the endothelial cells had taken up the Novazyme enzyme, ·
leaving little or none remaining to enter the lysosomes and clear glycogen.[4]

John said it was time to poll the group to make sure there was agreement. Still sitting, he went around the rectangular table asking the scientists if they agreed with the conclusions. Mattaliano, O'Callaghan, and the
rest of the Genzyme group nodded, smugly, and each gave a firm "Yes."

Finally, John reached Canfield, hoping the man who was always so
skeptical would challenge the way the experiments were conducted—that
he would find something wrong with the conclusions.

But Canfield, not lifting his gaze, nodded almost imperceptibly and
said, "The results speak for themselves."[5]

"Are you sure, Bill? Is there anything else you'd like to add?" John
pressed.

Canfield shook his head.

John stood up and thanked the group, and then said, gravely, "God
help us if we're wrong."

As John made the half-hour drive back to Genzyme's Cambridge headquarters, his mind raced to absorb the enormity of the implications.

With the easy-to-produce Mattaliano enzyme coming in such a close
second, John was almost certain it would be the chosen one. Pharming's enzyme would have to be shut down. Who would tell those patients that development of their drug was coming to an end? Chen's drug, which held so
much promise, would also have to shut down. They would keep a sample in
the freezer—just in case—but the multimillion-dollar contracts with manufacturers who were producing the enzyme would be canceled immediately.

Novazyme would be the hardest hit. Not only had the science that Canfield had worked eighteen months to develop—and nine years before that—
been challenged and received a crushing blow, there would almost certainly
have to be layoffs if the Novazyme enzyme was not going to be manufactured
immediately. If Canfield viewed him as a traitor before, it was nothing compared to what he and others in Oklahoma would think of him now.

And there was a final, bleakly inescapable fact: because "his" drug had
lost, John's hope of exerting his influence over how the clinical trials were
run, his hope of making sure Megan and Patrick were included, was lost as
well. Since Genzyme's drug would be picked, Genzyme's medical and reg-

ulatory affairs department would run everything. As medical director, Landy would be in the driver's seat for all clinical trials.

A few days later, John presented a drug development strategy to Henri and van Heek. John recommended investing $50 million to ramp up manufacturing of the Genzyme enzyme by building two new giant two-thousand-liter bioreactors in the company's Allston plant. If all went well, they should have enough of Genzyme's enzyme on hand by the summer to begin a clinical trial. He didn't say it, but he intended to use every ounce of influence he had behind the scenes to persuade Landy and whoever else was in charge to get Megan and Patrick into that trial.

John suggested also that they find savings of $20 million a year by immediately canceling the outside contracts to manufacture Chen's drug. He also recommended shutting down manufacturing of Novazyme's enzyme, which would save several million. Eventually, he said, they ought to also close down Pharming's manufacturing plant, but not until the next year—not until production of Genzyme's internally developed drug had been scaled up. For the next year, Pharming's rabbits would continue to supply drug to the nine patients on the treatment.

Instead of being moved into human clinical trials, Novazyme's technology and experimental enzyme treatments were being sent back to the research labs. Still a believer in Canfield's approach, John said he wanted to keep funding Novazyme's research in the hopes of developing a second-generation treatment that worked better. John was convinced that Byrne's and other results using an earlier version of Canfield's enzyme had been accurate. He believed something had gone wrong in the rush to make it with human processing enzymes and the new inhibitor—and to add more and more phosphate molecules. Somehow, the latest versions were being taken up somewhere else before reaching their intended destinations. Finally, John told Henri, Canfield would have the time he needed to work out the problems.

Henri listened carefully, nodding in agreement. For a nonscientist, Henri had a way of absorbing and extrapolating the meaning of scientific information that surprised even the most egotistical scientists. When John had finished, Henri honed in on the risks of going with Genzyme's enzyme.[6]

"We know how it works in animals, but we don't know how—or if—it works in humans. This enzyme has never been tested in humans where the Pharming and Chen enzymes have. What if it doesn't work? What happens if we're wrong?"

"That's our nightmare scenario, Henri," John responded honestly. "But I think it's reasonable to bet on the Genzyme product because it's so much easier to manufacture. We'll keep the Chen line in reserve. If the Genzyme treatment doesn't work, we can go back to the Chen product and figure out what to do."

Henri asked John to present the strategy to Genzyme's board of directors the next day. "And then, John, your job is just to go and get this done."

John wanted to bring the same sense of urgency to Genzyme that he had cultivated at Novazyme by inviting patients to talk to his employees. So in February, with Henri Termeer's go-ahead, he held what he called the Pompe Summit—bringing patients and their families to a luncheon at the Charles Hotel for all employees working on Pompe disease. Henri overruled members of the medical and regulatory affairs groups who paraded into his office worrying that their objectivity would be compromised, agreeing not only to attend the Summit, but also to give a speech. Like John, Henri believed in the power of inspiration to drive people to achieve the seemingly impossible.[7]

In the morning, before the patients arrived, about two hundred employees involved at all levels in the Pompe program—from machine operators to secretaries—heard Genzyme's senior scientists and regulatory officials present the drug development strategy developed by the Pompe leadership team. Mattaliano, in a PowerPoint presentation entitled "In Vivo Veritas"—or "the truth revealed in animal testing"—presented the results of the Mother of All Experiments. The title was a muted but obvious dig at Canfield, who had been so insistent prior to the experiments that his approach and his enzyme were superior.[8] It had been six months since the Novazyme acquisition, but tension still ran high between the Genzyme and Novazyme scientists. When the title slide came up on screen, John saw with a pang, Canfield winced and looked away.

Landy stood up and presented a plan to rush the Genzyme enzyme into clinical trial as soon as they had enough enzyme in storage to supply the trial patients for one year. Bill Fallon, the Novazyme manufacturing guru, gave an overview of the efforts under way to scale up production of large volumes of the enzyme by refurbishing a bioreactor in Framingham and building two new large reactors in Allston. Canfield, in his turn at the podium, explained Novazyme's scientific approach and held out the promise of a better second-generation treatment.

The patients, their families, and Henri arrived in time for lunch. John had strategically placed his own family at Henri's table. Beside Henri, Megan sat in her new pink wheelchair, which had just replaced the red one she had outgrown. Megan used the pink one inside the house and in crowded places like this where she couldn't bring her electric chair. John, Aileen, and Sharon filled out the same round table; Patrick, who didn't like crowds and grew agitated and fussy at attention, had stayed at home with a nurse.

Henri, in his dapper tweed sport coat and bright orange tie, leaned over to speak to John's daughter. "I've heard a lot about you, Megan," he said. "It's great to have your dad here." As John watched, Henri then rose and went from table to table, spending at least five minutes talking to each of the patients and their families. Seeing this, John told himself he'd made the right decision in selling Novazyme to Genzyme, despite his frustrations with the bureaucracy and his own lack of authority.

After an initial session of seating and mingling, John took to the floor to introduce the patients. "How many of you have ever met a patient?" he asked the assembled Genzyme group. Only a handful of the two hundred employees in attendance raised their hands.[9]

"Well, you are all going to meet some very special patients and families today," John said, beaming. "I myself know the first speaker very well. Greg Assink has flown here all the way from Michigan with his wife Deborah and their new baby Megan, who, I'm proud to tell you, is named after my own daughter. Greg and Deb have been strong supporters of the Children's Pompe Foundation. They are among the most committed parents I have ever met, and I am proud and pleased they have made the trip today."

Greg stood up, carrying four-month-old baby Megan in his arms, his wife smiling from the seat beside him. He told the assembled group that he had two daughters with the disease—the one in his arms and another at home. Kelsey, now eight years old, was too weak to travel. Their youngest had been tested and diagnosed only weeks after she was born. She was still able to hold her head up, but her mouth hung open and her tongue poked out a little, the telltale sign of the disease.

"I cannot tell you what it means to us to have all of you working on a cure for our children," Greg said, choking up. "Deb and I want to thank you from the bottom of our hearts—and for you to know that *we* know you'll be successful. We know Kelsey and Megan will be saved because of your work."

After several other parents spoke, it was Aileen's turn. "I think you all know who my husband is," she said dryly, drawing laughter and some scattered applause. "This is Megan here, our daughter, and Sharon, our nurse. We want to thank you all for your hard work. We're counting on you." Megan waved from her seat as the audience applauded.

Finally, Henri rose to address the patients. He gave a long and rousing speech, ending with an emotional declaration of his commitment. "I don't know how much better we can make your children," he said. "But I promise with every fiber of my being that we'll do our best to make it happen."

From the back of the room where he had been sitting, nervous at the prospect of patients being present, Landy jumped up as soon as the meeting ended. Inspired by the hope he heard in the voices of patients and their families, he forgot about how uncomfortable he had been at the very idea of the meeting. He rushed from one patient family to the next, introducing himself and thanking them for coming. Like most of the Genzyme staff there, he had never before met patients with Pompe.[10]

As Landy mingled, he saw a bioreactor operator named Patrick embrace John and say, "I've got a daughter, too, and I can't imagine what you go through. Your daughter is beautiful. I want you to know I will not let you down."

Landy, agreeing with Patrick, but not given to emotional declarations himself, simply shook John's hand and nodded, biting his lip.

John flew home to Princeton on a private jet that evening with Megan, Aileen, and Sharon, talking nonstop and excitedly. He was still coming down from the nervous state he'd hyped himself into in the days before the big summit.

"In just five months, I've formulated a strategic plan to move Gen-zyme's largest ever drug development program forward," he said. "It's been such hard work. I never would have thought it possible. Did you see how inspired people were at the end?"

"They sure were, John," Aileen said, leaning back in her seat and clos-ing her eyes. She, Sharon, and Megan had flown up that morning for the luncheon, and it had been an exhausting day.

"We built a consensus around the plan and, with the meeting today, we've begun to create a sense of urgency within the company to move quickly into clinical trials," he said. "I bet we can have Megan and Patrick treated by the summer," he added, with his customary confidence, and re-ally believing it himself.

"You really think so, Mister John?" Sharon interjected.

"I'm trying my damnedest," he said.

"You sure are," Sharon said, growing tearful. "I just can't wait for the day, Mister John. I am so proud of you."

Megan, who had been looking out the window, jumped into the con-versation. "Daddy, when did you say Special Medicine will be ready?"

"It's almost ready," John said. "Just a few more months, honey."

"I don't want it to be blue anymore—I want it to be pink," she said.

He nodded and said, "Okay, honey, we can make it pink."

"Will I be able to walk?"

To walk? When he had first told Megan a year and a half ago about a medicine he was making for her—then, as now, calling it Special Medicine—one of her first questions had been whether she would be able to walk. At the time, there had been reason to believe it was possible. Now, two years later, she and Patrick were so weak that the muscles in their legs and torsos were possibly too damaged to repair themselves.

Today, he would consider it a victory if the children's hearts were made healthy by the drug—and there was still a good chance that would happen. That alone would pull them back from the danger of heart failure, which was a risk the family now faced every day. He had to hold on to what might be, John told himself, not what could have been. If only he could help their hearts, he thought again, he would be happy.

"Daddy, will I be able to walk?" Megan asked again, interrupting his thoughts.

"I hope so, Megan," he said, haltingly. "But we don't know. I don't think it will happen right away. Special Medicine isn't magic, you know. You're going to have to work really, really hard to get stronger. Will you do that?"

She nodded, but possessed of her father's persistence, she pressed again: "But will I walk?"

It was a sensitive thing he was trying to do, resetting her expectations without taking away her hope. Hope, as he knew, was perhaps second only to love, the most powerful motivator in the world.

"I think you're going to get a whole lot stronger. I *know* your heart is going to get a whole lot stronger," he said. "I don't think you'll walk right away, Megan. But if you try really, really hard, you never know what can happen."

24. The Sibling Study

SPRING–SUMMER 2002
FRAMINGHAM, MASSACHUSETTS; CAMBRIDGE, MASSACHUSETTS;
PRINCETON, NEW JERSEY; OCEAN CITY, NEW JERSEY

At long last, the Pompe leadership team turned its attention to discussing the clinical trials on which Genzyme hoped to win FDA approval. At the group's meeting in the Framingham science building, Landy took the floor and used a flip chart to present his plan. It called for a single clinical trial in twelve patients who would all be less than a year old.[1]

John, stunned that Landy was conceiving of a trial that by design could not include his children, lobbed the first question. "Why are we testing in infants first?"

"There are several reasons," Landy said smoothly. "The main reason is that the life expectancy of infants is so short that we can demonstrate in less than a year that our therapy extends their lives. That's the gold standard for the FDA to approve a therapy," he finished matter-of-factly.

It was the same argument John had heard for four years from researchers at Pharming and Duke. That argument was why he had formed the Children's Pompe Foundation in the first place—to fund clinical trials in his kids' age group, which nobody else was planning to do. If now, at Genzyme, the first major trial of the treatment he'd been so desperately pursuing did not include his children, then the past four years had in many ways been an enormous waste of his time.

"Dr. Alfred Slonim has always recommended a new treatment be tested first in slightly older kids," John pressed. "Testing in infants first doesn't make sense because these kids are usually the sickest. You may have the perfect drug, but these kids may be too sick to ever be rescued."

"What you're recommending is Novazyme's strategy," Landy said.

"Call it what you want—the reality is this," John asserted. "These infants probably make no enzyme at all, so you may have the greatest drug and still not get clinical benefit because of the body's immune response."

"John, we may only include babies who are crim positive, and in case you don't know, that's medical terminology for a patient who naturally produces a small amount of active enzyme," Landy said, enunciating every word, his voice louder. "We have many factors to consider here in trial design, including the fact that we may be working with a very limited supply of enzyme and babies need the least amount of drug."

As he spoke, Landy grew steadily more red-faced and breathless. "Testing in infants is the fastest way to get the drug approved," he repeated. "You're proposing the Novazyme plan."

"That's because the Novazyme plan is the best goddamn plan I've seen," John retorted, refusing to back down. His hard-won credibility as head of the Pompe program depended on being seen as able to rise above his own needs as a father—to be coolly, serenely objective. After all this time, he wasn't always able to remember that.

In the quiet of his office after the meeting, Landy calmed. His anger at the challenge to his authority as medical director in front of the science team had caused him to lose any ability to sympathize with John. Now, mentally reviewing the meeting, Landy realized what had occurred almost immediately to everyone else—that though John didn't mention Megan and Patrick, he was arguing against a clinical trial plan that excluded them.[2]

Surely, Landy thought, there could be a compromise. He pulled the binder with the enzyme production and supply plans from his desk, and silently scrutinized the spreadsheets that predicted future drug supply. After a moment, he pulled a legal notebook from another desk drawer and began scribbling notes. Half an hour later, he opened a document on the computer and began typing, rewriting the clinical trial plan to include two trials—one in sixteen infants and another in sixteen young children.

It was asking a lot of the manufacturing team. Neither trial could begin until Genzyme had made enough of the enzyme—a little over a kilogram—to last a full year. It wasn't prudent to take the risk of running out, he believed, while the big, new bioreactors in Allston were still being built and the trial enzyme was going to come from three older ones at Genzyme's plant in Framingham. For Landy's new plan to work, four of the next five runs in the bioreactors needed to come out clean.

Still, he thought, it could work. It could be a way to help John's kids.

Unfortunately, almost everything went wrong during the next few weeks on the manufacturing front. The yield from the first run was less than the Pompe leadership team had predicted, in part because the portion of drug that needed to be set aside for testing to validate the new system had not been subtracted out of the supply calculation. Then several bioreactor runs failed. The final blow came in April when some glass vials in which Pharming's enzyme was stored cracked. A senior official recommended throwing out all the Pharming vials. John pushed van Heek to broker a compromise in which Genzyme would throw out only vials that were part of the production runs in which others had cracked. Still, it cost dearly. A third of the Pharming drug was lost. The first Genzyme drug made by the Framingham bioreactors had to be siphoned off to supply some of the Pharming patients who would need to be transitioned to the Genzyme therapy a year ahead of plan.

When the Pompe leadership team assembled three months later in May to finalize the clinical trial design, there was only half as much enzyme available as everyone had hoped. Red pen in hand, Landy stood before the group saying he needed to change the trial design to reflect the shorter supply. He wanted to keep the infant trial at sixteen patients because he thought that was the bare minimum needed to convince the FDA that the experimental drug worked. Most drugs were approved on the basis of testing in hundreds of patients.

John held his breath as Landy paused and turned the page of his flip chart. Had he canceled the second trial?

To John's relief, he saw that Landy still planned a second trial. But the relief dissolved in dismay as John saw how Landy had done it. He had limited participation to children younger than three years old, who would need less enzyme because they were smaller. Megan, five, and Patrick, four, would not qualify.

What could he say? What Landy had done was perfectly reasonable from a clinical and corporate perspective—and in the overall interest of speeding a treatment to market for all patients. As director of the Pompe program, John couldn't think of one single rational argument to make against it. But as a father, he longed to put up his hand and say, "What about Megan and Patrick?" The whole room knew his kids were dying. How could they put forward a plan that wouldn't include them?

Rage surged within him as Landy painstakingly described the dose levels for the trial and the clinical endpoints he would measure. But John reminded himself that he had sold himself to Genzyme as someone who could be objective and rise above his children's desperate need to run a program to benefit all patients. Landy was only doing his job.

Megan and Patrick were not part of his job description.

A few days later, with McKinney at the wheel, he and John rode to Genzyme's headquarters. McKinney tried to make small-talk, but John didn't engage, staring silently out the window ahead. McKinney was one of the few people at work with whom John spoke candidly about his fears for his children. McKinney knew that John found it excruciating to maintain his objectivity as leader of the Pompe program when his children's lives depended on its decisions, and often marveled privately to his wife that he didn't know how John carried it off.

When John finally spoke, his voice was dark and distant. McKinney was used to the young program director's quick wit and humor, his exasperation and impatience. He was ready for him to complain about Landy's insensitivity, but he didn't in any way expect to hear what John said next.

"You know, Tony, sometimes you get awfully tempted," John said, his face unreadable. "There's drug sitting there. You wonder if anyone would notice if some of it went missing."

John was actually suggesting stealing some of the drug and giving it to his children!

"I'm sure you think about it, John, but that's a dangerous road to start down," McKinney said, haltingly. "I'm sure we can find a better way."

"Of course," John said, sounding utterly exhausted. He leaned back and stared out the window again.

"I'm sorry, John," McKinney said softly. "I'm so sorry."

The two men were quiet for the rest of the ride. John's mind kept turning over the shock of Landy's announcements—and the thought of those bottles of enzyme, just sitting there. He'd thought about it before. His coworkers and his investors would be shocked if they knew how many times he'd thought of it before. What if he took several vials of drug? How would he give it to the kids? It had to be infused in their veins in a hospital every two weeks. The children needed to have an operation to have a tube installed so large volumes of enzyme could be safely infused. Should he take the drugs and fly the kids to Mexico?

It wasn't that simple. Nothing ever was. The children needed to be monitored by doctors who knew about the disease. What if they built up antibodies to fight the enzyme? He would never know if the right doctors weren't doing the right tests.

All the plans ended in failure. With a sigh, he turned back to face the road. He couldn't just take off with a few vials; he had always known that. He would have to find another way.

Back in his office, John pulled out the reports from the manufacturing team and a calculator and began to go over the drug supply numbers. He looked at Landy's latest plan and added up the amount of drug each patient needed. Landy's calculations were based on his assumption that the clinical trials couldn't begin until Genzyme had a year's supply of enzyme on hand. Maybe, John thought, he could persuade Landy to go with a nine-month supply instead. That way they could include bigger kids like Megan and Patrick.

Late that afternoon, John showed up at Landy's door. It was open a crack and he could see Landy seated at his desk, his sleeves rolled up, the knot of his tie loosened. Papers were spread all across the desktop. John recognized the same drug supply lists that he himself was clutching. He knocked and sat down at his small conference table, pulling out the legal pad on which he'd recalculated the supply.[3]

"Hal, I wanted to show you how, if we keep a nine-month supply of drug, we can include bigger kids in the trial," John said.

"I'm not comfortable with that," Landy said immediately. "You have to be conservative. Every time we turn around there's less drug. It would be an absolute disaster if patients were left without drug in the middle of the trial."

"But Hal, that's a risk many parents would take," John said, still not mentioning the names that burned on his tongue. "What's the alternative for the patients? Many of them will die if they have to wait longer."

The two men argued back and forth, until it became clear to John he was not making any inroads. Defeated, he picked up his papers to leave. He was starting to stand up when Landy said quietly, "John, I want to let you know I also want to treat Megan and Patrick."

The words stopped John cold. In the nine months they had worked together, Landy had never said the names of John's two sick children before. He had been longing to hear Landy's exact words for four long years, and now they had just been uttered in a quiet, matter-of-fact tone.

"What—what are your thoughts?" John said, struggling to maintain his composure.

Landy described a plan for John's kids that he had been putting together for several days, ever since he realized he would have to revise the trial in a way that would exclude them. He hadn't wanted to share it with John until it was all set. He told John that he preferred not to petition the FDA to give his kids the drug on a compassionate-use basis—a provision the federal agency sometimes approved to make experimental treatments available to patients who will otherwise die—because the company might face accusations of favoritism. Parents of children with Pompe called almost daily, begging for some of the enzyme. They had their senators and congressmen lobby Henri on their behalf.

To get around any possible nepotism charge, Landy had devised a scientific rationale for a tiny third clinical trial, calling it the Sibling Study. He would argue that it was necessary to help Genzyme understand not only why Pompe disease manifested differently in patients, but also why the enzyme treatment's effectiveness varied widely. Megan and Patrick had the exact same defect in the gene that coded the Pompe enzyme, and yet they had very different forms of the disease, Megan being much stronger than Patrick. Landy said he would argue that the Crowley siblings were ideal for an experiment aimed at finding the causes for the varying clinical manifestations of the disease and effectiveness of the treatment.

"When could we begin?" John asked, breathless.

"We can begin as soon as we've written a protocol, probably in about two months. Where would you like us to conduct the trial, John?"

"CHOP is close to our home and has the best doctors," John said immediately, using the acronym for the Children's Hospital of Philadelphia.

"Then I'll begin a dialogue with the hospital's clinical trial review board," Landy said. "As soon as they approve the trial, we can begin."

John sprinted back to his office and called Aileen. "Hal just told me they want to treat the kids," he blurted out as soon as she was on the line.

"What are you saying?" she asked. "When will it happen?" He could tell she was excited, but not quite believing what he was telling her.

He repeated everything he had heard from Landy. He thought they could get the children treated in two or three months.

"Two or three months," Aileen repeated, in a tone of wonderment and joy.

The next afternoon, John pulled up at the home his family had moved into only a month earlier. As the limousine drove away, John paused for a moment, staring up at the enormous white brick house with three turrets. He and his daughter both thought it looked like a castle, which was half the reason Megan loved it. It was a beautiful spring day, with a peaceful blue sky framed by tall trees. He stepped into the foyer from which two staircases rose gracefully on either side of the doorway leading to the great room. Megan, in her electric wheelchair, sped through that doorway and pulled up an inch from his feet.

"Hey, Mario Andretti, slow down," he said, jumping backward. Like the average five-year-old, she moved quickly when excited. Her electric wheelchair was big and black with a head support, a foot rest, and a pocket for her ventilator in the back. A seat belt kept her from falling out. She had grown so comfortable in the chair that it really had become an extension of her body. She could amble, speed, twist, and twirl in that chair.

"Megan, I have the best news for you," John said, the words bursting out. "Special Medicine is ready."

"Where is it?" she asked, backing up.

"It's in Cambridge, Massachusetts, where Daddy goes every week."

Megan considered. "Is it pink?"

"We'll have to see. I've told them in Cambridge that you want it to be pink and they're working on it."

"Who else is going to get it?" she wanted to know, mouthing and signing questions so fast now that he could barely keep up.

"You and Patrick."

"Hurray," she sang, pumping her arms.

Megan sped around John in circles, singing, "I'm getting Special Medicine." After a half-dozen circles, she zoomed toward the kitchen where her mother was reading to Patrick.

"John, tell Patrick," Aileen said. John bounded to Patrick's side and relayed the same news. Patrick waved his hands and squeaked as he always did when he saw his father. John was never sure how much his youngest child understood. He bent and kissed him on the forehead, content in his joy to take any reaction Patrick had.

John thought it should have taken Landy a couple of days to write the protocol—the detailed plan for conducting the clinical trial. But days flew by, then weeks. He wanted to order Landy and his team of clinical research assistants to work faster, but he felt he couldn't because they didn't report to him. Each time he inquired—and he did, every few days—they made clear they were swamped by work that was a higher priority. And from a corporate point of view, John couldn't deny that the two main trials that would form the basis of Genzyme's application for FDA approval ought to be a higher priority. As head of the Pompe program, how could he argue that his children's trial was more important than the trials on which a new treatment for all patients rested?

After an excruciating month, Landy's team finally submitted his children's trial protocol to CHOP. Now John waited for the hospital's clinical trial review board to meet and assess the protocol. Several more weeks went by. Finally, the board was set to meet in early August, two days into the summer vacation John and Aileen had planned with the family in Ocean City, New Jersey.

Before John left, he made arrangements with Dr. Richard Finkel of CHOP to relay the board's decision to him while he was in Ocean City. The famous neurologist was to lead his children's Sibling Study and had promised to call.

Aileen drove down first in the morning to buy food and set up the oceanfront house they had rented for two weeks. Anticipating the horde of relatives and flood of medical equipment that had to come with them, they'd gotten a six-bedroom house with an elevator and a four-car garage. John followed in the afternoon at the wheel of the handicapped van carrying Megan, Patrick, John Jr., Sharon, and all their medical supplies. It had taken a week of planning and three hours of loading to get the van ready with everything needed for the fortnight.

Aileen had chosen Ocean City, thinking that it would be easy for Megan and Patrick to ride in their wheelchairs along its big wide boardwalk lined with stores, restaurants, and a park featuring dozens of rides. But it was too hot the afternoon they arrived to take the children outside. Patrick watched television, and John and Aileen played a series of board games—Arthur's Library, The Princess Game, and checkers—with Megan and John Jr.

Soon the guests were arriving. Sharon's daughter Misty and three grandchildren had followed John's van. Aileen's parents came next, followed by her brother Brian, his wife Kim, and their three children. In addition to Sharon, two other nurses were there to share the round-the-clock care of the children. Altogether, there were nine kids and nine adults in the house, making it crowded despite the three floors.

When the temperature finally fell in the early evening, everyone spilled onto the boardwalk, heading for the rides. Megan led the way in her electric wheelchair, the other kids struggling to keep up on foot. Aileen pushed Patrick, talking excitedly about the rides. Megan declared the Ferris wheel was going to be the first stop.

"Aileen, tell her that nobody's going on the Ferris wheel," John said, pleading. "There are plenty of other fun rides that are safer."

Aileen, shaking her head, said, "John, I've promised the kids they can go on the Ferris wheel. We have to let them have fun."

The group reached the entry to the Ferris wheel and discovered two steep flights of steps leading to the launching area. John's eyes widened and he shuddered involuntarily. Aileen ignored him and carried Patrick up the stairs, Sharon following with his ventilator, Aileen's mother standing at the entrance guarding the wheelchair. Sighing, John followed with Megan in his arms, Aileen's brother Brian carrying the ventilator, and her father remaining beside the little girl's wheelchair.

In no time, they were flying high above the beach, Aileen and Patrick in the cart above John and Megan. Aileen peeked over the edge and saw John holding fast to Megan, his eyes shut. She burst out in giggles, suddenly remembering that years ago, before they were married, John had thrown up on a roller coaster, splattering the other passengers. John's reluctance to let the family get on the Ferris wheel hadn't been for the kids' sake—he was scared of heights. Megan looked up, saw her mother, and waved, running her finger over her cheekbone. When Megan was learning sign language years ago, Patrick had been fed through a tube in his nose, so Megan's sign for him, to distinguish him from everyone else, was to trace the path of the tube across the side of his face. Aileen leaned Patrick's head over in Megan's direction so they could see each other. As Megan waved, Patrick flapped his hands excitedly.

When the Ferris wheel finally came to a halt, John got off, mumbling, "I'm not getting on another ride." But minutes later, he was rolling down the tracks beside Megan on the train ride, Aileen and Patrick in the cart behind them. The vacation was off to a great start.

It was 9 P.M. when the group finally headed home on the boardwalk, Megan again in the lead. Somehow, her wheelchair got locked in an upright position. Each time she went over a bump, her head fell forward. John, walking beside her, had to lift her head back up.

"Megan, what are you doing?" he said, after several lifts.

"She can't do it by herself anymore," Aileen whispered, shushing him.

The information hit him like a big wave, knocking him out of vacation mode. He knew neither child could sit up anymore, not even with assistance. But he hadn't noticed that Megan had gotten so weak she could no longer pull her head up if it fell forward. Thank God she was going to be treated any day. As he patiently pulled Megan's head back up again and again, he thought of Dr. Finkel, who was supposed to call the next day to report on the board meeting. John silently prayed that there wouldn't be any further delays.

All day Monday, John played checkers with Megan and John Jr., while listening for Dr. Finkel's call. It was too hot again to take the youngest two outside, but John took a drive with little John to the liquor store to buy a bottle of his favorite Veuve Cliquot champagne, anticipating that at long last there would be some good news.

The next morning, after Aileen left for the beach, John dialed Finkel. The doctor took the phone, apologizing for not calling the previous day. He didn't have good news and hadn't wanted to ruin John's vacation. "There's some concern on the IRB about the ethical fairness of treating your kids. There's a concern about a conflict of interest."[4]

The thought that the hospital might actually turn down the trial had simply not occurred to John.

"Dr. Finkel, Megan and Patrick will be the twenty-sixth and twenty-seventh kids who will have received a Genzyme Pompe enzyme," he said, desperately. He knew to the digit the exact number of patients in the United States and Europe who had already received Chen's or Pharming's enzyme either in trials or with special permission from government agencies and Genzyme, known as compassionate use.

Finkel tried to reassure John. He said he had talked to the head of the review board, and he thought he could get the trial approved after making a few changes and resubmitting it for the September meeting.

Aileen came back from the beach and immediately asked John if the doctor had called. John took her into their bedroom and told her about the conversation.

"I'm not surprised," Aileen said bluntly. Without asking another question, she left the room and went downstairs, plunging herself into conversation with the other guests.

For the rest of the week, the house was packed with friends and relatives. They sat on the patio, drinking and talking late into the night. John found it hard to join in the fun. He wanted a quiet place to read and rest, and there was none. His head hurt, and his heart was heavy with disappointment. One night, as he lay in bed trying to sleep, the group on the patio was exceptionally loud. He couldn't escape the booming voice of Aileen's brother Marty, who had arrived that day. Frustrated, he walked out onto the patio and asked the group to lower their voices.

"Shut up," they yelled back tipsily. Several bottles of wine sat on the patio table, uncorked.

Aileen, who had been telling John all week to relax, let loose, and have some fun, flapped her hand at him and continued, "Get out of here, asshole."

When Aileen awoke the next morning, John exploded at her. "I rented this house and all of these people came down here," he shouted, so loudly that she pulled him into the bathroom to keep the others from overhearing.

"But you invited them," she said in a loud whisper. "You're waking everyone up." He was too upset to care.

John's relationship with his guests went from bad to worse. His mother arrived later that morning and gaily suggested they take a day trip. "How about we head up the road to Atlantic City and do a little gambling," she said. When he shook his head, she teased him, saying "Don't be an old fart." John bellowed in response, accusing her of not visiting her grandchildren enough. Soon they were yelling at each other and bringing up everything that had annoyed them in the past few years. She said she didn't feel comfortable in his house now that he was a rich big shot.

"Then leave—get out!" he said, unconsciously echoing his wife's words from the night before.

She drove off.

John woke up early the next morning, pulled on shorts and a tank top, and went for a run down the boardwalk. He felt lethargic and out of shape. Until a couple of years ago, he had run and lifted weights almost every day. Now the constant travel had thrown off his schedule; he rarely exercised these days, and he had several extra pounds around his middle. As he built up a sweat, he thought about how he was close to the emotional low of three years earlier, when the only road to happiness had seemed to be to divorce Aileen and live across the street. He reminded himself that his frustration was not Aileen's fault, not his mother's, not Marty's, and certainly not the children's. He was just tired—tired of living away from home, tired of trying to be the objective head of Pompe disease, tired of being on a quest to save his children that never seemed to end. He simply didn't want to do it anymore.

As the sun rose, he stopped and walked, breaking hard. He had been mulling for a long time whether to stay on at Genzyme, which meant moving his family to Boston, or whether he should quit after his children got treated. With his mind cleared from the exercise and the quiet of the predawn morning, it became clear to him that he should leave. As part of the sale to Genzyme, he had agreed to stay at the company for one year. Next month, that year would be up. When he returned to Cambridge, he decided, he would quietly tell van Heek that he planned to resign at the end of the year. That would give him enough time to get his kids treated and submit plans for the two main clinical trials to the FDA. All he had to do was get over the worst vacation of his life and hang on a little longer at Genzyme—just long enough to let Finkel work out the kinks in the Sibling Study at CHOP.

But two weeks later, Landy, who had sympathetically told John to let him handle communication with the Children's Hospital, was back on the phone with more bad news. A hospital board had met again, and still had not approved the Sibling Study. There were still too many questions about conflict of interest, Landy said. "You might want to have a Plan B."

"A Plan B," John said blankly. "Right. Yes, yes, we'll find a Plan B." He put the phone back into the cradle, gently, and lowered his head into his hands. He couldn't even summon the energy to be angry or disappointed. He'd been coming up with Plan Bs for four years now. It was probably time to just give up.

25. Plan B

FALL 2002
PRINCETON, NEW JERSEY; ROTTERDAM, NETHERLANDS;
GAINESVILLE, FLORIDA

A week later, John called Dr. Byrne, the University of Florida physician-researcher who had performed the laboratory experiment that appeared to show that Canfield's enzyme made mice stronger. Byrne had cowritten the plans for the animal studies and human clinical trial for Novazyme. As the doctor who would have been in charge of the Novazyme clinical trial, he had taken the design to his hospital's clinical trial review board a year ago and gotten approval.

John told Byrne his children were declining fast. "Megan can't even pull her head up if it falls forward. I know it sounds like a little thing, but it's that final piece of dignity. And Patrick's even weaker." John described plans for the Sibling Study and how they had been repeatedly turned down by the Children's Hospital of Philadelphia.

"I was wondering if we could do the Sibling Study at your hospital, Barry?"

"I'd love to help," Byrne said sincerely. "The geography's not the best, though," he said.

"Right now I'd go to the moon to get Megan and Patrick treated, so Florida is not that far away," John said, wearily. "You're right, Barry, the geography is not ideal. That's why I didn't think of you in the first place. But with all the trouble at CHOP, I'd just like to move this along quickly. I don't think the children can hang on much longer."

Byrne asked John to e-mail the Sibling Study protocol, and said he would use it to write an application to his hospital's clinical trial review board, which would meet again in October. He promised to call as soon as he had news.

John asked one of Landy's clinical research assistants for a copy of the study and e-mailed it to Byrne. Should he tell Landy about his conversation with Byrne? He decided to wait, concerned that Genzyme's scientists and doctors viewed Byrne unfavorably because he had been allied with Novazyme. But, more important, John knew Landy's team would go over the study submission—as was their job—and who knew how long they would take to pull the whole thing together? No, he wouldn't tell Hal Landy or anyone else, not until everything was settled. There was only one person he trusted to get this done quickly: himself.

A week later, in late September, John and a half-dozen other senior Genzyme managers and scientists flew to the Netherlands to explain their decision to drop the Pharming enzyme. Dutch newspapers had been filled with stories quoting panic-stricken patients and their families saying Genzyme was ceasing production of the very enzyme needed for their survival. "Do I have to be embarrassed of my son in my old age?" Henri's mother, who still lived in the Netherlands, had phoned him to complain.[1]

On the morning after they arrived, the Genzyme group—including John, Landy, van Heek, and McKinney—drove to Rotterdam and met with Dr. Arnold Reuser, the scientist who had developed the Pharming enzyme, and officials from Sophia Children's Hospital.[2]

In the afternoon, John and the team met with about forty patients and family members in a conference room at the medical faculty building at Erasmus University. The group was large. The incidence of Pompe appears to be higher in the Netherlands, although researchers say they can't be certain this is true. Before the presentations began, John went around the room introducing himself. He shook hands with a big man in a wheelchair who breathed with a ventilator. John also met the man's wife. Another woman introduced herself as the mother of a little boy who had done so well on the Pharming enzyme that he was now able to walk. A woman showed John pictures of her daughter who was being treated with the enzyme. A father of another child gave John a brief nod and looked away.

When everyone was seated, van Heek rose first to address the group, speaking in Dutch, promising that Genzyme remained committed to treating the patients—just with a different enzyme. He explained that Genzyme couldn't afford to take the four enzymes it owned into development and had done a wide-ranging study, the Mother of All Experiments, to determine which one worked best. Landy spoke next, showing a handful of slides summarizing the Mother of All Experiments.

John followed with the development plan. "We plan to conduct two clinical trials, one on sixteen infants, one on sixteen children aged three and younger," he said. "These are very difficult, time-consuming, expensive enzymes to make, but we're using the best technology in the world to do it." He tried to project confidence and authority into his voice, so that the assembled patients could hear that, even if they had to listen to a translator for the exact words. "Ultimately, this will be a more reliable and safer way to make enzyme."

An arm shot up in the audience. "How do we know the rat enzyme will work as well for my son?" the woman who had raised her hand asked angrily. In the morning meeting and now, the Dutch had been derisively calling the internally developed Genzyme treatment the "rat enzyme" because it was grown in CHO cells, taken from Chinese hamsters.

"As Hal just described, all our animal studies indicate it will not only work as well, but better," John said. "Let me also say our enzyme is not a rat enzyme. It is an enzyme made in a very sophisticated process using tissue from hamsters to produce human enzyme. The hamster cells are a production facility."

"Who is going to take responsibility if our children do not do well on the rat enzyme?" another parent challenged.

"This is not a decision we made lightly, believe me," John said, trying to convey his deep sympathy. "We made it based on scientific evidence. As Jan has said, new patients will not be put on our enzyme until we are sure we have enough in storage to supply your needs. We are making sure we have enough enzyme to supply each and every one of your needs—even though it means many other Pompe patients in the world will have to wait longer, and perhaps die, waiting to be treated."

"And Mr. Crowley, why don't you tell us when your children began receiving this enzyme?" the same parent asked accusingly. With a shock, John realized that everyone in the room knew about his own situation and assumed Megan and Patrick were being treated.

"When we're talking about supply issues, I know what we're talking about because I live it," John said. "I know about how drug supply affects everything you can do in drug development. My children are so weak they can't sit up or even hold their heads up for long anymore." His voice was shaking, and he paused to try to steady it. "They—they are in wheelchairs and on ventilators. They get weaker every day. And my children still have not received *one single drop* of enzyme."

When John sat down, still struggling to compose himself, there was absolute silence in the room. Nobody—not the parents, not the patients, not even the Dutch doctors and scientists—asked another question. After van Heek had thanked everyone for attending and the meeting had ended, the wife of the man in the wheelchair hugged John. "I hope your children get treated soon, Mr. Crowley," she said.

Finally, only John and McKinney remained in the room. "It just killed me to hear these people complaining about being put on a different treatment," John said bitterly. "If Megan and Patrick had gotten enzyme like they did three years ago, they might be running around like regular kids now. I've failed my children, Tony. I have failed my family. I don't know what I'm doing here anymore."

John arrived home after dinner on a Friday night soon after to find a message from Dr. Byrne. He stepped into his study and dialed him back.

"This rarely happens, but our application went up and down in one day. We got the green light from our review board," Byrne said. "We're set to go. We could probably get this together in two weeks."

For once in his life, John was amazed at the speed with which something had happened.

"Can I come down tomorrow?" he asked, sounding a little dazed. "Yes, yes, I know it's a Saturday but I'd like to come and talk face to face."

John arose at 3 A.M. the next day to catch the first flight from Newark to Jacksonville. On the plane, he read the new protocol Dr. Byrne had gotten approved by his review board and e-mailed back the night before. John saw that Byrne had avoided the conflict of interest by writing a study for six children so that Megan and Patrick were not the only patients. Byrne had combined elements of both his original Novazyme application and Genzyme's Sibling Study. John knew now that Landy would have real trouble with this protocol, but again, he decided that he would think about that later. For now, he would go to Florida and get everything set up. If he had enough momentum, Landy and others at Genzyme would piss and moan but would eventually get out of the way.

John drove the two hours from Jacksonville to Gainesville, forcing himself not to speed, despite his excitement. He remembered Aileen's embrace when he told her the night before, and Sharon's scream and Megan's eagerness to get to Disney World. It was seventy degrees and sunny as he drove on the wide, palm tree–lined roads toward the brick buildings that made up the University of Florida campus and hospital. John parked in a garage and made his way across the street and up in an elevator to a conference room where Byrne and Dr. Carolyn Spencer, also a pediatric cardiologist, awaited him.[3]

The two doctors were warm and enthusiastic as they explained the trial protocol they had designed together. They walked him through sliding glass doors and into the bright new clinical trial research center where they said Megan and Patrick would receive their infusions of the experimental medicine. Children had painted bears, dolphins, and their names—Michael, Jessica, Melanie—on the ceiling tiles. What a wonderful place for his children to finally be treated.

That afternoon, Byrne's head nurse, Julie Berthy, drove John around Gainesville for several hours to look at apartments. He found one—a three-bedroom unit on one level for $1,100 a month—that he decided would work just fine.[4]

Back at his hotel, John bought five blue and orange Gators T-shirts for the family. If they were going to live in Gainesville for a while, they would have to become University of Florida football fans. No team could ever supplant Notre Dame as the Crowley family's favorite football team, but the Gators were becoming a close second, at least for John.

That night, John chatted with Drs. Byrne and Spencer at the sunken sports bar at the Hilton Hotel where he was staying, a football game playing on the thirty-five-inch television.

"How soon can we begin, Barry?" John asked.

"We need to schedule a surgeon, an anesthesiologist to implant the ports," Byrne said, referring to the tubes that allow regular infusions without sticking patients each time and stressing their already fragile veins.

"Getting the contracts signed by company and the university usually takes some time," Spencer added.

"I'm in charge of the program, and I'll make sure it gets done quickly," John said firmly. Then, with a little less certainty, he asked, "Can we stick a needle in their arms and infuse them first and do the surgery later?"

"We could. But why would you?" Byrne asked slowly, putting his drink down on the table.

"Once the children are infused with enzyme, the trial has officially started and nobody is going to stop it. Until then, I'm worried someone at Genzyme or somewhere else is going to think of some reason again for a delay."

"I don't know if I can get everything lined up to begin the trial next week," Byrne said, after a pause. "But I'll give it a shot."

On Monday afternoon, John was in his Princeton office, talking on the phone making arrangements to rent medical equipment and a handicapped van in Gainesville, when Landy called.

"How are you, Hal?" John said, trying to sound casual as he covered his eyes with his free hand. God, he hoped the news of the Florida trial hadn't yet traveled to Cambridge.[5]

"Not well, John," Landy said. His voice seethed with barely contained rage. "We just got a call from Barry Byrne's office about shipping drug to Florida. What is the meaning of this? What the hell do you mean by doing this?" It was Landy's job, not John's, to write and submit applications for clinical trials.

"Hal, you knew we were looking for Plan Bs," John said weakly.

"I didn't know you'd gotten hospital approval," Landy snapped. "I haven't even seen the protocol. John—what the *fuck* are you doing?"

"Calm down, Hal," John said. "I'll come up there and we'll work this out."

"'*Calm down*'?!" Landy erupted. "You have no idea. People here are very upset. You have no idea of the trouble this is causing. This place is in an uproar!"

"I'm sorry, Hal," John said quietly. "Of course we want your approval and guidance. I'm sure we can work this out. I'll come up in the morning and we'll figure this out."

"'*Work this out*'?" Landy repeated incredulously, shouting again. "You have no idea—you have *no* idea what you've done. John, you may have jeopardized your chances of ever getting your kids treated."

26. "You Can Tell Megan"

FALL 2002

CAMBRIDGE, MASSACHUSETTS; PRINCETON, NEW JERSEY

The next morning, Dr. Landy sat in his office shaking his head as he read the protocol that had been approved for the clinical trial in Florida. His anger had subsided, and he was beginning to blame himself for what had happened. He should have gotten John's kids treated sooner. It was actually remarkable, he thought, that John had maintained his objectivity for so long. How could he have missed the fact that John was going over the edge?[1]

But the more he read of the Florida protocol, the more certain he became that he could not go along with it. It was markedly different in several areas from the Sibling Study he had put together—most notably in the number of patients that would be enrolled. Byrne's protocol said they would enroll up to six patients, when the Sibling Study was set up for just two.

While he scrolled through the document, John appeared at his door, looking downcast and apologetic. "John, this protocol is completely different," Landy burst out, pointing to his computer screen. He scrolled down the document to highlight each section that varied. "You can't just submit things. We have standard protocols. We have quality control checks. This is not the Sibling Study."

"But this will solve the conflict-of-interest question," John said.

"But we don't have drug for six kids," Landy said heatedly.

"We do have extra drug—one of the children in the Duke trial died. We don't have to enroll all six children at once. We could start with three and add more if the drug supply improves. There's every indication it will. The bioreactors are producing drug well."

Landy shook his head. He pointed to other differences. "The preclinical section describes results of animal experiments using the Novazyme enzyme instead of Genzyme's," he noted, angry again.

"We can fix everything. I'll make all the changes you want. I'll make it two patients, I'll take out the Novazyme animal stuff, I'll change the cardiac end point," John said, pleading. "It'll take me an hour on the word processor."

"You can't do it. We have strict protocols," Landy said, adamant.

"Okay—let your team do it. Barry says he can send a notice of amendment to his review board this week," John said.

"We don't have the resources to do it so quickly," Landy said. "We're stretched to the limit with 1602 and 1702," the two main clinical trials whose protocols the company planned to submit to the FDA the next month.

John stopped, realizing suddenly that Landy had meant what he'd said the previous night. He didn't intend to allow the Florida trial to go forward. And he, John, didn't have the power to force Landy's hand—at least not without some help.

John walked up the stairs to van Heek's office, hoping to convince him to overrule Landy. Van Heek listened as John described what had happened, not asking a single question. When John had finished, van Heek said soothingly but unconvincingly, "I'm sure, John, that we can work this out." Then he stood up, signaling he had another meeting. As John walked out of the office, he knew van Heek was not going to come to his rescue this time.

What John didn't know was that Henri and the rest of Genzyme's senior management had already heard about the Florida mess. Henri had personally phoned Landy to reassure him that he—and not John—had authority over all clinical trials involving Pompe disease, including the Sibling Study. "John can't be trusted on this one—you are going to have to hold the line," Henri said. "We agree with you that John has gone too far this time."[2]

* * *

The next evening, the phone rang in Genzyme's satellite office, the same colonial on Nassau Street in Princeton that John had rented for Novazyme. It was Genzyme's soft-spoken general counsel, Tom DesRosier, delivering "an off-the-record heads-up" that two other lawyers would be calling in a few minutes to ask him some questions. Before long, the attorneys were on the line telling John they were following up on complaints he'd violated company rules by submitting the protocol to the University of Florida without getting the required sign-offs.

"Guys, off the record—I think this is bullshit," John fumed. But for the next fifteen minutes he patiently answered their questions.[3]

John sat at his desk for the next hour, uncertain what to do. As a lawyer himself, he knew the questions about violating internal rules would go nowhere. But he realized not only had he lost the Florida battle, but his credibility as a leader of the Pompe program had also taken a big hit. Unless he pulled back, he would lose his job—and his influence, however small, over the clinical trials of the Pompe drug. He sat down at his computer and began typing, pausing with every few words.

"I know there has been a lot of discussion regarding the treatment of my children. I'm sorry for any confusion it has caused," he wrote. "As we all know, the most important thing is that the entire program continue to move forward. There is a perception that my children's trial is interfering with the larger program. I will let the doctors in Florida know we are withdrawing the request for treating my children. We can revisit the Sibling Trial after the 1602 and 1702 studies have been submitted to the FDA," he finished.[4]

By the time John had finished, the rest of the staff had left for the day and the office was quiet. He read over his e-mail again, staring at the screen, not wanting to give up on the Florida trial that had seemed so close only two days ago. Finally, he looked at the clock and saw it was 6:30 P.M. As usual, he was late heading home. He hit the "send" button and left the office. More than anything that had happened on this horrible day, he dreaded the task that lay ahead.

* * *

John arrived at home and went right to his study. Aileen, who usually let him stay there, stepped inside and stood by his desk until he looked up from his computer.

"How was your day?" she asked tentatively, having picked up on his vibes enough to know something was wrong—again—with the trial plans.

"Long day," he said noncommittally, looking back at the computer screen.

"What's the deal with Florida? Sharon and I have been packing all day. We need to know when we're leaving."

"We'll get the kids treated, but not now. Just give me more time," he said, still avoiding her eyes.

"How much time?" she asked.

"I don't know," he said, wearily. "At least another month until I can get another study up and running."

He sighed and looked up. Aileen's green eyes glazed and then hardened. "Okay, John, two things," she said, her voice thin and without emotion. "Next time, just tell me when we're ready to get in the car and drive to the hospital." She turned to walk briskly from the room.

At the door, she paused. "And one more thing—you can tell Megan." Without looking at him, she walked out the door and disappeared.

John followed her to the playroom, where Megan sat at the computer playing a Barbie Princess game. He pulled up a chair beside her and reminded himself not to get too emotional.

"Honey, you know we're really, really close to getting you Special Medicine," he said.

Megan backed up her chair quickly and swirled around to face him. "Yes, we're going to Florida," she said, nodding.

"Well, Special Medicine is almost ready, I'm just trying to make it perfect," he said. "I just wanted to tell you that Special Medicine is taking a little longer to get ready so we won't be going to Florida this week. It's going to take a little more time."

Megan lowered her chin on her hand and rested it there, sitting silently for a minute, eyes lowered.

"I'm sorry, honey," John said.

Without a word, Megan turned and resumed her game.

As John walked slowly across the kitchen back to his study, his heart raced and his stomach tightened. He had trouble catching his breath. A wave of nausea swept over him, a mix of anger and anxiety. Someone at Genzyme should have been forced to tell Megan. Why couldn't Aileen or someone else have helped out by telling her? Why did everything end up on his shoulders?

The phone was ringing in his study. He picked it up, knowing it would be van Heek, who had been trying to reach him all day. "John, I've got a bad feeling about all of this," van Heek said. "I'm so sorry, I wish there was something I could do to help. I wish I could help, but my hands are tied."[5]

"It's all right, Jan," John said tiredly. Even soothing other people's consciences came down to him. "I know it's not your fault."

The weekend was a struggle. Aileen had arranged for the family to go to pick pumpkins as they did every year, but even she wasn't able to get up much enthusiasm. The family returned home Saturday afternoon with ten pumpkins but absent the annual picture of everyone in the pumpkin patch.

John barely slept Saturday night and awoke Sunday to the sound of a car horn. He raced down the stairs in his boxers to find the day nurse blaring her horn trying to get someone to wake up and let her in.

"Couldn't you knock?" he said to her. She ignored him and started up the stairs. A few minutes later, John overheard her admonishing Aileen for locking the door that was usually left open. John's temper flared and he marched down the hall shouting, "Get the fuck out. Now. And I promise you, you will never, ever return here." She'd been with them for almost four years.

Megan, who was in the room with the nurse, began to cry, and John regretted having lost his temper. "Oh Megan, it's okay," he said softly, giving her a hug. "Even big people have disagreements."

An hour later, John Jr. noticed someone missing in the usual Sunday lineup and asked, "Where's the nurse?"

"She quit," John said, the words tumbling out before he realized he was lying in the presence of a rather outspoken witness.

"Oh no, that's not what happened," Megan said, wagging her finger at him slyly. "Daddy told her, 'Get the fuck out of here.' "

John did a double-take, then laughed out loud. "You stop that, Megan," he said, as seriously as he could, "before I tell Mommy what word you just used."

"Don't tell Mommy," she said, nervously. "Please, please, Daddy, I won't ever say that word again."

By firing the nurse, John had ruined Aileen's plans for the two of them to take John Jr. on a trip to her nephew's sixth birthday party in Scranton, Pennsylvania. Now Aileen (a better nurse than John) had to stay home with Megan and Patrick while he went to the party with John Jr.

But even backing out of the driveway proved too much for John that day. He heard a crunch and then a loud pop, jumping out of the car to find he'd driven over the portable TV set for the handicapped van. He kicked the back bumper, shouting, "I hate this car, I hate the nurses . . . I hate this disease."

Aileen came over from the doorway, where she had been waving good-bye, and wordlessly pulled John into her arms. They stood together, clinging to each other, until John Jr. climbed out of the backseat and flung himself at them, shouting, "Cool—group hug!"

27. Ready to Run

WINTER 2002–SPRING 2003
CAMBRIDGE, MASSACHUSETTS; NEW BRUNSWICK, NEW JERSEY;
PRINCETON, NEW JERSEY

On Monday morning, Dr. Landy sat in a conference room in Genzyme's headquarters in Cambridge with a dozen other members of the Pompe leadership team, waiting for John to show up. John was usually the first one there, ebullient, chatty, teasing McKinney or telling a funny story about his kids until the full team was assembled. They had read John's letter that morning with relief and sadness. Landy wondered what shape John would be in. An uneasy silence prevailed.[1]

When John finally appeared—a quarter hour late—he looked tired and drawn. He was dressed impeccably in his usual navy suit and red tie, scrubbed, every hair combed into place, but Landy could see plainly that his eyes were sunken, his posture was slumped and weary, his skin had broken out in acne. He went briskly to the podium, unsmiling and business-like, and then led the group through the usual round of updates from subcommittee chairmen on manufacturing and clinical trial planning. The bioreactors were working well. The clinical trial protocols were almost ready to be mailed to the FDA. Dr. Kishnani, who was running the clinical trials at Duke, was reporting very encouraging results in her eight-patient trial at the end of one year of therapy. John played a video she had sent that showed two one-year-old boys in diapers, sitting, standing, walking, and even climbing up stairs.[2]

The news was almost all positive, but there were few questions and no laughs. Like Landy, most people in the group had come to like John and they were embarrassed by the Florida debacle. John made only one reference to what had happened, about an hour into the meeting. "We'll deal with Megan and Patrick after we get the filings done on the two main trials," he said crisply, echoing the e-mail from Friday night that they had all read by now.

Landy approached John during a break and said, "Thanks for sending that e-mail. I think it was the right thing to do." When the meeting was over, he asked John if he would come to his office and apologize to some members of his staff who were still upset. John hated the idea, but dutifully followed Landy around his department, thinking he had no choice if his children were to stand a chance of being treated. "I'm sorry if I let you down and put you in a difficult position," John said to one person after another.

Landy's anger had subsided, and he felt mostly sorry for John. He hoped John's apology would calm some of the younger people in his department who were still consumed by a self-righteous rage that John had gone behind their backs to set up the trial for his children. Perhaps, thought Landy, only those who had children and experienced firsthand the depth of a father's love could appreciate why John Crowley had gone to Florida. The more he thought about it, the more he appreciated the restraint it took for John to wait as long as he had for a treatment. By this point, John had been at Genzyme almost thirteen months.

That afternoon, determined to find a way to treat John's kids, Landy called members of Genzyme's sales team in New Jersey and asked if they would check with doctors and hospitals they worked with in the Princeton area to see if any might be willing to run the Sibling Study. Then he returned to his main job—trying to finish and submit the protocols for the two main clinical trials to the FDA for approval.

As always, another crisis erupted, this one having nothing to do with John. A health minister from Spain was on the phone, begging Landy to send some of the extremely scarce experimental treatment to a baby dying of Pompe disease in Madrid. Desperate entreaties from parents were an almost daily experience for Landy and others at Genzyme. He politely told the minister there was barely enough experimental drug to run the upcoming clinical trials. "I'm very sorry to tell you Genzyme will not be able to provide drug for this child."[3]

But the Spanish health officials didn't stop there. They called Henri; they reached out to van Heek; they beseeched John. Soon the U.S. ambassador to Spain was calling all of them. European governments not only were more lenient in their approval of the use of experimental treatments on dying patients, they were not above pressuring companies to make medicines available. European health officials held enormous sway over drug approval—and pricing—and the company couldn't afford to alienate them. Genzyme's leadership worried that the company would face retribution—that their drug approval would be held up or their pricing questioned—if they didn't figure out a way to get drug to the child.[4]

Van Heek told John to make the arrangements to send a shipment of the Pompe enzyme to Spain. Scarcely a month earlier, at van Heek's instruction, John had coordinated another shipment, under pressure from the government of Italy. The Italian media had been carrying almost daily stories about a couple who had chained themselves to the gate of a hospital and were vowing to starve themselves until Genzyme produced some of its experimental medicine to save their two-year-old daughter Rosella. Pictures of the health minister presenting the Genzyme enzyme to Rosella appeared everywhere.[5]

Back in September, John had been excited for Rosella and also for himself, believing Megan and Patrick would be next. But now there were no immediate plans for his children, and he was being asked to ship more of the scarce enzyme to someone else's child.

The Spanish press covered police escorting the Genzyme officials carrying the drug to Gregorio Maranon Hospital to save the baby. The irony consumed and depressed him. He could be a hero to a kid he'd never met thousands of miles away when he couldn't do the same for his own children. Genzyme and the Children's Hospital of Philadelphia were trying so hard to avoid being accused of favoritism—and yet here were other families using political influence to get to the front of the line. Influence peddling pervaded life. Would his children have been already treated if he'd gone on a hunger strike instead of starting a drug company? Had his position as head of the Pompe program at Genzyme become more of an obstacle than a stepping-stone to a treatment for his children?

*   *   *

Days later, John was jolted out of his self-pity by an e-mail from a relative of Greg Assink saying his daughter Kelsey had died. She was nine years old and had the same nonclassical infantile form of Pompe disease as Megan and Patrick.

John and Aileen decided to attend her funeral. Not only was Greg a long and ardent supporter, having flown to a fund-raiser carrying $20,000 in checks, and attended the Pompe Summit at Genzyme, but John and Aileen also considered him to be their friend. They were about the same age, and John and Greg had an easy understanding.

Because of John's schedule, he and Aileen flew separately to Grand Rapids, Michigan. They met at the airport and drove together to the wake in Hudsonville, a suburb. As they neared the town, John told Aileen he had thought of a way to offer some hope to the Assink family. Greg and Deborah's youngest, the baby they had named after the Crowleys' Megan, had also been diagnosed with Pompe. "Think how thrilled they would be if they knew Genzyme planned to begin clinical trials early next year," John said. "Think how thrilled they would be if they knew their Megan would definitely qualify." Genzyme, like most drug companies, kept plans for trials quiet—particularly because the company hadn't even submitted its application to the FDA. "I'm thinking of telling them about the trials and guaranteeing them a place for Megan," John said.

"Are you sure you should do that?" Aileen asked. She knew firsthand the agony of dashed expectations, and she had also learned how little John really controlled what happened at Genzyme.

Before he could answer, the car pulled up outside the funeral home. Inside, they joined the end of a long receiving line. Hundreds of people were in attendance. As the line wound its way around the room, John and Aileen stared at Kelsey's life documented in poster-sized pictures propped on easels.

There she was, a blond, blue-eyed one-year-old, sitting up and looking almost normal except for the usual sign of Pompe—her tongue not quite fitting in her mouth. Just like Megan and Patrick.

There she was as a five-year-old in a wheelchair, tubes coiling from the tracheotomy in her throat to the ventilator propped underneath. Just like Megan and Patrick.

There was Kelsey on her Make a Wish trip to Disney World, surrounded by her parents, siblings, grandparents, and nurses. Just like Megan and Patrick.

The parallels between the two families were unavoidable. John and Aileen couldn't look at each other. They stood, holding hands, wiping away tears. They were thinking the same thing: unless their children got a drug soon, they would be at the front of a receiving line like this. It was only a matter of time—weeks or months.

It took an hour for John and Aileen to reach the front of the line. Greg threw himself into John's arms and wept. As they hugged, John whispered, "Please keep this quiet, Greg, but a study next year is going to be for kids under age three. It'll begin in just about two months. And I promise you, your little Megan will be in the study."[6]

"Oh my God," Greg burst out, immediately forgetting John's urging to keep the news to himself. "Deb, Mom, Dad, everyone, this is John Crowley and this is Aileen Crowley. John has some wonderful news for us. The clinical trials are going to start in the next few months and our Megan will definitely qualify. We don't know how to thank you."

On the drive back to the airport, Aileen asked, "How the hell are you going to guarantee Megan Assink a placement? Aren't there always a million criteria for determining who qualifies? Isn't this all up to Hal and those other people at Genzyme? You can't even get your own kids treated."

"I don't know how, Aileen, but I know I'm going to do it," John said. "I can only imagine Hal's horrified reaction if he ever knew. But you know what—it felt so good to be able to offer hope to that good and very decent family that I just don't care what Hal or anyone else thinks."

A few days before Thanksgiving, Landy called John and asked him to send Megan's medical records to a physician at Saint Peter's University Hospital in New Brunswick, New Jersey, named Debra-Lynn Day-Salvatore.

"And John, you need to stay out of it and let us do everything," Landy said, his voice firm.

John—being John—drove Megan's medical records over to the hospital himself the next day. It was only about twenty miles from his home in Princeton. Carrying a big cardboard box, he wound his way through the corridors to Dr. Day-Salvatore's office and knocked on the door.

The door opened to reveal a tall, slender woman with the unconscious grace of a ballerina.

"Hi, I'm John Crowley. I'm just dropping off my daughter's medical records," John said.[7]

"I'm Dr. Day-Salvatore," the woman answered, her voice just a little louder than a whisper. "Please, come on in."

John dropped the box beside the desk in Day-Salvatore's tiny office. The office shelves were filled with books and pictures of her patients, some of whom John recognized as children with Pompe. She seemed as curious about him and his children as he was about her and her hospital. She asked not only about Megan's and Patrick's medical history, but also about their day-to-day lives.

"Is Megan in school?"

"She just started kindergarten this fall. She loves it and the kids love her," John said. "She's so popular. Our nickname for her is 'The Mayor.' She likes to be in charge, and she bosses everyone around. She has lots of friends. The kids seem to treat her just like any other kid, even though she's in a wheelchair and has her nurse with her at all times, of course."

"I can see you're very proud of your daughter," Day-Salvatore said, chuckling kindly. "How about Patrick? I know he's weaker. Does he go to school, too?"

"He's in preschool three days a week. Tollgate Grammar School. They have a handicapped program in Hopewell."

"I see," Day-Salvatore said. She cleared her throat, looking sympathetically at him across the piles of papers on her desk. "I know you've had some real challenges getting your kids the drug." She had heard from Landy about the debacle at Children's Hospital.

"Yes, it's been really hard," John said without elaborating. There was so much history involved with explaining to anyone the obstacles he'd overcome in his fight for his children—only to have more thrown his way—that these days it was just easier to agree. "I just want to get my babies better."

"I'd very much like to treat your children," Day-Salvatore said, as John struggled to compose himself. "Our clinical trial review board is going to meet on December 19 to review your children's protocol."

The next morning, John called van Heek to say he wanted to leave Genzyme a couple of weeks earlier than he'd planned. He told van Heek he wanted to be sure he was no longer a Genzyme employee when the St. Peter's board met to review the clinical trial. Van Heek, who had known John intended to leave at the end of the year, understood completely. The two men then negotiated the terms of John's severance package, the combination of benefits corporations often give senior management on leaving a job. John proposed a year's salary and, most important, an extension of his family's health benefits during that time. On joining Novazyme, he had held on to excellent health coverage at Bristol-Myers under the federal government's COBRA program, which allowed people leaving jobs to continue their health insurance at the same level of coverage for one year, plus another eleven months if they were disabled. Before joining Genzyme, John had negotiated for comparable health benefits for his children, and now he was hoping to extend those for another nearly two and a half years—one year through the severance package, and another year and a half through COBRA. Van Heek eventually agreed. The quarter after John left, Genzyme claimed a charge of $4.2 million against John's severance package—$4 million of that for the children's future medical expenses, each estimated at nearly $1 million annually.[8]

On December 24, a Christmas card containing several sheets of paper arrived at the Crowley house addressed to John. On the front was a picture of the Virgin Mary in blue, clasping a sweetly sleeping baby Jesus to her breast, smiling and shining with the promise of salvation. "You asked for something to put under your Christmas tree," the note accompanying the card said. "I hope the enclosed approval letter will help fill that void." It was signed, "Dr. Debra-Lynn Day-Salvatore." Inside, the doctor had enclosed a copy of her hospital review board's two-page letter approving the clinical trial for Megan and Patrick. Her hospital was willing to take the risk—the trial would begin on January 9.[9]

When John had wiped the tears from his cheeks, he put the card and approval letter back in the envelope and propped them prominently on a branch of the tree.

That night, after the children went to bed, John and Aileen sat down at their enormous new round dining-room table with Aileen's parents, her brother Brian, cousin Kevin, and their wives Kim and Lisa. John stood up and made a toast.

"Here's to a year of good health for all," he said. "And I have a little something to share." John began to read from Day-Salvatore's card. Before he finished, the relatives were crying and hugging John and Aileen.

On January 9, 2003, Megan and Patrick, wearing matching baby blue hospital gowns printed with red clowns, lay in rooms next to one another in the pediatric intensive care unit at St. Peter's. They had undergone surgery days earlier to have tubes inserted in their chests to make regular infusions possible. They had had biopsies performed on their legs to have a little muscle removed so the amount of glycogen could be measured and compared after they finished a year of treatment. The surgeries had been exhausting for them and for their surgeons. Megan's muscles were so badly degenerated that it took the surgeon two hours to find a piece he could remove. Patrick's blood pressure had fallen so low that he almost died during the grueling, three-hour procedure. Seeing Aileen waiting alone outside the operating room, the surgeon pointed his finger in her face and said, "This was a terrible thing to do to that baby. You better tell me this treatment is going work."

At 9 A.M., Aileen, John, Sharon, and a dozen family members and friends crowded into Megan's room, waiting expectantly. Megan was supposed to get her infusion first because she was the more communicative and could better report any immediate side effects. Aileen's parents and John's mother and stepfather had come, as had Aileen's cousin Kevin, brother Brian, and their wives and children. John told them all that his father would have turned sixty-three today, had he been alive. John's friend Ed held the video camera, poised to record the event they had awaited, prayed for, and dreamed of for five long years.[10]

A nurse hung a plastic bag filled with a clear liquid on an IV post to Megan's right. Day-Salvatore nodded that they were ready to go. Megan sat propped up in bed, a pink stuffed dog named Nosey that Ed had given her tucked under her knees. "Who wants to press the button?" the doctor said. John pointed to Aileen.

"Oh, no—you're going to be the one, John," Aileen said. John took a deep breath, looked around the room, and lifted his right hand to a switch and pressed the "on" button. He saw the switch open and the clear liquid begin dripping. He looked at Aileen, her eyes full of tears, and without a word pulled her into his arms and kissed her.

Megan's heart monitor began to beep and the parents realized that their little girl, overwhelmed by the emotion of the moment, was also starting to cry. As they rushed to either side of her, she lifted one arm and waved apprehensively, and soon everyone was laughing through their tears.

"Now for our little redheaded stepchild next door," Aileen said, still sniffling. She and John led the entourage into the next room and waited for a nurse to bring in Patrick's bag of medicine. As a male nurse put a clear plastic bag on the IV pole to Patrick's left, John joked, "Careful there. That bag cost $200 million," his estimate of what Genzyme had spent developing the drug.[11]

When Day-Salvatore signaled they were ready to go, Patrick lay in bed, not even registering the presence of the group, his eyes trained on a Sponge Bob cartoon on the television monitor overhead. In one hand, he clutched his favorite toy, a little stuffed Santa Claus. "He hates all the noise and attention," Aileen explained to the group, bending down to kiss his forehead. "He's pretending we're not even here." She stepped forward and pressed the button on his IV, beginning the infusion. Then she turned to kiss John again. As they hugged, Ed put the camera down and went over to embrace them.

Later that day, as Ed and John stood chatting in the corridor outside the children's rooms, Ed said, "You and Aileen look happy again, John. I'm really happy to see that."

John nodded, quiet for a few seconds, and said, "You know, I don't really know how it happened, but somehow I stopped blaming Aileen. Not immediately, but very slowly, over time, we forgave each other. Never in a million years could I imagine myself with anyone else. Not after what we've been through."

"I have to say, I wasn't sure today was ever going to happen, John," Ed said. "This is really an incredible day."

"It's different from how I had imagined it so many times over the years," John said. "There are no bells, no trumpets, no bright lights. There are just two little sick kids who desperately need some Special Medicine. No more—no less. And that's how it should be."[12]

The children's first infusion lasted four hours. They both grew flushed and peed nonstop, but that was the only side effect. An hour into Megan's infusion, the phone rang on the table beside her bed. Aileen picked up and passed the phone to Megan. Her kindergarten teacher, Mr. Fletcher, was on the line, with her eighteen classmates by his side, waiting to talk to her.

"Oh, hi, Mr. Fletcher," Megan said, holding the receiver. "Everything's going fine here. Can I talk to Sophie? Okay, good, Sophie. Can you put Carly on the phone?" And down the line Megan went for the next half hour, talking to every classmate.

When the infusions ended, the children were so energized they couldn't sleep. Megan sat up and played with her Barbie dolls with Aileen until past midnight. Day-Salvatore said it was a good sign. It meant the experimental enzyme was metabolizing glycogen and turning it into energy. Aileen beamed, thinking that perhaps this was the first time since the children were born that they were experiencing a sugar rush, like any other kid who ate too much ice cream. The next day, the children stayed in the hospital to be sure there weren't any side effects. They would need to return to St. Peter's for an infusion every two weeks for the foreseeable future.

For the next few weeks, the big question behind each child's every movement was how well Special Medicine was working. In the trials thus far using Chen's and Pharming's version of the enzyme, it had worked on some children but not on others. It appeared to be more effective if the children produced at least a little bit of naturally active enzyme so that the body didn't greet the infused enzyme as a foreign substance. That was a hopeful sign for Megan and Patrick, who both made a minuscule amount of active enzyme. But also in the trials, the children who received the enzyme therapy when they were only a few months old—before their muscles were substantially damaged—seemed to do far better than those who were treated as toddlers and older, which didn't bode well for the Crowley children. It didn't appear that muscles damaged beyond a certain point could regenerate. The first round of tests was scheduled for early April, three months after the first infusion.

That winter and early spring, John accompanied Megan to school on some days and played nurse for Patrick on others, trying to make up for the lost time with them during the past three years. "You should come on a day when I have P.E.," Megan said. "P.E.'s my favorite."

So the next Monday, a P.E. day, John followed Megan onto the handicapped school bus that picked her up at 8 A.M. in front of the house. She wore her new Nike sneakers and a pink sweat suit, even though she knew she wouldn't be getting out of her wheelchair that day. "Wrong shoes," she told her dad, frowning at his loafers.

Megan's kindergarten class was taught by a distinguished, grandfatherly, and very funny teacher named Mr. Fletcher. He'd been around the school so long and was so beloved that the parents and his colleagues just called him "Fletch." He was a veteran teacher who swore every year would be his last. Sitting in a rocking chair in the front of the room, he spent the morning reviewing the days of the week with the children.

"What comes after Tuesday?" he asked, looking around at the students seated in a circle around him.[13]

John looked over at Megan, in the back row to his left, and saw she was staring out the window.

"Hey, Gertrude," Mr. Fletcher called, picking up on the name Sharon had called Meagan for so long no one remembered exactly why. "Why don't you help us here?" Mr. Fletcher knew Sharon well since she usually accompanied Megan to school.

Megan looked at him with a blank stare.

"Did you hear the question?" he asked.

"No," she admitted, shaking her head.

"I asked you what day comes after Tuesday. What's the matter, Gertrude, are you deaf now, too?"

"Oh, that's easy. Wednesday," Megan responded, oblivious to Mr. Fletcher's sarcastic reference to her handicaps. John laughed, delighted.

The wiseass in him liked the teacher's sense of humor and the way he held Megan accountable.

At P.E. time, John watched Steve Hennessey, the gym teacher who moonlighted as a guitar player at children's parties, divide the students into two teams, wearing either red or blue mesh jerseys. John, standing a few feet behind Mr. Hennessey, couldn't follow the rules, but the kids seemed to know what they were doing.[14]

Mr. Hennessey blew the whistle, and Megan, with her blue teammates, raced across the gym. When a child tripped and fell in front of Megan's wheelchair, John held his breath, waiting for the crash and the screams that would surely follow. But she swerved left and out of the way, careening into the path of some other kid, who screamed, "Watch out! Megan!" The whole group on Megan's left leaped out of the way.

Megan approached the wall at a sprint, brought her chair to an abrupt halt, holding her head with her left hand as she spun around, and accelerated back.

"We won," she yelled from the end of the blue line, pumping her left arm and looking at her dad.

John waved, giving her a thumbs-up. Mr. Hennessey turned to John and smiled. "She's a chip off the old block," John said proudly.

That night, as he and Aileen ate dinner, John said, "You know, watching Megan in P.E., I realized that she really doesn't see herself as handicapped in any way. She thinks she's just like the rest of them."

"Are you kidding me? She doesn't think she's just like them," Aileen laughed. "She thinks she's a little superior!"

In early April, John and Aileen sat with Dr. Day-Salvatore in a corner of the large, second-floor hospital room where the children were receiving their now-regular infusions, oblivious to the import of the day. Day-Salvatore held up an echocardiogram that showed Megan's heart before the infusion—swollen to twice the normal size for a child her age. In the second picture, Megan's heart had shrunk to nearly a normal size. Her liver, so swollen with glycogen that she had had an enormous Buddha belly, was inside the normal range, too. She'd lost eight inches from her waistline.[15]

Day-Salvatore had painstakingly measured the strength of Megan's skeletal muscles before her infusion and again last week. The scale ran from one to five, a one indicating a flicker of movement, and a five for normal strength. Before the infusion, Dr. Day-Salvatore had measured Megan's neck muscle at a two. Now it was at a three. Megan's shoulders had gone from a two and a half to a three. Even her very weak legs had shown a little improvement—her ankles had increased in strength from one to one and a half.

"The results for Megan are very promising," the doctor said.

"This is great news, Dr. Day-Salvatore," John said.

"What about Patrick?" asked Aileen.

The doctor hesitated and then said, "Unfortunately, Patrick's results are less promising." Patrick's heart, like Megan's, swollen to twice its size, had declined in size, but only slightly. His skeletal muscles had registered virtually no gain in strength. "He may just be slower to respond, so I'm not giving up hope yet," the doctor said. "But we don't have the same results for him that we have for Megan."

John and Aileen sat silently for a second, feeling both elated and deflated. The news was so good for Megan that they wanted to celebrate; but it was so disappointing for Patrick that they wanted to cry. And yet they were not surprised. Megan's progress had been plain for everyone to see. As her liver shrunk, her belly had gone down in size daily—Sharon had measured the decline with a tape. Everyone had noticed that Megan could once again hold her head up and sit unassisted. She was making remarkable progress.

Patrick, on the other hand, didn't seem markedly different in his physical abilities. Everyone hoped that even though there was no outward difference, good things were happening inside to his heart and liver. But Day-Salvatore's results made clear that was not the case—at least not yet. She had opened up the chilling possibility that their children were heading in different directions. One might live and one might die.

Even the bad news for Patrick couldn't contain John's excitement over Megan's good results. He carried the echocardiogram over to her bed to show her how much her heart size had declined. "See Megan, this is how big your heart was before Special Medicine," he said, holding the picture in front of *Chrysanthemum*, the book she had been reading. "See here, this is how much smaller it is now." He hugged her and said, "You know what this means? It means you're gonna live to be an old lady."

Aileen went over to Patrick, who was pretend fighting with two little plastic action figures. She picked up his hand, kissed it, and said, "Now Patrick, you just tell that heart of yours to listen to what Special Medicine has to say, okay? We need to get Special Medicine working a little better in you."

For the rest of the spring and summer, Megan continued to gain strength. Aileen called John down to the kitchen one afternoon to show him that Megan could sit unassisted on a barstool. When Megan raised her hand to answer a question in class, Mr. Fletcher pointed out to Sharon that her arm shot straight up in the air where before she could only raise her hand shoulder high. "Next time I look around, Gertrude, you're going to be touching the ceiling," he said.[16]

Taking a family picture one day, John saw through the digital camera lens that Megan's cheeks were raised into a smile for the first time in two years. Aileen insisted she saw a difference in Patrick as well, not so much in physical strength, but in mood. He seemed more comfortable, more communicative; he now actively played with his toys more than passively watching TV.

After five grueling years, John suddenly had no job, no schedule. His last day at Genzyme, December 19, had been a quiet affair—no big luncheons or speeches. A few colleagues stopped by to shake his hand and wish him well as he packed his pictures of Aileen and the kids and some mementos. Now, his tiny office forever behind him, he had more free time than he knew what to do with. He volunteered to teach Megan's religious education class at St. Paul's, signed up for Italian lessons, and began training for the Marine Corps Marathon. He indulged his passion for fine cars—adding a Mercedes E55 Sedan to the Jaguar convertible he had bought a few months earlier. He and Aileen took long weekends away in Tucson and Las Vegas. They even left the kids for a full week and flew to Ireland with Aileen's parents and John's Uncle Jim and Aunt Marie.

And one bright July afternoon, as John washed the convertible in the driveway, Megan came whirring out in her wheelchair to watch.

"I wanna go for a ride," she said, "but *first* you have to finish cleaning your car."

It had been years since John had taken Megan out alone in her handicapped van, let alone a car. She had been too weak to sit up even in a toddler car seat, and there were too many things that could go wrong with a child on a ventilator and the only adult occupied with driving. John studied her for a long moment. Megan seemed so much stronger he thought it was worth a try.

"Well, Princess, you arrived at just the right time," he said, with an exaggerated bow. He ran to the basement, brought up her old car seat, and strapped it into the passenger side of the car. Then he lifted Megan out of her wheelchair, strapped her into the seat, and pulled the car around to the front doorway.

When Aileen heard the horn blaring, she got up from the kitchen table where she was doing homework with little John while Patrick napped upstairs. She stepped out of the front door to find father and daughter in the convertible, smiling and waving. Her heart lurched to see them looking so happy and beautiful—her handsome husband with his youthful smile and thick, dark hair, and her spunky daughter with her naughty brown eyes and her penchant for pink. Aileen cupped her hands to her mouth and blew them a kiss.

"Ready, Megs?" John asked.

"Yeah!" his daughter said, motioning for him to turn up the sound on the CD player. Laughing, John amped up the volume and hit the accelerator. From the speakers, the Dixie Chicks sang out with exhilarating abandon.

The car pulled out of the driveway and peeled down the street, the riotous notes of Megan's newest favorite song, "Ready to Run," dissolving behind them on the warm summer air.

Afterword

I first met the Crowleys on April 27, 2001, when I visited them to write a story on Novazyme for the *Wall Street Journal*. I arrived at their two-story brick colonial in Pennington, New Jersey, in the late morning. John, preppy and enthusiastic in a blue polo shirt and khakis, burst out the front door and ran to the curb to greet me. His personal exuberance was so great that it actually caught me a little off guard. He led me into the den, where Megan, four, and Patrick, three, sat on a couch watching Barney on TV. It was a scene out of any suburban household—except that both kids had tubes coming out of their necks connected to microwave-sized ventilators on the floor, breathing for them.

Aileen appeared for a minute, smiling politely if distantly, and disappeared upstairs with Patrick. Megan gestured toward the front door and said something in a muffled voice. "Her electric wheelchair has just arrived and she wants to go outside and try it out," John translated. Sharon came in to attach Megan's ventilator tube to a smaller, portable one, and followed John and Megan outside. Her legs hung limply, swaying with the movement, as he carried her.

John fastened Megan into the seat belt of the bulky black wheelchair parked inside the garage. He explained the workings of the joystick near her right hand. "When you want to go left, you push that way. To go right, this way," he said, gesturing as he spoke. "For straight ahead, you push straight ahead."

Before he could finish, Megan took off. With John running behind— shouting, "I haven't showed you how to stop yet!"—Megan sped down the sidewalk, her powder blue cotton dress billowing in the wind. Her fearlessness and zest for life were striking even then.

I wrote a first story about the Crowleys and Novazyme that appeared in the *Wall Street Journal* in July 2001. And over the next year and a half, I called John every month asking about the children and how close they were to being treated. During that time, he sold Novazyme, became chief of the Pompe program at Genzyme, tried and failed to get his children into multiple clinical trials, and then finally resigned. His voice grew more strained, angry, and even desperate as the months went by.

Finally, in January 2003, an ebullient John called to say that Megan and Patrick were going to get their Special Medicine the next week. He invited me to join them for the first infusion in St. Peter's University Hospital in New Brunswick, New Jersey, a short train ride from Manhattan.

That August, two years after my first piece appeared, I wrote a second, longer one about the children being treated and growing stronger. It appeared on the front page of the *Wall Street Journal* and told of John's struggle against conflict-of-interest accusations and Genzyme's own internal protocols to get the experimental medicine to his children.

Readers wrote in for weeks, deeply moved, sympathetic, and awestruck. The story is a "testament to the strong undying drive of devoted parents," wrote one man. After reading the first few paragraphs, "I set my bag back in the trunk of my vehicle and proceeded to read the entire article leaning over my vehicle in the middle of the parking garage. As a doctoral student in the biomedical sciences with venture capital aspirations, your work touched a note on multiple bases beyond emotion," said another. The idea came up that it would make a wonderful book.

In January 2004, I began reporting and writing this book, and I've spent the past two and a half years interviewing the Crowleys, their friends and family, and almost everyone trying to develop a Pompe treatment. My daughters, Tatyana, eight, and Aleka, six, have accompanied me many times, playing with the Crowley kids while I talk to their parents.

"Megan is so cool," Tatyana said on the train home from our first visit, after a marathon game of hide and seek. A side benefit of the Crowleys' huge house is that Megan can actually find places to hide in her wheelchair. Indeed, Megan made using a wheelchair look like so much fun that Tatyana, as she reached the top of the steep flight that leads up to our apartment, turned around and asked, "If I fall down there and break my leg, can I get a wheelchair like Megan's?"

So much has happened since that summer afternoon in 2003, where the book ends, that I could easily fill a sequel—and maybe someday I will. But in the meantime, here's a synopsis of the past three years. They are, like this book, about the pace of biological discovery and the power of the profit motive to speed science into medicine, but equally, if not more important, about the resilience of hope and the enduring force of parental love.

For the first six months after receiving their Special Medicine in January 2003, Megan and Patrick continued to grow stronger. But toward the end of the year, the gains slowed, and by early 2004, John and Aileen noticed a slight decline in the children's skeletal muscle strength. When Megan stopped too abruptly, her head, once again, fell forward. She needed to use her hands to push her head back up. Patrick began to struggle again to grip his favorite Power Ranger figures to make them fight one another.

"Why aren't you getting stronger?" John found himself thinking, frustrated. Then he would remind himself that his children's hearts, so swollen before treatment that they posed the biggest risk to their survival, remained substantially stronger. Perhaps the drug had done all that it was meant to do—it had bought the children time.

With the well-known "success" of building and selling Novazyme, John was eagerly recruited by biotech and venture firms in the months after leaving Genzyme. He thought about retiring on his $6 million, but it wasn't in his nature to throw in the towel at the age of thirty-six. Besides, he had the children's future health care costs to think of.

In mid-2003, John began working with Domain Associates in Princeton, New Jersey, one of the oldest health care–focused venture capital firms in the country, as chief executive of a tiny start-up firm in which the fund had invested to develop obesity drugs, among others. This job is simple, he told me at the time with his boyish grin. "It's a helluva lot easier when it's just business and my kids' lives aren't at stake."

John's Novazyme and Genzyme experiences also made him the go-to guy for anyone with a potential treatment for Pompe. Even as he ran the two start-ups, he was in Florida one week, checking out Dr. Byrne's gene therapy; Utah the next, interrogating scientists about stem cell therapy; and Milwaukee at the end of the month, investigating an idea for improving enzyme replacement therapy.

Before long, John was on the boards of seven fledgling companies, five of them developing treatments for genetic diseases like Pompe. In the spring of 2004, the investors at one, Amicus Therapeutics in New Jersey, asked him to take over as CEO. He demurred, unwilling to back just one horse when he wasn't sure which one had the potential to win. There was too much at stake, and, as he told me, "I'm also emotionally not quite ready to get back into genetic diseases and Pompe every day." But he did agree to consult for Amicus one day each week to develop a strategic plan and lead the search to find a CEO.

The more John learned about Amicus's science, the more excited he became about its potential to help his children. As he'd known, most patients with Pompe don't entirely lack the acid alpha-glucosidase enzyme, they make it incorrectly, with the end result being that the body misidentifies and eventually discards it. Instead of trying to find a way to replace it, as Dr. Canfield had been, Amicus's founding scientists tried using chemicals that stabilized the acid alpha-glucosidase enzyme so that it isn't identified as errant and degraded. Scientists call these chemicals pharmacologic chaperones, because they bind to the defective enzymes, enabling them to survive and travel to the region of the cell where they are needed.

About 80 percent of Pompe patients, including Megan and Patrick, have imperfectly produced acid alpha-glucosidase enzyme. Most human genetic diseases involve similarly defective proteins.

In October 2004, John led a strategic planning session for the Amicus board in which they discussed the potential of pharmacologic chaperones to treat not only genetic diseases but many other disorders like Parkinson's and Alzheimer's. When the board again asked John to consider taking over as CEO, he couldn't turn it down. "Emotionally, I still really don't want to have to do this," John told me at the time. "But I think I have to. This technology could save the kids."

John described how, when he told Aileen he wanted to take the Amicus job, she took a deep breath, grew tearful, and said, "Here we go again. You know I'll support you in anything that could help the kids."

John phoned Henri Termeer, Genzyme's CEO, wanting to be the first to tell him he would be heading a company with a competing technology, but the older man surprised him. "I hear you're going to take the job after all,"[1] Henri said with a chuckle when he came on the line, beating John to the punch line.

"Word sure gets to you fast, Henri," John said, rueful and amused. Henri wished him well.

When John assumed the job of Amicus's CEO on January 3, 2005, the company was already fairly well funded. It had $15 million in the bank, even though there were only eight employees. Just as he had at Novazyme, he hired the consulting firm Health Advances to help write a business plan. Then he set off on a hiring spree. In the fifteen months since he started, John has brought in fifty new people, thirty-two of them Ph.Ds. Among his hires are several Novazyme alumni, including the new chief of biology, Hung Do, who was one of Canfield's top molecular biologists; the new corporate counsel, Doug Branch, the former Novazyme attorney; and the new chief of drug development, Pedro Huertas, who had been medical director at Novazyme.

Also in 2005, John raised $55 million for Amicus from several large venture capital firms. Sherrill Neff, who left Neose a few years ago, runs the venture fund that led the round. Neff joined Amicus's board. Stuart Kornfeld, Canfield's mentor and one of the discoverers of enzyme trafficking in lysosome, joined the company's scientific advisory board. His laboratory and Dr. Byrne's are performing experiments testing the potential of chaperone technology in different diseases. John hoped to take Amicus public in the summer of 2006 to raise another $75 million, with Morgan Stanley and Goldman Sachs as the lead bankers.

For John, even as the job is exhausting, it is also therapeutic, containing his frustration—and fear—at his children's slowly declining strength. Knowing he's doing everything he can to find a treatment to make them stronger, he can relax enough to let go of his fear of losing them and enjoy them.

"There are two differences from last time around," John told me. "I think this time, I actually know what I'm doing, from people to science to finance. I haven't screwed this one up," he said with a self-effacing laugh. "It's been stressful, but for general business reasons. Because of Megan and Patrick, there's a sense of urgency behind it, but I have a little different perspective. I realize the battle against Pompe is really a marathon and not a sprint. If you make it a sprint, you make mistakes and you burn out yourself and your team. I still set aggressive goals, and nobody in this company ever worked harder, but not in the exhaustive sense that the kids are going to die tomorrow if we don't do it. It helps that the kids have been relatively stable for the past two or three years. I also appreciate just how complex this disease is."

Amicus is already testing one of its potential chaperone drugs in patients with Fabry disease, a related disorder. John plans to begin trials in Pompe within the next year, and he hopes Megan and Patrick will be included.

Sharon still lives with the Crowleys during the week and commutes home to her husband and extended family in New England on most weekends. She is now over sixty years old, and it's becoming harder for her to lift Megan and Patrick as they keep growing. She recently hired Mr. Hennessey, Megan's P.E. teacher, to come over two afternoons a week and serve as her personal trainer.

About once a month, Sharon stays over the weekend so that Aileen can join John on a business trip. So far this year, Aileen has flown with John to San Diego and Las Vegas. For their fifteen-year anniversary last summer, Aileen joined John on a business trip to France, and they spent several days afterward touring Normandy.

"If you knew when we met what you know now—that all of this would happen to us—would you have still married me?" John asked Aileen one evening as they were falling asleep in their hotel room.

"Yes," Aileen said without missing a beat. "How about you?"

John was silent for a few seconds, and then replied, "Yes, Aileen, I would, too. I wouldn't give up these kids and this life with you for anything."

While they have come to accept that this disease may define the rest of their lives, they are content to find joy where it comes to them—in the long weekends Sharon's kindness allows them to take; in their children's enjoyment of each day; in the continued celebration of birthdays and holidays and the forward motion of their lives.

This past spring, Genzyme received approval from both the FDA and European regulatory authorities to market the Pompe therapy that Megan and Patrick continue to receive every two weeks. "This is a very special day for people across the Pompe community and at Genzyme who have worked together for many years and overcome enormous challenges so that patients with this devastating disease now have a chance," Henri Termeer said, in announcing the U.S. approval of the drug to be called Myozyme.

Even before the Pompe therapy was approved, Genzyme had vastly expanded the number of patients treated with Myozyme as production improved exponentially from the tough days of John's tenure there. More than two hundred and eighty patients have received the drug in trials and on compassionate use. Genzyme reports spending more than $500 million since 1998 in the development of the treatment, which Wall Street expects will be priced in the same range as the company's other genetic disease therapies—about $200,000 for the average patient annually.

Dr. Kishnani, of Duke, reporting on the trial in older babies and toddlers, said sixteen of the twenty-one (more patients were enrolled than planned) were still alive after a year of therapy. Ten had gained so much strength they could perform new motor functions—like holding their heads up, sitting, or even walking. Eleven were still able to breathe independently.[2]

But even in the trial results, it was clear that Megan and Patrick are not unique. Eleven children did not gain sufficient strength to perform new motor functions; five children died, and five who could breathe on their own at the start of the trial needed ventilators before the year was over. The results also show "that early initiation of (therapy) is of paramount importance in maximizing the chances of a favorable motor outcome," Dr. Kishnani wrote. Her results underscore what John and Aileen already know—that it is likely that Megan and Patrick would have gained much more strength on Myozyme had they been treated when they were younger and stronger.

Dr. Canfield remains a scientist at Genzyme, running the Glycobiology Research Institute, the name given to the former Novazyme business. Hung Do, before moving to Amicus, worked with Canfield and others at Genzyme to develop what they believe is a better version of Myozyme.

The results of the experiments they conducted may eventually vindicate Canfield about the importance of having the right carbohydrate chains—in this case, mannose-6 phosphate—attached to the enzyme for it to be taken into the lysosomes of muscle cells. The problem with Dr. Canfield's earlier version of the enzyme, scientists at Genzyme now believe, was that other sugars attached drew it elsewhere before it could get to the lysosomes of muscles. Besides avoiding that pitfall, the new enzyme is easier to produce. The carbohydrate chains are chemically fused onto Myozyme. In mouse experiments, the new version appears to be absorbed three to five times better.[3] Genzyme scientists say this is one of several new approaches that may evolve into a better second-generation treatment.

Tiffany House, who grew weaker when she was first moved off the Pharming enzyme and her dose was decreased, is feeling stronger on a higher dose.[4] She graduated last year with honors from the University of Texas in San Antonio, and this year enrolled in a master's program in English. She's still in a wheelchair and needs breathing support at night, but she's becoming more independent. Her parents drop her off at school, and she's on her own between classes, eating lunch and socializing, until she's picked up in the afternoon. She hopes to eventually gain enough strength to go to law school.

Lindsey Easton, still only able to move her eyes, mouth, and thumbs, is now nineteen years old. She graduated last year as covaledictorian from Glenpool High School. Her speech, read by her grandfather, brought the audience of students and their families to their feet. "Physically I am weak, but I have met that challenge by utilizing my strength—my mind. I have experienced numerous adventures through reading that I cannot enjoy physically. When you meet a roadblock, don't give up, look for alternatives or solutions to those dead ends," her grandfather read for her. When I last spoke to her mother in April, she said Lindsey was taking classes online at the local community college. Lindsey hadn't received the Genzyme treatment yet, but she was hoping to begin therapy soon, even though she was uncertain how much of her lost muscle strength the medicine could restore.

True to his word, John did ensure that Megan Assink was one of the first patients treated in Dr. Byrne's trial for older babies and toddlers. At the time she was treated, in the spring of 2003, she was one and a half years old, still able to sit and eat, but losing strength. She couldn't crawl and her tongue protruded slightly, just like her namesake, Megan Crowley, and her late sister Kelsey.

Today, at age four and a half, Megan Assink looks like any other kid. Her tongue doesn't protrude and she can smile. And Megan, with braces on her legs, can walk. She's still working on speaking clearly; though she can enunciate single words, her speech is difficult to understand when she talks fast and in complete sentences. Her father, Greg, says that it is improving steadily.

"She's a miracle child," he says. "I will never be able to thank John enough for making this happen." Greg and Deborah recently sent John a thank-you card and a tape of their daughter walking. After watching it, Megan Crowley wheeled up to her father. "That's great," she said flippantly, "but why aren't I walking?"

Before John could think of the right answer, Megan sped away, heading for the toy room. As always, she didn't pause for long to think about her disability.

Megan Crowley is now in third grade at Johnson Park Elementary School, the public school in Princeton. She loves to read Junie B. Jones and Nancy Drew books. She takes violin lessons at school and played the moneychanger in the Dr. Seuss play. Her favorite subject remains P.E., still taught by Mr. Hennessey. For her ninth birthday, her parents gave her a cell phone, which she carries with her in a pink sequined case. It was only when they got Megan's first cell phone bill that her parents realized just how much time she spent on the phone. As usual, John had used about six hundred minutes, Aileen a little over seven hundred. Megan had talked for 1,921 minutes in January. "I'm going to have to get her a new plan," John laughed. And then, unprompted, he added, "You know, the kids aren't walking, but they sure as hell couldn't be happier."

John Jr. is in fourth grade, in a special education program. He still struggles with hyperactivity and dyslexia. His best friend in class is a boy disabled by a brain tumor. "He and I are good friends because he's different, like me," little John told his mother recently. In March, Aileen and John spent the afternoon watching John Jr. and his friend anchor the school's TV news program, which is played in all classrooms at the end of the day. "He had a petrified look on his face, but he did great," Aileen said.

When I last talked to John and Aileen, they were excited about Patrick's eighth birthday party. He's in second grade at the same school. For his party, he invited all nineteen of his classmates to his house. Aileen used her digital camera to take pictures of every child with Patrick and had them all framed and ready to take home after the party. As she was printing out the pictures, Aileen told me, she noticed that Patrick's tongue was protruding much more than usual. "The little wiseass was sticking his tongue out in every picture," she said. "I couldn't believe it!"

As he gets older, he's becoming more communicative, and his family is discovering that the apple doesn't fall far from the tree—he has the same irreverent sense of humor as the rest of them.

As John has thrown himself back into the race for a cure, Aileen has stuck by her mission—to keep the kids happy. And certainly, being rich has helped. In recent years, the Crowleys have hosted annual Halloween parties at their house, inviting several hundred guests, including friends from high school and college, extended family, and also the children's nurses, therapists, teachers, and doctors, as well as Novazyme alumni and Amicus employees. There are always jello shots, a DJ, and a dance floor. At the last party, John and Aileen, along with Sharon and her husband Eddie, were the last ones shimmying on the back deck under the floodlights.

As if the demands of Amicus and family weren't enormous enough, John took on one more role, accepting a commission as an officer in the U.S. Navy Reserve. He is assigned to the Office of Naval Intelligence. "When I voluntarily resigned from the Naval Academy over seventeen years ago, I wrote in my separation letter that at some time and in some way I would again serve my country when it was needed most," he wrote in his application. For him, after September 11, that time had come.

John's best friend Ed Devinney, now a commander in the Navy, swore him in on a high floor of an office building overlooking Ground Zero. John spends one weekend each month and several weeks a year away from home working on a variety of Navy intelligence projects.

When I interviewed her years ago, Dr. Nina Raben, the biochemist from the National Institutes of Health, said something about the Crowleys' journey that I have continually found to be true. "This is a very American story," Dr. Raben told me, having grown up in the former Soviet Union. "It's about hope, it's about willpower, it's about money. It's about a belief in happy endings."

As human beings, we are defined at our cores by how we respond to hardship. Writing about the Crowleys has taught me that there isn't one right way, but that each person must find her own path, drawing on her own unique strength, passion, and resources. Who can say whether John's or Aileen's role is more important? Fueled by love, each of their journeys is tough, vital, and courageous. Knowing that each day really may be their children's last, they live with abandon, throwing themselves into every birthday party, trip to Broadway, weekend in Ocean City. Knowing so intimately the tenuousness of life, they instinctively understand what most of us forget—that all they really have, and all they are really pursuing, is time—time with the people they love. And so they grab onto each precious moment, cherish it, celebrate it, laugh at it, cry in it, and hope for another—even as they continue on the journey into the unknown and the unknowable that we call life.

GEETA ANAND
New York City
May 2006

Timeline of Major Events

December 16, 1996 Birth of Megan Crowley.

June 5, 1997 John Crowley graduates from Harvard Business School.

March 6, 1998 Birth of Patrick Crowley.

March 13, 1998 Dr. Daniel Birnbaum diagnoses Megan with Pompe disease.

May 21, 1998 Aileen Crowley and the children move to her parents' house in Rumson, New Jersey.

Week of July 6, 1998 Dr. Y. T. Chen calls with blood test results indicating Patrick might have Pompe disease.

July 27, 1998 John begins work at Bristol-Myers Squibb Co. as a field marketing director in neuroscience division.

Mid-August 1998 John travels to the Netherlands to meet with Pharming officials about their Pompe disease trial.

September 14, 1998 Megan is admitted to Monmouth Medical Center with pneumonia; she is later moved to the Pediatric Intensive Care Unit.

October 26, 1998 Megan is released from the rehabilitation center and family moves into new home in Pennington, New Jersey.

December 3–5, 1998 John attends National Institutes of Health conference in Bethesda, Maryland, where he first meets Dr. William Canfield.

June 3, 1999 Chen begins his first clinical trial, infusing baby John Koncel with the enzyme replacement therapy.

November 1999 John and Aileen host the Children's Pompe Foundation fund-raiser at the Millennium Hotel in Manhattan.

April 4, 2000 John begins work with Canfield's company, later named Novazyme.

September 12, 2000 Novazyme closes first round of financing, raising $8.3 million, with Perseus Soros, HealthCare Ventures, and Catalyst as investors.

December 14, 2000 John and Tony McKinney present the results of their "proof of concept" experiments to Neose.

December 31, 2000 Canfield successfully clones human phosphotransferase (PTase).

January 8–11, 2001 H&Q meeting in San Francisco. Neose and Perseus Soros representatives discuss the possibility of fraud at Novazyme.

January 16, 2001 Venture investors and Neose question John and Canfield about the disastrous scientific presentation made by John and McKinney on December 14.

February 8, 2001 Novazyme dedication of Lindsey Paige Easton Biologics Manufacturing Facility.

March 17–24, 2001 Crowley family participates in Megan and Patrick's Make-A-Wish Disney trip.

April 4, 2001 John and Canfield meet with Genzyme and present Novazyme's plans to develop a next generation Gaucher treatment.

June 18, 2001 Novazyme board decides to sell to Genzyme.

August 8, 2001 Genzyme signs definitive merger agreement to acquire Novazyme.

September 26, 2001 John begins work at Genzyme as senior vice president and head of the Pompe disease program.

January 31, 2002 Results of Genzyme's "Mother of All Experiments" presented.

February 28, 2002 John holds Pompe Summit for Genzyme employees to meet patients.

April 1, 2002 Crowleys move to new house in Princeton.

Week of August 5, 2002 Board at Children's Hospital of Philadelphia meets to review Dr. Hal Landy's Sibling Study, and raises questions about John's conflict of interest.

September 2002 John and a team of Genzyme employees meet in Rotterdam with families of Pompe patients on the Pharming enzyme.

October 4, 2002 Dr. Barry Byrne calls John to say his Institutional Review Board (IRB) has approved his revised Sibling Study trial.

October 7, 2002 Landy calls John to admonish him for submitting the application for Byrne's study; subsequently, John drops the plan.

October 29, 2002 John and Aileen attend family visitation at funeral home for Kelsey Ann Assink in Hudsonville, MI.

December 19, 2002 John's last day at Genzyme.

December 24, 2002 Dr. Debra-Lynn Day-Salvatore's Christmas card arrives at the Crowley house with trial approval and a start date for the Crowley kids.

January 9, 2003 Megan and Patrick receive first infusion of Special Medicine.

Acknowledgments

I want to thank John and Aileen for trusting me enough to share the full story of the struggle to save their children—not just the times they responded heroically, which are many, but also when they stumbled, compromised, or tried to escape. I want to also thank their children, Megan, Patrick, and John Jr., for allowing me to become part of their lives during the five years I spent reporting and writing this book and two earlier articles for the *Wall Street Journal*. Without the openness of the Crowleys and their wide network of family and friends, this book would not have been possible. I also want to acknowledge the vital cooperation of William Canfield, John's partner at Novazyme Pharmaceuticals and now a scientist at Genzyme Corporation, as well as Henri Termeer, Genzyme's longtime chief executive, and several other current and former officials at the company, in telling the story that is described here. Dr. Canfield and Mr. Termeer sat down repeatedly with me, and relived the journey they took with John, which tested the limits of their own courage, compassion, and resolve. Jan van Heek, Bo Piela, Bob Mattaliano, Mike O'Callaghan, Ed Kaye, and Frank Ollington gave generously of their time to make sure this book was accurate. Hal Landy's candor and thoughtfulness give this book a depth it would otherwise have lacked.

I want to thank Randall, Marylyn, and Tiffany House for spending two days talking about their Herculean efforts to push Pompe research forward—and how their paths crossed with John, often fraught with tension. Given that they have often jousted with him, it is a testament to their graciousness that they spoke to me about their experiences. This book, which focuses on John's story, does not do justice to the enormity of the

Houses' contribution toward advancing the development of a treatment for Pompe. Somebody needs to write their story, which is, in many ways, just as incredible.

I am grateful also for the input of Deborah and Greg Assink, the parents of Megan, who is thriving, and her big sister Kelsey, who passed on in 2002. And I want to thank Laurie Easton for talking to me about her irrepressible daughter Lindsey and sharing her graduation speech.

I need also to acknowledge the generosity of two other families who shared their stories after having lost children to the disease. Barry and Deb Koncel took time to tell the story of their son John's participation in the first clinical trial of Dr. Chen's enzyme, and Carolann Elmore talked with me many times about her son Niko's participation in the same trial. Both John and Niko have since passed on, but their courage and their parents' extraordinary dedication remain sources of inspiration to the doctors and nurses who met them along the way.

I want to thank Tony McKinney, Hung Do, Bill Fallon, Julie Smith, Pedro Huertas, and others from the Novazyme team who helped shape this book. The venture investors, Gus Lawlor, Dennis Purcell, Steve Elms, Josh Phillips, and Dave Alberts, as well as the company's lawyer, Doug Branch, spent many hours with me, and for that I am very grateful. Sherrill Neff and Stephen Roth, who used to run Neose, were invaluable in describing some of John's and Novazyme's biggest debacles. John Frick, whose firm didn't invest, took time to explain his decision.

Drs. Barry Byrne and Carolyn Spencer at the University of Florida were immensely helpful, as were the National Institutes of Health scientists Nina Raben and Paul Plotz, who allowed me to spend a day with them. Dr. Arnold Reuser and Dr. Rochelle Hirschhorn gave me insight into the scientific breakthroughs that made a treatment possible. I tremendously enjoyed visiting with Dr. Slonim and Dr. Martiniuk. This book would not have been possible had Duke University Medical Center's Dr. Chen and Dr. Kishnani not spent hours explaining their research. The dedication of these physician researchers to their patients is nothing short of extraordinary.

Sharon was not only a wonderful source of information but made the book writing process a whole lot more fun with her terrific sense of humor. I am also deeply indebted to Aileen's parents, Marty and Kathy; her

Uncle Charles and Aunt Sandra; her brothers, Brian and Marty; their wives, Kim and Kate; her cousin Kevin and his wife Lisa; and the many other relatives and friends who took time to talk about Aileen. John's mother Barbara and brothers, Joe and Jason, deserve my gratitude as well, as do John's best friend Ed and buddies Karl Palasz, Mike Ostergard, Andy Singer, Bradley Campbell, and John Gordon. Brian Markison, John's former boss at Bristol-Myers, could recount verbatim his conversations with John back then.

Much of this book was written in diners and coffee shops in Manhattan, as I strove to find a quiet place, away from my family. I want to thank Juan and Maria, the waiter and restaurant manager, respectively, at Euro Diner; the staff at the Starbucks at Third Avenue and Twenty-eighth Street and at Lexington Avenue and Fortieth Street; and Pete, the waiter at Frontier Diner on Third Avenue and Thirty-ninth Street. All of them were gracious when I stayed at my table for far longer than was profitable or proper, laboring over this book.

I want to thank my dear friend and former *Boston Globe* editor, Sarah Snyder, who read initial drafts of each chapter, tore them to shreds, and recommended better structure. This book wouldn't be as well organized if it weren't for her. I want to thank Bob Dow, whom I first wrote about when covering the September 11 tragedy, in which he lost his partner, Ruth Ketler. Bob, an enormously talented creative writing professor at the University of Massachusetts in Amherst, read an early draft and helped me put more voice into the pages of this book. This book may never have come about were it not for Stephen Gendel, Novazyme's publicist, who introduced me to the Crowleys in 2001 for the first story I did for the *Wall Street Journal*.

I also want to thank my sister, Mona, my parents, Mohan and Mary Donna, and two of my friends, Deepika Mehra and Mary Silver, for reading early drafts and offering encouragement. Mary's eleven-year-old daughter Natalie came up with the title. My college roommate, Ana, swept into New York City in March and April and took my kids to movies, bookstores, and ice cream parlors so I had time to make the final editing changes. My old friend and former *Boston Globe* colleague Kate Zernike, one of the best writers I know, polished my last draft. I also had better appreciate my husband Greg's candid early readings, which were immensely helpful in improving the book. Greg took care of our children on many weekends over the two and a half years it took to write this book, and I am not exaggerating to say he never once complained. I couldn't ask for more support than he gave me.

I need to thank my *Wall Street Journal* editor, Elyse Tanouye, for encouraging me to write the first two stories in the newspaper that led to this book. She and the *Journal*'s top editors, Paul Steiger and Dan Hertzberg, deserve my gratitude for giving me eight months off to write the first draft. Ron Winslow, Carrie Dolan, and Amy Stevens, who edited the front-page piece on the Crowleys, asked smart questions that helped shape my thinking.

Thank you to my book agent, Joelle Delbourgo, who was a constant source of encouragement. And thanks to my editors at Regan: Cal Morgan, whose wise letter after the first draft served as my guide in rewriting the book, and Alison Stoltzfus, who put her heart and soul into every page. A writer cannot ask for more than a passionate editor, and she was that and more.

Notes

PROLOGUE

[1] Dr. Priya Kishnani explained that the difficulty in speaking clearly for patients with Pompe disease is due to weakness in the oropharyngeal muscles, the ones involved in speech, in an interview March 30, 2006, and follow-up e-mail exchange.

CHAPTER 1

[1] Barbara Valentino Crowley, in an interview on February 26, 2004.

[2] Details here are from interviews with John, Barbara and Joe Crowley in 2004.

[3] Interviews with Mike Ostergard, Harvard Business School classmate, on October 26, 2004; John Gordon, another former classmate, October 27, 2004; and Karl Palasz, also a former classmate, October 28, 2004.

CHAPTER 2

[1] Dialogue and detail in this scene are based on the recollections of John and Aileen in interviews in 2004; Dr. Kong, in an interview on June 14, 2006, said his medical records from 1997 and 1998 were in storage and he no longer had a clear recollection of his meetings with the Crowley family.

[2] Dialogue and details are based on Dr. Daniel Birnbaum's recollections in an interview on November 24, 2004, and also on John and Aileen Crowley's recollections in interviews in 2004.

[3] Dialogue and details in this section are based on recollections of John and Aileen in interviews in 2004.

CHAPTER 3

[1] Dialogue and details are based on recollections of Dr. Birnbaum in an interview in 2004, and John and Aileen in interviews in 2004.

[2] The incidence of Pompe disease is still not certain. Dr. Arnold Reuser, a professor at

Erasmus University in Rotterdam who has researched the disease for decades, said in an interview on May 12, 2006, that the best estimates range from one in 40,000 people to one in 100,000 people worldwide affected with the disease.

CHAPTER 4

[1.] Information in this section on scientific history of development of a Pompe treatment is from *The Metabolic and Molecular Basis of Inherited Disease*, Eighth Edition, McGraw-Hill, New York, chapter by Hirschhorn R, and Reuser AJJ: Glycogen Storage Diseases Type II.

The scientific history is also based on interviews with Dr. Y. T. Chen on April 15, 2004 and April 9, 2006; Dr. Rochelle Hirschhorn on May 10, 2006; and Dr. Arnold Reuser in 2004 and on May 12, 2006.

[2.] Hers HG: Alpha-glucosidase deficiency in generalized glycogen-storage disease (Pompe disease). *Biochem J* 86:11, 1963.

[3.] Dr. Hirschhorn interviewed May 10, 2006, and Dr. Reuser, interviewed in 2004 and again on May 12, 2006, confirmed this description of their race to clone the gene, which is backed up by their papers, listed below.

Martiniuk F, Mehler M, Pellicer A, Tzall S, Gundula LB, Hobart C, Ellenbogen A, Hirschhorn R: Isolation of a cDNA for human acid alpha-glucosidase and detection of genetic heterogeneity for mRNA in three alpha-glucosidase deficient patients. Proceedings of the National Academy of the Sciences, 1986.

Hoefsloot L, Hoogeveen-Westerveld M, Kroos M, van Beeumen J, Reuser AJJ, Oostra BA: Primary structure and processing of lysosomal alpha-glucosidase. *The EMBO Journal*, 1988.

Martiniuk F, Mehler M, Tzall S, Meredith G, Hirschhorn R: Sequence of the cDNA and 5'-Flanking Region for Human Acid Alpha-Glucosidase. *DNA and Cell Biology*, 1990.

[4.] Jan van Heek, in an interview on May 26, 2004, recalled meeting with Chen and Reuser in the 1990s and not doing any deal because the project seemed too risky.

[5.] Duke University Medical Center press release from February 1998, provided by Duke University Medical Center Press Office.

[6.] Duke University Medical Center press release from February 1998.

[7.] Dialogue and details in this section are based on an interview with Dr. Alfred Slonim on March 15, 2004, and interviews with John and Aileen that year.

[8.] Dialogue and details of this meeting are based on interviews with Randall House on December 6 and 7, 2004; an interview with Slonim in 2004; and interviews with John and Aileen in 2004.

CHAPTER 5

[1.] In interviews on May 19, 2006, Brian Markison, John's boss at Bristol-Myers, and Sandra Holleran, Aileen's aunt, confirmed this account of how John got his first interview at the company.

CHAPTER 6

[1.] Information from interviews with Randall, Marylyn, and Tiffany House on December 6 and 7, 2004, and Marylyn and Tiffany again on May 22, 2006.

[2.] Dialogue is based on John's recollection of the conversation; Randall in interviews in 2004 did not recall the conversation but says it may have occurred and escapes his memory today; he and Marylyn agreed in interviews that they were unhappy that John was starting his own foundation, believing it would be a distraction and take resources away from their own.

[3.] Dialogue and description in this scene are based on John's recollections; I tried in vain to reach Gerben Moolhuizen by phone and e-mail at work at OctoPlus, a drug development firm in Leiden, Netherlands, in May 2006.

[4.] Information in this scene is based only on the recollection of John.

   I made several failed attempts to reach Moolhuizen by phone and e-mail at his job at the Dutch firm OctoPlus.

   Rein Strijker declined to be interviewed for the book, saying this in an e-mail about John's visit described in this scene: "I indeed clearly remember his visit to Geel during which he offered a large amount of money if his children could participate in an early clinical trial. At that time we took the position that money was not a good criterion for inclusion in such a trial. If I remember correctly his children had a somewhat atypical form of Pompe disease and could not be included in the early study. He later became involved with Novazyme and Genzyme and was, in that context, closely involved with the situation that led to the (almost) going down of Pharming. As you may imagine, I do not have much respect for the way he has operated in this matter (even though I have sympathy with and feel sorry for the situation with his children). Hence, I do not wish to spend more time on contributing to a book that pays tribute to Mr. Crowley."

   Since I couldn't speak to Strijker, I wasn't able to try to reconcile his recollections with John's.

CHAPTER 7

[1.] Markison and John, in interviews in 2006, provided these details of his job at Bristol-Myers.

[2.] Dialogue and details are based on interviews with Dr. Marc Hofley on April 7, 2004, and Marty and Kathy Holleran on March 5, 2004, as well as on interviews with John, Aileen, and Joe Crowley in 2004 and 2005.

[3.] Dialogue and details are based on interviews with Greg Assink in 2005 and Greg and Deborah Assink on April 9, 2006, and interviews with John in 2004.

CHAPTER 8

[1.] Dr. Nina Raben in an interview on March 29, 2005; Marylyn and Randall in interviews in 2004.

[2.] Dialogue and details are based on John's recollections; Randall does not recall the details described here, but says the conversation may have occurred; he and Marylyn agree with the basic point, which is that they didn't want John to start his own foundation, believing it would be a distraction and take resources from their group, and that they were doing everything possible to move research forward.

3. Dr. Paul Plotz, in an interview on March 29, 2005, said he believed anybody who wanted to attend an NIH-sponsored event should be allowed to do so, and he may have made the phone call to Randall or Marylyn, but he couldn't specifically recall doing so. Marylyn, in an interview in 2006, said she recalled Dr. Plotz insisting John be allowed to attend.

4. Marylyn, in interviews in 2004 and 2006, agreed she didn't want John to attend but relented and allowed him to do so, under pressure from Dr. Plotz. She confirmed John's recollection of this phone call, and said she was mean and intimidating. She says she found him pushy, unprofessional, and interfering and worried he would disrupt the plans in place for her daughter to be treated in Pharming's clinical trial, expected to begin soon. In retrospect, now that tempers have cooled, she said she understood why John pushed so hard to attend.

5. Dialogue and details that follow are based on John's recollections in interviews in 2004.

6. Dialogue and descriptions in this scene based on John's recollections; I tried in vain to reach Gerben Moolhuizen by phone and e-mail at work at OctoPlus, a drug development firm in Leiden, Netherlands, in May 2006.

7. Dialogue and details are based on recollections of Dr. Alfred Slonim and John in interviews in 2004.

8. Dialogue and details are based on the recollections of John in interviews in 2004 and Reuser in an interview in 2006.

9. Description of presentation is based on recollections of Dr. Y. T. Chen and John in interviews in 2004 and checked with Chen in another interview on April 9, 2006.

10. Description of presentation is based on recollection of Dr. Frank Martiniuk in an interview on January 17, 2006, and John in interviews in 2004.

11. Description of William Canfield's presentation is based on interviews with him on May 5 and July 9, 2004, and recollections of Slonim and John in 2004.

12. John remembers meeting Canfield at this meeting, although Canfield, in the interviews in 2004, said he didn't recall being introduced to John at that meeting. Slonim, in his interview in March 2004, said he remembered introducing them.

13. Dialogue and details are based on John's recollection. Randall, in interviews in 2004, said he didn't recall stopping John from getting on the bus, or saying the quotes attributed to him. He said he may have kept John off the bus and said these things and simply doesn't remember. In retrospect, Randall said he understands why John was trying to get into the meeting and believes he was doing the right thing, but he found John's efforts threatening at the time because Tiffany was so sick and plans for her to get treated in Pharming's upcoming trial were so tenuous. Randall said he worried that John's aggressive efforts to save his own kids would derail the plans to get Tiffany in the Pharming trial.

CHAPTER 9

1. Dialogue and details in this chapter are based on John and Aileen's recollections of what happened and what they said at the time.

2. Dialogue and details are based on recollections of Ed and John in interviews in 2004 and 2005.

CHAPTER 10

[1.] Dialogue and details are based on recollections of Sharon Dozier, John, and Aileen in interviews in 2004.

CHAPTER 11

[1.] Slonim, in an interview in 2004, recalled describing Martiniuk this way to John; John, in interviews in 2004, remembers Slonim describing Martiniuk this way.

[2.] Dialogue and details in this scene are based on recollections of Martiniuk in an interview in 2006, and John in interviews in 2004.

[3.] Dialogue and details in this scene are based on an interview with Martiniuk in 2006 and interviews with John, Aileen, and John's mother Barbara in 2004.

[4.] Dialogue and details in this scene are based on recollection of Chen in interviews in 2004, and John in interviews in 2004.

[5.] Dialogue and details are based on John's recollection in interviews in 2004 and recollections of Deb and Barry Koncel in an interview on November 27, 2004.

[6.] Dialogue and details are based on John's recollections of the meeting. The Koncels recall the visit, but not the detail.

[7.] Dialogue and details are based on recollections of the Koncels in an interview in November 2004; Chen, in interviews in April 2004; Slonim in an interview in March 2004; and John and Aileen in interviews in 2004.

[8.] Dialogue and details are based on recollections of Chen in interview in April 2004, and John in interviews in 2004.

[9.] Details of Bristol-Myers's assistance were provided by Markison and John.

[10.] Dialogue and details are based on recollections of Greg Assink, John, and Aileen in interviews in 2004 and 2005.

CHAPTER 12

[1.] Dialogue and details in this scene are based on Chen's recollections in an interview in 2004, and John's in interviews in 2004; Brian Markison, in an interview in 2006, confirmed that Bristol-Myers pulled the manufacturing plant off the selling block, but he said the decision was based on several factors, including John's idea for manufacturing the Pompe enzyme at the facility.

[2.] Dialogue and details in this scene are based on John's recollection in interviews in 2004. Deb and Barry Koncel, who were not in the room when John visited, said in an interview they weren't aware John stopped by that day.

[3.] Details are based on interviews with Martiniuk in 2006, John in 2004, and Emil Kakkis on June 15, 2006, who said he also grew unsure the science would work.

[4.] Dialogue and details are based on interviews with Martiniuk in 2006, and John in 2004.

[5.] Martiniuk, in a 2006 interview, agreed he didn't give John regular updates on his work but said it was because John stopped funding his program. He said he couldn't remember how much of the $180,000 John actually paid, but said he didn't receive all of the money promised. John said he didn't send the final check because Martiniuk wasn't keeping him abreast of his work and he had no idea whether he was making progress toward beginning a trial.

6. Dialogue and details are based on interviews with Canfield and John in 2004.

7. Dialogue and details are based on recollections of Canfield in interviews in 2004, and Doug Branch on May 4, 2004.

8. Quote is based on recollections of Marty Holleran and John in interviews in 2004.

9. Dialogue and details in this scene are based on recollections of Canfield and John in interviews in 2004.

10. Dialogue and details in this scene are based on recollections of John and Slonim in interviews in 2004.

11. Dialogue is based on John's recollection in interviews in 2004, and Andy Singer's in an interview on May 10, 2006.

12. Dialogue and details based on interviews with Doug Branch and Canfield in 2004.

13. Dialogue and details in this scene are based on recollections of Canfield and John in interviews in 2004.

CHAPTER 13

1. Dialogue and details are based on recollections of John and Canfield in interviews in 2004; and Tony McKinney in interviews on February 25, April 21, and April 26, 2004, and again on April 9, 2006.

2. Dialogue and details are based on the recollections of John in interviews in 2004, and John Frick, in an interview on May 18, 2006.

3. Information from Dr. Stephen Roth and Sherrill Neff in interviews on January 4, 2005, and interviews with John in 2004.

4. Information from Roth and Neff in interviews in 2005.

5. Dialogue and details of this scene are based on recollections of Roth and Neff in interviews in January 2005; and John, Canfield, and Doug in interviews in 2004.

6. John, in interviews in 2004, said he recalled this conversation with Markison when things were going badly at Novazyme. Markison, in an interview in 2006, confirmed having had this conversation with John.

7. Canfield, in interviews in 2004, said John didn't tell him he had mortgaged his house. John, in interviews in 2004, said he put the money in the Children's Pompe Foundation and brought Canfield a check from the foundation. John said he didn't want Canfield to know he'd been reduced to borrowing on his house to get money for the company.

8. Gus Lawlor, in an interview on July 19, 2004, said that when he read the agreement John struck with Neose, he saw it was so one-sided in Neose's favor that it made him question John's abilities and whether to even invest in Canfield's company. It was only when Neose's Neff agreed to renegotiate the deal that Lawlor moved ahead and invested in the firm. Terms of the Neose deal are based on recollections of John and Neff.

9. Details from Josh Phillips in an interview on July 21, 2004, and John in interviews in 2004.

10. Copy of Novazyme business plan from 2000. Dialogue and details in this scene are based on interviews with Josh and John in 2004.

11. Details based on recollections of Josh in an interview in 2004, and John in interviews in 2004.

12. Details based on recollections of Dennis Purcell in an interview on November 5, 2004; Lawlor in an interview in 2004; Steve Elms in an interview on May 9, 2006; and John in interviews in 2004.

CHAPTER 14

[1] Dialogue and details are based on interviews with Canfield in 2004, Hung Do in 2006, and John in 2004. Laurie Easton, interviewed on April 7, 2006, provided additional dialogue and details, as did Hung in interviews in 2005 and 2006.

[2] Canfield shared this view in interviews in 2004.

CHAPTER 15

[1] Canfield in interviews in 2004.

[2] John and McKinney in interviews in 2004 and 2006.

[3] McKinney in interviews in 2004 and 2006.

[4] Interview with Barry Byrne on April 21, 2004; Raben in an interview in 2005; and McKinney in interviews in 2004 and 2006.

[5] Dialogue and details are based on McKinney's and Canfield's recollections in interviews.

[6] Canfield in interviews in 2004, and Hung in interviews in 2005 and 2006.

[7] Canfield in interviews in 2004, and Hung in interviews in 2005 and 2006.

[8] Canfield in interviews in 2004, and McKinney in interviews also in 2004.

[9] Dialogue and details are based on recollections of John in interviews in 2004, and McKinney in interviews in 2004 and 2006.

[10] Dialogue and details of the meeting are based on interviews with Neff, Roth, McKinney, and John in 2004 and 2005.

[11] Dialogue and details in this scene are based on recollections of Canfield and Roth in interviews in 2004 and 2005, respectively.

[12] Dialogue and details in this scene are based on recollections of Canfield and Doug in interviews in 2004.

CHAPTER 16

[1] Dialogue and details are based on recollections of Gus in an interview in 2004.

[2] Dialogue and details are based on recollections of Gus and John in interviews in 2004.

[3] Gus, in his interview in 2004, said it wasn't that he disagreed with the investment in the manufacturing plant, it was the fact that John didn't confer with his board before spending the money that bothered him.

[4] Dialogue and details are based on recollections of Gus and John in interviews in 2004.

[5] Steve, in an interview in May 2006, said he liked the idea at the time because he believed a diversified company made for a safer investment, though in retrospect, he thinks Gus was right that Novazyme didn't have the resources to handle more than one drug development project.

[6] Dialogue and details in this scene are based on recollections of John; and Canfield, and Dennis Purcell in interviews in 2004; and Steve Elms in an interview in 2006.

[7] Dialogue and details are based on interviews with Roth, Neff, and Gus in 2004 and 2005.

[8] Dialogue and details are based on interviews with John and Dennis in 2004.

CHAPTER 17

1. Dialogue and details of this scene are based on interviews with Gus, Lawlor, Dennis, Canfield, Roth, Neff, and John in 2004 and 2005.
2. Dialogue and details are based on recollections of Pedro Huertas and Gus in interviews in 2004.
3. Dialogue and details in this scene are based on interviews with Gus, Dennis, John, and Canfield in 2004, and Steve in 2006.
4. Dialogue and details in this scene are based on interviews with Gus, Dennis, and John in 2004, and Steve in 2006.
5. Dialogue and details are based on interviews with Gus, Canfield, and John in 2004.
6. John in an interview in 2004, and Byrne in an interview in 2004.

CHAPTER 18

1. Bradley Campbell, in an interview on May 21, 2006, confirmed this account from John and Aileen of how he arranged with his father for Textron to lend its jet to take the Crowley kids on their Make-A-Wish trip.

CHAPTER 19

1. Details from Henri Termeer in interviews on May 26 and September 21, 2004; and John and Canfield in interviews in 2004.
2. Figures are based on recollections of Canfield, Gus, Dennis, and John in interviews in 2004, and Steve in an interview in 2006.
3. Information from John, confirmed by Termeer in interviews in 2004.
4. Susan Ferris of BioMarin, confirmed that the stock price soared over $1 billion; John, Gus, Josh, Dennis, and Steve, provided investor perspective.
5. John, in interviews in 2004, said this was his thinking at the time. Genzyme's annual revenue from Cerezyme in 2000 was $540 million, though it is now substantially higher.
6. Dialogue and details in this scene are based on recollections of Canfield and John in interviews in 2004.
7. Dialogue and details are based on recollections of Jan van Heek in an interview on May 26, 2004; and John in 2004 interviews.
8. Copy of presentation made to Genzyme; quotes and details of the visit to Genzyme are based on recollections of Canfield, John, and van Heek in interviews in 2004.
9. Canfield, John, and McKinney in interviews in 2004; and Hung in interviews in 2006.
10. Copy of presentation made to Genzyme; dialogue and details of visit to Genzyme based on recollections of Canfield, John, and van Heek in interviews in 2004.
11. John and Canfield, in interviews, recall van Heek pacing as described. Van Heek, in an interview in 2004, didn't recall this detail, but said it sounded accurate.
12. Numbers in this scene are based on John and Canfield's recollections in interviews in 2004; Termeer and van Heek, in interviews the same year, declined to confirm the earlier offers they made for Novazyme, citing company policy of not discussing negotiations. Other dialogue and details here are based on recollections of all four men.

[13.] Dialogue and details in this section are based on recollections of Gus, Canfield, and John in interviews in 2004.

CHAPTER 20

[1.] Termeer in interviews in 2004, recalled his thinking.

[2.] Bob Mattaliano and Mike O'Callaghan, interviewed on September 21, 2004, relayed the perspective they shared with Henri and others at Genzyme. Termeer recalled their perspective in interviews in 2004.

[3.] Termeer shared this perspective in interviews in 2004.

[4.] Dialogue and details in this scene based on interviews with van Heek and John in 2004.

[5.] Dialogue and details in this scene are based on recollections of John, Gus, Dennis, Josh, and Canfield in interviews in 2004, and Steve in an interview in 2006.

[6.] Dialogue and details of the negotiations back and forth are based on interviews with John; Termeer and van Heek, citing company policy, declined to confirm the numbers of the negotiations.

[7.] Details of Genentech offer are from John and Canfield in interviews in 2004. Joe Mc-Cracken of Genentech confirmed in an e-mail on May 21, 2006 that the deal details are consistent with his recollection.

[8.] Bohmer, Richard M.J., and Bradley Campbell. "A Father's Love: Novazyme Pharmaceuticals, Inc." Harvard Business School Case 603-048.

[9.] Dialogue and details of the meeting are based on interviews with John, Gus, Josh, and Dennis, in interviews in 2004, and Steve in an interview in 2006.

[10.] Josh, in an interview in 2004, said that in retrospect, he thinks it was a great decision to sell. He said he didn't know at the time how much Canfield was struggling to produce his enzyme with human PTase and kifunensin. If he had known, Josh says, he would have favored selling the company. He said he also didn't know that John no longer expected to make the timeline to go into clinical trials in September.

CHAPTER 21

[1.] Dialogue and details based on recollections of John and Termeer in interviews in 2004.

[2.] Dialogue and details are based on recollections of Hal Landy in an interview on July 20, 2004, and several interviews in 2003; and John in 2004.

[3.] Dialogue and details in this scene are based on recollections of Landy in interviews in 2003 and 2004; and John in 2004.

[4.] This is John's impression of the Genzyme management structure, shared in interviews in 2004.

[5.] Canfield described his reaction to being left off the leadership team in interviews in 2004.

[6.] Based on interviews with John, Canfield, McKinney, Mattaliano, and Mike O'Callaghan in 2004.

[7.] Landy described his reaction in an interview in 2004; Termeer and John explained what had happened in interviews in 2004.

[8.] Dialogue and details of this meeting are based on recollections of John, Landy, Mattaliano, O'Callaghan, McKinney, Julie Smith, and Bill Fallon, in interviews in 2004 and 2005.

[9.] Tape of *Today* show episode from November 2001, provided by John and Aileen.

10. Landy, in interviews in 2003 and 2004, described his feelings and actions during and after that first leadership team meeting.

CHAPTER 22

1. John provided the information on how much money he, Canfield, and the venture investors made on the sale. Elms confirmed the Perseus Soros part. The actual sale price of Novazyme was $116 million because it was a stock deal and Genzyme's stock price had fallen in the post-September 11 downturn in the market.
2. Dialogue and details are based on interviews with Termeer and John in 2004.
3. Termeer shared this perspective in interviews in 2004. Henri Blair, Genzyme's cofounder, confirmed this in interviews in 2005.
4. Information on the children in the trials described by John was confirmed in interviews with Drs. Chen and Kishnani in 2004 and 2006, as well as in interviews with the Koncel family those years.

   In addition, the trial results are described in this paper: Amalfitano, Andrea, et al: Recombinant human acid alpha-glucosidase enzyme therapy for infantile glycogen storage disease type II: Results of a phase 1/11 clinical trial. *Genetics in Medicine* March/April 2001.
5. Dr. Kishnani, in an interview in 2006, described the trial design, as did John in interviews in 2004. Even though the trial was designed to include only babies who made a small amount of enzyme, two babies who made no enzyme ended up in the trial. In addition, Kishnani said three babies in the trial were older than six months old. Two of the older babies were eight months old and one was 14 months old at the start of the trial.
6. Study results described by Dr. Arnold Reuser, John, and Landy in interviews in 2004. The study results were also published in the following paper: van den Hout JMP, Reuser AJJ, de Klerk JBC, Arts WF, Smeitink JAM, van der Ploeg AT: Enzyme therapy for Pompe disease with recombinant human alpha-glucosidase from rabbit milk. *Journal of Inherited Metabolic Diseases* 24 (2001) 267–275.
7. Information based on interviews with Reuser, John, and Landy in 2004; also based on interviews with Tiffany House and Randall in December 2004.
8. Information based on interviews with Tiffany in December 2004.
9. Information based on interviews with Termeer, Landy, John, and Randall in 2004.
10. This is the view of the leadership of Genzyme, shared by Termeer, van Heek, John, and Landy in interviews in 2004; Reuser and House disagreed that the approach was impractical and risky, believing it could have been improved over time.
11. In fact, several patients didn't do as well when they were switched from the Pharming enzyme to a lower dose of another enzyme made by Genzyme, according to Landy, Tiffany and Randall in interviews in 2004. The Houses blamed the leadership of Genzyme, including John, for making a hasty decision. These patients eventually improved when Genzyme increased the dosage of the new enzyme they received. Hung Do, who worked under Canfield and is now a scientist at Amicus Therapeutics, said in interviews in 2005 and 2006 that in subsequent experiments in recent years, he and others learned that the Pharming enzyme was more effective in treating humans than appeared in the Mother of All Experiments because of the limitations of animal experiments.

[12.] Canfield and John, in interviews in 2004, described Canfield's view of the various enzyme treatments in 2001; Hung, in interviews in 2005 and 2006, also shared his and Canfield's analysis of the enzymes back in 2001.

[13.] Dialogue and details in the exchange in this scene are based on interviews with Canfield and John in 2004.

CHAPTER 23

[1.] Based on interviews with Mattaliano, O'Callaghan, John and Canfield, 2004 and 2005, and Hung, Mattaliano and O'Callaghan in 2006.

[2.] Details of the results and the meeting provided by Mattaliano, O'Callaghan, and John in interviews in 2004 and 2006.

[3.] Results described in interviews in 2004 by Mattaliano, O'Callaghan, Canfield, and John.

[4.] Mattaliano described his explanation in an interview in 2004; John and O'Callaghan confirmed this is what Mattaliano's understanding was at the time and what he articulated the day of the meeting.

[5.] Canfield, in interviews in 2004, said he agreed with the results of the Mother of All Experiments at the time they were presented. But in the interviews, he said he had later begun to believe his enzyme would have done better if it were given as a continuous infusion into the mice rather than as a single injection. If given as an infusion, the enzyme, after filling the receptors that were attracting it first, might have eventually gotten into the intended target—the lysosomes of muscle cells—in greater numbers.

[6.] Dialogue and details in this scene are based on interviews with Termeer and John in interviews in 2004.

[7.] Termeer, in interviews in 2004, described the reaction of his medical and regulatory employees to the summit and his decision to support it and speak at it.

[8.] Mattaliano, in the interview in 2004, agreed the title was a dig at Canfield, but said Canfield had seemed supercilious about his approach in the past.

[9.] Dialogue and details in this scene are based on recollections of Termeer, Landy, van Heek, John, McKinney, Canfield, Aileen, Dozier, Greg Assink, and Fallon in interviews in 2004 and 2005.

[10.] Landy, in an interview in 2004, shared these emotions and recollected his actions and observations that day.

CHAPTER 24

[1.] Dialogue and details of this meeting are based on interviews with Landy, Smith, Fallon, McKinney, and John in 2004 and 2005.

[2.] Landy, in an interview in 2004, described his feelings and thoughts after the meeting.

[3.] Dialogue and details in this scene are based on recollections of Landy and John in interviews in 2004.

[4.] A spokeswoman for the Children's Hospital of Philadelphia said in an interview in 2003 that a hospital board questioned the fairness of a study that included as patients only the children of a senior official at Genzyme, the company sponsoring the study. The board was concerned that the conflict of interest could skew the trial, the spokeswoman said. She said Dr. Richard Finkel was unavailable for comment.

Dr. Edward Kaye, a Genzyme official who had previously worked at CHOP, told me in an interview in 2004 that he had tried to intervene on John's behalf with hospital officials. He said they told him they really wanted to help, but they couldn't overlook the conflict of interest questions that arose because John, a senior Genzyme official, was the father of the children in the trial.

CHAPTER 25

1. Termeer, in interviews in 2004, recalled this conversation with his mother.
2. Dialogue and details are based on recollections of John, van Heek, McKinney, and Landy in interviews in 2004, and Reuser in an interview in 2006.
3. Dialogue and details are based on interviews with Byrne and Dr. Carolyn Spencer on April 21, 2004, and interviews with John.
4. Details from Julie Berthy, interviewed on April 21, 2004.
5. Dialogue and details in this scene are based on Landy and John's recollections in interviews in 2004.

CHAPTER 26

1. Landy, in an interview in 2004, shared this perspective. Dialogue and details of the next scene based on interviews with Landy and John in 2004.
2. Termeer, in interviews in 2004, recalled making this phone call to Landy, although Landy doesn't recall the conversation, but he says it may have occurred and escaped his memory.
3. Dialogue and details are based on John's recollection; Termeer said he didn't recall the details and said he couldn't discuss internal legal matters anyway. A Genzyme spokesman said Tom DesRosier did not recall this specific conversation, but he and another Genzyme lawyer did have conversations with John from time to time "about situations in which his inexperience or questionable judgment led him to do something we would consider problematic." The spokesman declined to allow me to speak to DesRosier, saying he didn't recall the conversation I was referencing in this scene.
4. Contents of John's e-mail are based on his recollections of what he wrote; he didn't keep a copy and Genzyme wasn't able to provide me with one.
5. Dialogue and details are based on an interview with van Heek in 2004 and interviews with John the same year.

CHAPTER 27

1. Dialogue and details in this scene and section based on recollections of John, Landy, and McKinney.
2. Details on the video are based on recollections of Kishnani, in an interview in 2006, and John in 2004.
3. Landy, in his interview in 2004, recollected receiving this entreaty and others.
4. Information on entreaties from officials in other countries is based on interviews with Termeer, van Heek, Landy, and John in 2004.

5. Detail from van Heek and John in interviews in 2004; Genzyme supplied copies of the articles in the Italian press about Rosella's plight.

6. Dialogue and details in this scene are based on interviews with Greg Assink in 2005 and 2006 and John and Aileen in 2004.

7. Dialogue and details in this scene are based on the recollections of Dr. Debra-Lynn Day-Salvatore, in interviews in 2003 and 2004, and John.

8. On March 5, 2003, Genzyme reported annual earnings for 2002, listing, among special expenditures: a $4.2 million severance charge associated with the departure of John Crowley, former chief executive officer of Novazyme Pharmaceuticals Inc. The charge primarily reflects the cost of medical insurance continuation for Mr. Crowley's children, who both have Pompe disease.

John provided the estimate of nearly $1 million annually for the medical care of each of his children.

9. A copy of the card and review board letter was provided by John and Aileen.

10. Dialogue and details are based on my observations, since I was present this day.

11. Genzyme, counting the acquisition cost of Novazyme as well as Pharming's and Chen's enzymes, estimates the cost of developing the treatment, Myozyme, at $500 million by the end of 2005.

12. Dialogue and details based on interviews with John and Ed in 2004.

13. Dialogue and details in this scene are based on John's recollections.

14. Dialogue and details are based on interviews with John in 2006, and with Steve Hennessey on March 14, 2006.

15. Details of test results are based on interviews with Dr. Debra-Lynn Day-Salvatore in 2003, and John in 2003 and 2004. Dialogue and details of the scene are based on recollections of Day-Salvatore and John and Aileen.

16. Dialogue and details are based on recollections of Dozier in interviews in 2004.

AFTERWORD

1. John wasn't looking to sell the company to Genzyme because he believed any additional acquisitions of genetic disease companies by the bigger company risked being seen as anticompetitive. After the Novazyme acquisition, Genzyme faced a lengthy review by the Federal Trade Commission, concerned that the bigger company was buying up all potential competitors in violation of the antitrust laws. The commission eventually decided not to sanction Genzyme, but another acquisition might result in a different ruling.

2. Kishnani presented these results at the American Society for Medical Genetics meeting in San Diego in March 2006.

3. Results of these experiments were confirmed by Hung, Mattaliano, and O'Callaghan.

4. Hung says he and others performed experiments in the years after the Mother of All Experiments and found that the Pharming enzyme worked better than initially realized. The Pharming enzyme did have some phosphate molecules on the carbohydrate chains, but the phosphate molecules were covered by other molecules. So in mouse experiments, Pharming's enzyme wasn't well absorbed. But it turns out human beings have uncovering enzyme on the cell surfaces, which exposes the phosphate in the carbohydrate chains, enabling the enzyme to be well absorbed. "We're so arrogant as scientists," he told me. "At any point in time, there's so much that we don't know."